STAGE COMBAT ARTS

'In our current academic environment that favors radical specialization, this compendium stands apart, boldly focusing on the *integration* of craft, and the reunification of a performer's body, mind and spirit. Mr. DuVal has successfully blended the systems he espouses here, and in so doing, he has also brought together Eastern and Western practices, traditions, and philosophies. This is an invaluable resource for any student or teacher delving deeply into their study of performance and the martial arts.'

Adam Noble
Associate Professor of Acting & Movement – University of Houston
Fight Director & Southwest Regional Representative, Society of
American Fight Directors

'Acting is said to be the physical manifestation of an internal world. Christopher DuVal's innovative approach nudges the actor out the safety of the cerebral and in to the dynamic tangibles of breath, voice, speech and movement. A must-have teaching resource for the 21st century!'

Anne James
Associate Professor, California State University, Fullerton
Associate Teacher, Fitzmaurice Voicework

'This book is an invaluable resource for those who teach voice, stage violence, or acting. Mr. DuVal approaches the integration of voice and violence from a practiced, careful, generous perspective. The methodical, logical progression of concept to video demonstration to application through text examples and exercises is brilliant. Anyone serious about the craft of acting should have this book on their shelf!'

Jonathan Cole, PhD
Associate Professor, Willamette University
Certified Teacher, Society of American Fight Directors

'This book is a holistic approach to the skill of acting – calling upon the actor to approach their craft like an athlete in training. Each structurally consistent chapter gently invites the reader to develop a curiosity for their often unconscious physical and mental habits that limit their abilities on the stage. There is then a strong motivation to apply the subsequent exercises which effectively raise awareness, release tension and re-direct focus for optimal connection on stage and off. Chris DuVal's thorough, disciplined and gentle approach to the skill of acting is a rare and welcome teaching agent for acting students at any level.'

Nancy Lee-Painter
Professor of Theatre
National Playwriting Program Chair Region VII,
Kennedy Center American College Theatre Festival
Lewis-Clark State College

'Chris DuVal has managed a rare feat in writing a manual that is clear, enlightening, creative and ultimately, immensely useful, that can, and will, be used extensively by teachers of Stage Combat, Acting, Movement and Voice alike. There is much in this book to recommend. It deserves a place front and center on every theatre artist's bookshelf and desk.'

Robin McFarquhar, PhD
Professor and Chair of Acting, University of Illinois, Urbana Champaign
Fight Director/Teacher, Society of American Fight Directors
Alexander Teacher, AmSAT

STAGE COMBAT ARTS

ARTS

An Integrated Approach to Acting,
Voice and Text Work + Video

CHRISTOPHER DUVAL

Bloomsbury Methuen Drama
An imprint of Bloomsbury Publishing Plc

B L O O M S B U R Y
LONDON · OXFORD · NEW YORK · NEW DELHI · SYDNEY

Bloomsbury Methuen Drama

An imprint of Bloomsbury Publishing Plc

50 Bedford Square
London
WC1B 3DP
UK

1385 Broadway
New York
NY 10018
USA

www.bloomsbury.com

Bloomsbury is a registered trade mark of Bloomsbury Publishing Plc

First published 2016

Copyright © Christopher DuVal 2016

British Library Cataloguing-in-Publication Data
A catalogue record for this book is available from the British Library.

PB: 978-1-4725-2665-6
ePDF: 978-1-4725-3255-8
ePub: 978-1-4725-2216-0

Library of Congress Cataloging-in-Publication Data
A catalog record for this book is available from the Library of Congress.

Typeset by Integra Software Services Pvt. Ltd.
Printed and bound in India

CONTENTS

ABOUT THE AUTHOR

Christopher DuVal is on the faculty at the University of Utah, where he teaches Acting, Stage Combat, and Voice in the Actor Training Program. Chris has worked at the Oregon Shakespeare Festival for over fifteen years, teaching stage combat, and working on many productions, including *The Heart of Robin Hood*, *Troilus and Cressida*, *The Three Sisters*, *The Cherry Orchard*, *The Trip to Bountiful*, *Dead Man's Cell Phone*, *Comedy of Errors*, *Twelfth Night*, *Henry V*, *Love's Labour's Lost*, *The Tempest*, *Othello*, and *Henry VI Parts I*, *II*, and *III*. He has also extensively acted, taught, and fight directed at other regional theatres and universities across the country, including at the Dallas Theater Center, Sacramento Theatre Company, Laguna Playhouse, Shakespeare Orange County, Utah Shakespeare Festival, Syracuse Stage, Pioneer Theatre Company, Idaho Repertory Theatre, South Coast Repertory, Stanford University, Chapman University, San Jose State, California State University Fullerton, University of Idaho, and many others. He received his MFA from the University of California, where he studied acting with Dr Robert Cohen and voice/speech with Dudley Knight. Chris is a Certified Teacher with the Society of American Fight Directors, a Senior Level Instructor of Theatrical Combat with Dueling Arts International, an Associate Teacher of Fitzmaurice Voicework®, and holds a 2nd degree black belt in Aikido.

Video demonstrators

Michael T. Brown is a graduate of the Actor Training Program at the University of Utah where he received his HBFA in Theatre. While in Utah, Michael appeared in a variety of professional productions, including:

One Man Two Guvnors, at Pioneer Theatre Company, *The Skin of Our Teeth* (The Grand Theatre), and *Who's Afraid of Virginia Woolf* (Pinnacle Acting Company). Favourite university credits include: Romeo in *Romeo and Juliet*, Leo in *In the Next Room (or the Vibrator Play)*, Will in *Blue Stockings*, and Tournel in *A Flea in Her Ear*. Michael then moved to Kentucky where he was an Apprentice at the Actors Theatre of Louisville, for their 2015–2016 season. Michael now lives in New York City.

Brian Evans teaches voice and speech, stage combat, and acting in the School of Dance, Film and Theatre at Ohio University. He is an Associate Teacher of Fitzmaurice Voicework and a Certified Teacher with the Society of American Fight Directors. As an actor, he has worked at venues including Human Race Theatre, the Colorado, Illinois, and Oxford Shakespeare Festivals, South Coast Repertory, Porthouse Theatre and CATCO. Television credits include *Chapelle's Show* and *Judging Amy*. He produced and directed award-winning theatre while working in Los Angeles, at theatres including the Raven Playhouse, Metropole Theatre Works and Elephant Stage works. Locally, Brian is a proud member of Brick Monkey Theatre Ensemble. He received his MFA in Acting from UC, Irvine. Brian is a member of SAG-AFTRA and Actors' Equity Association.

Sensei Michael Friedl is a 7th degree black belt in Aikido. He also studied Shorei/Kempo Karate and Tai Chi. Friedl Sensei began his Aikido training in 1972 under Clyde Takeguchi Sensei in Madison, Wisconsin. Friedl Sensei became a live-in student (also known as an uchi deshi) for Takeguchi Sensei from 1975 to 1977 in Charleston, South Carolina. Friedl Sensei affiliated with Frank Doran Sensei in 1979 and has since been a student of his. Friedl Sensei was uchi deshi for Saito Sensei in Iwama, Japan from 1981 to 1983. There he studied weapons intensely and the Iwama style of weapons remains a strong influence in his weapons style to this day. Friedl Sensei has served as President of the California Aikido Association. He conducts seminars throughout the United States and Canada.

Sifu Jerry Gardner teaches courses in movement to students in the Actor Training Program at the University of Utah. He holds a PhD in Buddhist Studies with an emphasis in ritual and meditation from the

Ngagyur Samten Chockhorling Institute, located in the city of Manali in Himachal Pradesh, India. He performs and teaches numerous movement systems including Butoh, Viewpoints, Noh Theatre, illusionary and corporeal mime, mask work, ballet and contemporary dance, Pilates, Laban/Barteneiff, and the martial arts of Karate, Kung Fu and Tai Chi. Dr Gardner is the co-owner, director, and master instructor of Red Lotus School of Movement where he teaches advanced courses in Wing Chun Kung Fu and Tai Chi Chu'an.

Bonnie Johnson is a vocal coach with thirty years of experience. In the 1980s and 1990s, she performed with the Utah Opera Company and the Utah Symphony. In 2000, she became a Musical Director and directed over seventeen musicals. She trains actors for the High School Shakespeare Competition in Cedar City, Utah. In 2008, Bonnie became an Associate Teacher of Fitzmaurice Voicework (FV). Since that time, she has taught FV workshops throughout Utah including workshops at the Utah Advisory Council of Theatre Teachers and the Utah Theatre Association Conference. Bonnie has used FV in a number of innovative ways including working with young singers and actors, athletes and is currently teaching a young man with a spinal cord injury (SCI) to find his singing voice.

Heidi Wolf lives in Seattle, WA, and is a Certified Teacher with the Society of American Fight Directors. She has taught stage combat and movement at Cornish College of the Arts, Ear to the Ground Theatre, Freehold Studio, St. Lawrence University, University of Idaho, University of North Carolina School of the Arts, University of Puget Sound, and the University of Washington School of Drama. Heidi has produced stage combat classes and workshops in Seattle since 2006 as the founding member of Comrades At Arms, and she continues to train in stage combat, voice, dance, and non-western movement forms. Her current and recent activities include dramaturgy, fight direction, and ensemble performance projects. Her latest research publication was 'Take Up the Sword of Justice: Sword-Wielding Women in the Propaganda Images of WWI'.

FOREWORD

Chris DuVal's *Stage Combat Arts: An Integrated Approach to Acting, Voice, and Text Work* is unique in the canon of books about the stage combat arts. There are many texts that focus on stage combat technique for various weapon disciplines: What are the mechanics of footwork? How does one execute a Counter Parry 2? What are Capo Ferro's principal guards for the Rapier and Dagger? Chris has penned a book about *acting* and in so doing approaches the teaching of combat arts as an advanced acting class requiring the integration of movement, voice, and acting training. This book addresses the teaching of:

- Functional approaches to movement, ease, and the use of the self in the performance of staged violence.

- The actor's connection to breath, vocal ease and power, and the integration of breath, body, and text to safely create vocal expressiveness in scenes of extreme physical/emotional commitment to action.

- Specific explorations that encourage the actor to engage imaginatively with the given circumstances, psycho-physical action, and text of a fight scene with physical and vocal ease coupled with a commitment to extreme actions, heightened emotional stakes, and acting challenges specific to acting a fight (e.g. scoring the action, focus on the other, playing wounds, thought and action, winning and losing, death and dying, etc.).

Chris' gem of a book outlines a progressive approach to the means whereby one teaches stage combat as *an integrated acting discipline* drawing on his extensive experience and training as a professional actor, a martial artist, a teacher of acting and stage combat, and as an Associate Teacher of Fitzmaurice Voicework®. Each chapter builds upon the last, encouraging the development of awareness and skill to prepare the actor to perform scenes of extreme physical/emotional violence safely with a sense of ease and the appearance of reckless abandon.

Chris does this through a series of extremely well-designed exercises meticulously described for the teacher with easy to follow step-by-step instructions to help guide students through the process. These are accompanied in many cases by drawings and video to clarify and demonstrate both the teaching of the techniques and the execution of the exercises by students. The book is skilfully organized to allow each exercise to provide a foundation for the next, resulting in a blueprint for teaching the acting of a fight in any weapon style or discipline. Chris provides exercises in various weapon styles throughout the book including unarmed technique, single sword, broadsword, and knife. But whichever style is being used for a particular exercise, the focus of the lesson is on acting.

In preparation for writing this Foreword, I had the opportunity to incorporate many of these exercises into the class I am currently teaching in Rapier and Dagger with impressive results. My students are progressing through the class with a heightened awareness of physical and vocal ease and a focus on the class as an advanced acting class as opposed to a 'special skill'.

As an Alexander Teacher, I particularly appreciate Chris' emphasis on ease of use through the incorporation of Fitzmaurice and Aikido/Tai Chi exercises focusing on breath, the extension of energy, open attention, and working with a partner. After introducing these concepts, Chris applies the lessons learned both to the execution of stage combat technique and the speaking of text.

Chris consistently encourages students (and the teacher) to focus on process as the best means to achieve product rather than 'trying hard' or 'getting it right'. I have often seen beginning students of acting the stage combat arts – or any new skill – employ so much excess straining in their efforts to learn that they actually incorporate harmful habits of misuse into their execution of the techniques being taught. I'm reminded of F.M. Alexander himself commenting on this end-gaining approach to learning, stating, 'Doing in your case is so "overdoing" that you are practically paralyzing the parts you want to work'. Chris' pedagogical approach provides a paradigm for teaching that, in the hands of a skilful teacher, will help students prevent or eradicate this harmful tendency from the first day of class. Beyond the teaching of acting stage combat, Chris is actually teaching students *how to learn without excess tension*, a skill transferrable to learning or performing any discipline.

While this book is an excellent 'how to' manual for teachers of physical acting, it is also a valuable resource for students, professional actors, directors, teachers of the performing arts, and anyone wanting insight into the learning process. I wish this book had been available when I first began studying the movement arts nearly thirty years ago. Due to the clear descriptions of each exercise, it is a perfect practical resource to help a student or professional actor continue the daily practice and study of Chris' approach beyond the college class or professional workshop.

Finally, I'd like to talk a little bit about Chris DuVal. Chris is an extraordinary teaching artist, fight director, actor, and human being. He is truly a gentle soul, a renaissance man of integrity, and humility, possessed of a passionate curiosity about what it means to be human. I respect and trust Chris as a colleague and friend. I would love it if we worked together at the same university, town, state, or region, close enough so I could collaborate with and learn from him on a daily basis. That not being the case, at least I can now pick Chris' brain through the pages of his book.

Chris' gentle approach to teaching and coaching actors permeates every page and every exercise outlined in the book. I recently read an old article in *American Theatre* magazine based on interviews with six actors who teach that asked the question 'what makes a good acting teacher?' One of the actors interviewed, the late Marian Seldes, replied in part:

> I think it's all a question of giving the young actor confidence and the place in which he or she can develop without humiliation, without terror, without any of those things people warn you about.

If you've ever seen Chris teach, worked with him on a production, or taken a class with him at a workshop or university you know that personifies exactly what Seldes describes in the quote above. He is 'an actor's fight director'. His teaching is student-centred and he creates an atmosphere in the classroom or rehearsal that is challenging and encouraging, rigorous and safe. Chris loves actors and it shows. And he loves storytelling. His extensive experience as a professional actor gives him insight into the actor's process and the importance of physical action advancing the plot, revealing character and relationship, and having an emotional commitment to the heightened circumstances.

So, whether you are an aspiring actor, a teacher of stage combat, a professional fight director, or an acting teacher (and if you've made it this far in this foreword), I encourage you to add this book to your shelf today. It is an indispensable asset and an invaluable tool for integrating acting, voice, and movement technique in teaching the combat arts.

Paul Dennhardt

Professor, Illinois State University
M. AmSAT Teacher of the Alexander Technique
Society of American Fight Directors – Fight Director/Certified Teacher
Dueling Arts International – Master Teacher/Master Fight Director

ACKNOWLEDGEMENTS

This book would not have been possible without the generous support, advice, and editorial assistance of David Carey and Rebecca Clark Carey, co-authors of *The Vocal Arts Workbook*, *The Verbal Arts Workbook* and *The Shakespeare Workbook*. I am grateful to have received their invitation to contribute this work.

There are many people to thank within the development of this book, not the least of which are my many teachers in the Society of American Fight Directors, Dueling Arts International, and the Academy of Theatrical Combat. For video assistance, proofreading, and advice, a special thank you to: Paul Dennhardt, DC Wright, and Suzie DuVal. Particular thanks to Brian Evans for his assistance in the video and work as a contributing author in Chapter 3, Stage Combat Arts and Voice, and to Heidi Wolf for her assistance in the video and proof-reading skills. Thank you to John Sipes, Jason Spelbring, Michael Harding, Mike Brown, David Lee-Painter, Michael Polak, Ted Sharon, Jan Gist, Jack Greenman, Phil Thompson, Andrea Robertson, Bonnie Johnson, Sarah Shippobotham, Jerry Gardner, Sandra Shotwell, Ana Lemke, Kalika Rose, Ben Rosenbaum, and cinematographer, Anthony Sams. As an Aikido 7th degree black belt master teacher, Sensei Michael Friedl's generous teaching of Aikido-based exercises on the videos offers a deeply significant contribution to this work. His teaching has inspired me throughout my work. In addition, I am grateful to Jon Toppo – Resident Fight Director and Actor at the Oregon Shakespeare Festival – for the many years I have enjoyed co-teaching and collaborating with him on many projects.

My gratitude to Catherine Fitzmaurice and Saul Kotzubei, who have transformed my work as an actor, fight director, and teacher. I continue to be inspired by Fitzmaurice Voicework®. This approach to voice work has informed a great many of the exercises in this book. Fitzmaurice Voicework is an in-depth and deep study. The work presented here is only a very small portion of the many helpful benefits that this approach holds for actors studying the Stage Combat Arts.

I owe a large debt of gratitude for the inspiration that has been provided by the many teachers I have been fortunate to learn from, spanning a variety of theatrical and martial disciplines. While I have carefully endeavoured to honour my teachers and colleagues from whom much of my work has been inspired, any errors within the exercises or narrative are solely my own.

All my thanks to my partner in life – Suzie – and our daughter Megan, for the long hours of writing this book and without whom, there is nothing worth fighting for.

INTRODUCTION

Framework

The art of armed and unarmed stage combat thrills actors and audiences alike. The cut-and-thrust athleticism of fights in movies, stage productions, and in television can be tremendously appealing. While the specific techniques of performing stage combat effectively and safely are an in-depth study, the primary goal of this book is to introduce you to the art of stage combat as a training tool that uniquely integrates the body, voice, and the imagination within the actor-training curriculum. The text offers an approach that is meant to be used by a variety of readers – from the student actor who is new to stage combat and how it relates to acting to the teacher of stage combat seeking to incorporate further exercises that support acting, voice, and text work within fight rehearsals. This book is also for those teachers at high schools, community colleges, and universities who are looking for additional approaches to teaching voice, movement, and acting. The emphasis throughout is on exploring acting and voice methods as viewed through the lens of stage combat.

All actors working in professional theatre and in the diverse world of film and television recognize that developing physical awareness and skilful dexterity is an essential component of the training processes. Combat scenes can often be very demanding for the actor – physically, vocally, and emotionally – and for this reason the art of stage combat hones and tests the actor's integration of skill and craft. However, in the performance of scenes that require physical action, the abilities of the actors to specifically engage their imagination, voice, and responsiveness to text, as well as to develop interactive, creative choices within a fight scene may lag behind their physical proficiencies. How to integrate the mind, the spirit, and the body into a cohesive artistic instrument of flexibility, focus, and responsiveness is a process that requires frequent practice. This book will give you the tools to further develop this ability.

Three primary disciplines are used to serve as the foundation of all the exercises that are described: Stage Combat, Aikido, and Fitzmaurice Voicework.

Stage combat as the actor's tool

Stage combat as a training tool for actors has long been associated with deepening the performer's ability not only to perform the illusion of violence safely and effectively but also to deepen connections with an acting partner, to more fully pursue the practice of playing objectives, to engage with an embodied commitment to the playing of dramatic conflict, and to enable the actor to emotionally release with both freedom and energy. In this book, the training of stage combat is fundamentally used as a tool for actors working with text rather than solely as a physical discipline of athletic theatrical illusion.

The question that is frequently asked amongst stage combat students is: 'Is stage combat a "movement skills" class or an "acting" class?' I would propose that there ultimately is no separation between the various actor-training disciplines practiced by professional actors. The study of theatrical movement *is* the study of acting and therefore the study of human behaviour. Stage combat, without the direct application to the acting process within the training, can quickly be reduced to a series of standardized physical 'tricks' that, if not practiced often, are ultimately forgotten by the actor. However, this is not to minimize the importance of the acquisition of the skills of stage combat. For safety and effectiveness, a high level of proficiency in technique is required, and yet 'technique' cannot be the be-all and end-all. The techniques of stage combat need to be connected to acting, voice, and text work. Ultimately, perfectly placed parries and perfectly targeted attacks alone do not create a good fight. The specificity of the acted choices within every moment within a fight, using the techniques required for safety and effectiveness, is the ultimate goal.

In addition, the study of stage combat is potentially beneficial for students as a laboratory for voice work. The actor who is challenged to vocalize with freedom and expressivity will also not be able to create the illusions of violence convincingly or with appropriate vocal safety in a fight scene. A stage combat class specifically highlights areas of the actor's process that are in need of additional training or focus.

Aikido in actor training

Aikido, literally meaning 'The Way of Love and Harmony with Energy', is a Japanese martial art developed by Morihei Ueshiba in the 1920s and into the 1930s. Morihei Ueshiba achieved prominence as a powerful practitioner in many hard fighting styles of the martial arts, through which he gradually developed a physical system that intends to protect the attacker as much as it protects the one who is attacked. The foundation of the art is focused on harmonizing with an attacker, connecting to the breath, and dispelling the conflict by physically blending with an attack rather than by clashing.

This is not to say that Aikido is necessarily the 'best', and certainly not the only, movement system worthy of the actor's study for cross-training purposes. There are a great many martial and movement systems that provide helpful complements for the actor's training. One such art is Aikido in its emphasis on connecting, blending, and extending with a partner's energy, which can be a useful psycho-physical training tool for the actor. One of the primary areas of investigation in this book is about deepening your ability to remain connected to your breath and energized ease within a potentially tension-producing environment of theatrical physical conflict. The tensions induced by being on stage are similar to the tensions created by a physical attack in Aikido. Connecting with an acting partner through the mind, spirit, and body is an aspect to an actor's training that can be further developed from an exploration of martial systems of training.

It is important to note that, though Aikido exercises are demonstrated in this book, the goal of the work throughout this book is not intended to develop or hone martial effectiveness. In particular, the video demonstrations of Aikido throws should only be practiced under the guidance of a qualified teacher of Aikido. Their inclusion in this book is for the purpose of being a supplementary aid to your training with a teacher of this martial art rather than used as a tool to explore on your own. Serious injury can result from unsupervised training or unqualified instruction in the martial art of Aikido. The wide varieties of exercises in this book are all intended to aid your artistic exploration as actors and to develop creative possibilities within your embodied imagination.

Breath and Fitzmaurice Voicework

Fitzmaurice Voicework, an internationally recognized system for voice training, provides many beneficial exercises and approaches for the actor studying stage combat. Catherine Fitzmaurice, the Founder and Master Teacher of this work, developed a teaching method that emphasizes the actor's deep connections to the breath and the body in relationship to the voice and text. Through influences of Yoga, meditation, Shiatsu, and classical training methods, Fitzmaurice-certified Teachers work with actors in the development of increased creative responsiveness, vocal flexibility, clarity, and presence.

Many exercises in this book are intended to free the body from habitual tensions that inhibit the breathing and thereby inhibit vocal and physical expressiveness within a fight scene. The goal is to develop an integration of the breath and body so that physical and vocal skills are informed by spontaneity, flow, and emotional availability. The flexibility of the breath, skilfully coordinated, allows the fullness of your work to be shared with clarity and intent but without push or strain. With an increased connection to your breath in the demands of a fight scene, physical tensions are released, resonance increases, emotional availability deepens, and an authentic presence is more fully revealed through the precise techniques of stage combat.

Stage combat students can become frozen or forced physically, vocally, and emotionally from the anxiety of a skills test fight[1] or within the context of rehearsal and performance. If theatrical violence is taught solely as a series of illusions and tricks that allow the actor to hide behind tense 'martial postures', the breath has a tendency to become inhibited and the voice tightens as a result of unnecessary physical tensions. This pattern often results in physical tensions that have reduced resonance and inhibited effectiveness.

Benefits of the Stage Combat Arts

Throughout the book, I will occasionally use the term 'Stage Combat Arts' referring to the art of stage combat as potentially integrated with a wide variety of acting, voice, and movement teaching methods. However, it is very important to remember that stage combat training is a specific discipline in and of itself – in much the same way that disciplines of voice, acting, and movement training offer unique perspectives within their own particular methods. The intention within this book is not to conflate stage combat with other theatrical disciplines of training or with the martial arts, which are all worthy of intensive and independent study. Rather, my hope is to further remind the reader of the similar underpinnings of a variety of disciplines within actor training. The focus throughout is on offering experiential explorations in the areas of acting, movement, and voice using stage combat or basic martial techniques and philosophy as a potential aid within this development. While the book does not focus on the overall development of stage combat skill, the Appendix and the Bibliography offer many resources for the reader whose interest lies primarily in the acquisition of physical proficiency. Within the context of this book, the actor's work on the voice and with text is also considered part of the arsenal of tools for the student studying stage combat. The term 'Stage Combat Arts' assumes that the actor's work on the breath and voice is not disconnected from the physicality required within a fight scene.

In addition, this book does not attempt to introduce a complete overview of the many acting, voice, and movement systems that can be usefully integrated within a stage combat training curriculum. Many recognized teachers of stage combat have developed unique acting, voice, movement, and stage combat integrations that have not been described in this text. Contact information for these teachers and their specific teaching specialties can be found by following the links in the Appendix.

The benefits of the Stage Combat Arts are numerous and address many of the top priorities within actor training. The study aids the actor with the following tasks:

- Eases and eliminates excess tension and emotional, physical, and vocal blocks.

- Encourages the interactive process of engaging with an acting partner rather than allowing the actor to retreat within self-absorption.

- Deepens the actor's listening and response skills to physical, vocal, and verbal stimuli.

- Leads to the development of intention-based acting while still remaining flexible, free, and safe.

- Allows actors to powerfully and safely release into the heightened realities of both 'winning' and 'losing' within both fight work and scene work.

- Develops a vocal instrument capable of both extreme and subtle engagement without a loss of control, flexibility, or availability to spontaneous response.

- Informs the actor of the necessity of physical economy and of playing one action at a time.

- Engages the actor with a psycho-physical understanding of the integration between the body and the emotions.

- Integrates the actor's connections between skill and spontaneity, between craft and the actor's availability to impulse.

The Stage Combat Arts workbook: An overview

Each chapter focuses on individual topics designed to aid students' development of connecting the Stage Combat Arts to the overall tasks of actor training. Chapter 1, **Breath and Connection**, establishes the foundation of allowing the breath to be a vital component within fight sequences. In this chapter, specific exercises are explored that free the breath within the physical demands of the Stage Combat Arts. Chapter 2, **Intention and Focus**, aids the actor to more deeply connect to physical control, economy of action, and embodied intent within staged fights. Through a series of exercises, the actor is brought into an awareness of how the breath might be released and productively engaged within solo

Stage Combat Arts drills. Chapter 3, **Stage Combat Arts and Voice**, connects the actor to vocal possibilities within the heightened demands of theatrical violence, placing a focus on the development of a free, flexible instrument capable of authentic expression within heightened moments of violence. The focus of the exercises explores allowing the breath and the voice to be engaged but without push, strain, or unnecessary tensions in dramatic conflict. Lastly, Chapter 4, **Acting the Fight**, offers creative acting-based choices that are available when performing fight scenes. The actor is engaged with specific 'acting the fight' exercises in which the released breath, the voice, the text, and the body are further integrated.

Each of the four chapters will introduce readers to basic examples of safe and effective stage combat techniques. Elements from the theatrical disciplines of Unarmed, Single Sword, Single Rapier, Quarterstaff, Knife, and Broadsword will be explored through the combination of exercises and online video tutorials. The techniques include basic solo and partnered drills of choreographed sequences. In addition, the theatrical techniques of kills and evasions will be learned and demonstrated within the text and supported by the online video links. The video tutorials are intended to demonstrate an integrated approach to stage combat as a tool for actors working to deepen their connections with their acting partners, with their voices, and with their relationship to the text.

If you or your partner are new to stage combat, proceed through the choreography in extreme slow motion, at (or under) the speed demonstrated in the video tutorials, and only under the supervision of a qualified instructor. All video tutorials demonstrate a slow and neutral variation of each technique rather than an up-to-speed performance level of energy. These stage combat exercises are intended to be of a basic nature to ensure that you are able to explore the purpose of the exercises as they primarily relate to the acting process and voice work rather than explore them as choreographic or production options.

Each chapter consists of the following sub-sections: *Framework; Exploration; Exercises; Follow-up;* and *Further Reading.* An *Appendix* provides links and resources for further exploration. Additional *Teaching Tips* are frequently provided throughout each chapter to aid the process of the reader who is organizing the material within a course setting.

The following is a brief description of each of the chapter sections:

Framework

Each chapter begins with a *Framework* that provides an overview and summary of the chapter's contents. The *Framework* not only prepares the groundwork for the work that is to follow, but it also helps to contextualize the chapter within the greater context of actor-training. It is best to read through the entire chapter, starting with the *Framework*, to get an idea of how the work proceeds through the sequential building blocks of the exercises.

Exploration

The *Exploration* section of each chapter specifically prepares you for the type of work that will be more deeply explored in the chapter. The focus of the *Exploration* exercises is to develop one's curiosity about the work by connecting the imagination to the body and voice. Developing a curiosity about the work, as a daily creative habit, is the focus of the *Exploration* exercises. By carefully working through these *Exploration* exercises and prompts, it is possible to take what you have learned directly into the *Exercises* that are to follow. Allow these early prompts to further engage the possibilities that exist in your own work, and take note of these insights as you continue to work through the exercises in the remainder of the chapter.

Exercises

The majority of each chapter is comprised of a series of *Exercises* designed to explore, free, or refine the physical process of connecting the Stage Combat Arts to your acting process. Each set of *Exercises* is grouped under specific headings that address individual topics.

The Stage Combat Arts are very physical. Ensure that the exercises are approached with the utmost respect and care for the safety of yourself, your partners, and the space. These physical exercises require open, high-ceilinged spaces (at least 15′ high with no low-hanging lighting fixtures or other obstructions), supportive athletic closed-toe footwear, and comfortable workout clothing. Be sure to remove all jewellery – including bracelets, watches, earrings, necklaces, and rings prior to the exercises. Fingernails should be trimmed, and ensure your hair is tied back and out of the way. Work in well-ventilated, well-lit spaces, with floor space intended for movement as the optimal surface. Avoid hard cement or tile floors, as they cause increased stress on the knees and back. Sprung floors or floating floors are optimal. Ensure that tables, chairs, and other physical items in the space have been cleared away and that you have adequate space to explore without danger of making accidental contact with any other items or students in the space. Always maintain a safe distance from your partner of *at least* 6˝–10˝ at the furthest extension of any weapon. In addition, for safety considerations, each student needs 250 square feet when working on a solo weapon drill, and each pair of students needs 500 square feet of distance when working with armed stage combat techniques. Never cross the face of any partner with any weapon. (For more information, refer to the *Teaching Tip* found prior to the exercise 'Basic Parry System' in Chapter 1.)

Teaching Tip:
(https://vimeo.com/132084602)

(This video is intended for demonstration purposes only and should not be attempted or explored without the guidance of a qualified teacher of Aikido. Serious injury can result from attempting these techniques without proper instruction and training.)

Many of the exercises will seem very simple. In Aikido, for instance, one of the foundational techniques, *Shomen Uchi Irimi Nage* (a front strike followed by a blending defence), is often referred to as the 'twenty-year technique'. On a first encounter, the action appears to be relatively simple and yet within this simple martial technique, there are infinite variations and subtleties that are possible to explore. Similarly, many of these exercises presented in this book have a unique economy of movement, but they are far from 'simple'. Explore how the work specifically resonates for your students, and allow the possibility that students can engage with the exercises deeply and thoroughly.

Follow-up

Through additional questions and added exercises, this section is designed to help you further integrate your work with the exercises. The goal of the *Follow-up* section is to deepen how the work of the exercises engages your creative process. This section asks you to connect the work of the chapter to your everyday life of moving, breathing, and speaking. The more you develop a curiosity about your physical instrument on a day-to-day basis, the more you will engage with your unique artistry at more meaningfully creative levels within fight scenes.

The Stage Combat Arts video links

Stage Combat Arts movement is challenging to describe with written words alone. For this reason, an accompanying video component is a supplementary teaching tool of this book. Imagine trying to describe the process of what physically occurs within an activity as common as walking. The description would be long and overly complicated, when simply seeing a video of the action would immediately suffice. Similarly, some of the exercises in this book may read as more complicated than they are in physical practice. The suggestion is to read through the chapter, watch the video links, and then refer back to the written description of the exercise as you work to incorporate the physical patterns. In many exercises, there is an icon provided that directs you to an online video tutorial. Read through the exercise and then watch the video to ensure that all steps are being followed carefully and precisely.

The instructions in the stage combat video tutorials are particularly focused on the neutral slow-motion demonstrations of the safety elements of partnering, targeting, distance, eye contact, cues, and footwork as outlined within the individual exercises. However, the explorations regarding the acting, vocal, and textual choices within the stage combat exercises are purposefully not demonstrated in the video tutorials. These are elements that will be very unique to each student and are often best overseen within the context of a stage combat course or acting workshop.

> *Teaching Tip:* Many of the exercises are specifically written as 'solo-based explorations'. Without a qualified and experienced instructor present, learning partnered stage combat from a book is potentially a very dangerous activity and should not be undertaken. It is also important to note that in some of the exercises – and only with those that are engaged with opening the body to the breath and voice – the Yoga-like physical postures shown on the video are primarily suggestions to physically guide your students' work and do not require an overly strict adherence to the form shown. Each individual's body – its flexibility, previous injuries, and comfort zones – is unique.

Working with the Stage Combat Arts workbook

This book will ask that you engage with an openness and curiosity to developing new patterns of the body and the breath. Thinking of yourself as being in 'exploration mode', rather than checking to see if progress is being made, will ultimately provide a greater environment for inhabiting the work fully. Approach the work carefully but also with a sense of creative play. Much of the work will result in easily understood practices and skills, while other exercises begin to develop deeper questions and possibilities for your future exploration. Changing the patterns of physical self-use requires time. By acknowledging that there are patterns that you become newly aware of while working through the book, you will begin to create an environment of positive change.

> *Teaching Tip:* If you are leading a class and a student feels unwell for any reason, there are helpful alternative approaches with many of the body/voice work exercises in this book. On the other

hand, at times it may be best to ask students to carefully proceed through the occasional discomforts that arise when first exploring the breath. Create an environment in which the students approach the work with patience, curiosity, and a sense of joyful exploration even within the rigorous demands of the work. Care must also be taken to ensure students identify the differences between *pain* and *physical discomfort.* Pain is the result of torn ligaments, overly stretched muscles, and damage to bones, joints, and tissues. Physical discomfort, however, can be a common sensation within the training in the Stage Combat Arts. Slight stinging sensations in the hands or large muscle groups, muscles sore from use, unfamiliar sensations that arise out of newly found connections to the body and breath – are all examples of physical discomfort. These sensations are often a sign that the body is developing a more healthy engagement within the work itself. In addition, all of these exercises are equally adaptable to differently abled students. Without exception, the Stage Combat Arts are universal art forms that are available to any body.

An important aspect in training within the Stage Combat Arts is that various students of both genders can often have both conscious and unconscious reactions to physical touch. At times, some students may experience reactions connected to learning the illusions of violence that are uncomfortable or result in emotions that are surprising to the individual. It is important to be sensitive to the issues of physical connection and students' individual histories that can be brought to the surface within the training of stage combat. With all physical contact, it is important to establish 'safe zones' of physical contact. These areas that can be contacted are to be individually decided by the student and communicated to the partner within the exercise. This can be easily accomplished by having a student take the hand of their partner and make contact with various parts of the body that are deemed acceptable within any given exercise that asks for appropriate physical contact to occur.

There are as many ways to safely teach stage combat, as there are safe teachers of the art. Every experienced and qualified teacher will have subtly different teaching styles and preferences for how to teach the work. Explore the exercises you find listed here while remaining open and flexible to other related, but safe, approaches to stage combat that you may encounter.

It is the premise of this book that the basic physical foundations of the Stage Combat Arts are available to everyone studying the art of acting rather than a select few who have committed their lives to the exploration and refinement of these arts. The overarching goal of the book is to aid the training actor in the development of creative freedom, increased flexibility, greater release to spontaneity, deeper availability to responding to impulse, heightened ability to connect to a partner and to images, and a further understanding of creative play – all skills that are honed and aided through the application and exploration of the Stage Combat Arts.

Note

1   Many stage combat organizations sponsor 'skills test fights' in which students perform a choreographed fight, often accompanied by a scene from a dramatic text. Upon successful completion of a skills test, the student may receive a certificate as having demonstrated proficiency in the weapon style that has been studied.

1
BREATH AND CONNECTION

Framework

(This chapter draws inspiration from the teachings of Saul Kotzubei and Catherine Fitzmaurice. See the Appendix and the Bibliography for more information.)

Movement and breath are inextricably linked. To be engaged, connected, open to stimulus and emotionally available, the breath must be not only free but also productively engaged. The balance between an appropriate amount of physical engagement and excess tension can be a challenging mixture to find. The subtleties of where in our bodies we breathe, how much our breath is restrained through tension, and whether we are really breathing much at all significantly affects our availability as actors to both an emotional and physical life on stage.

The craft of stage combat physically integrates and complements work on voice, speech, and acting methods. And just as these theatrical disciplines have breath in common as their foundation, so too does stage combat require connecting movement to breath. This allows the actor's physical and emotional life to become more full, responsive, safe and creatively effective. In stage combat scene work, there is a tendency for actors, often unknowingly, to allow the breath and the body to become held and rigid with muscular tension. As a result, the responsiveness and engagement of authentic connections can decrease within scenes of dramatic physical conflict. This increased tension develops a compromised ability to fight effectively and safely, and reduces the level of connection between acting partners.

When human beings are faced with even the illusion of physical conflict, as we are in stage combat, the body reverts to an ancient autonomic 'fight, freeze, or flight' response that can result in the unconscious introduction of unnecessary physical tensions. These tensions can reduce the actor's grounding, focus, and overall ability to fully communicate within physical and emotional responses to stimuli. And this is to be expected. When the body is placed into postures of aggression and conflict, the breath is naturally affected. Actors' understandable fears of hurting another actor and of looking foolish or not tough enough can restrict the breath and the body. This breath-holding pattern, unconscious as it may be, limits the actor's availability and creativity.

When working with the breath and exploring violence, dual systems need to operate in harmony. The individual must deeply care about ensuring the safety of their partner. At the same time, the actor must be able to engage in physical conflict that very nearly can seem to overwhelm the character with passion. How to balance these two seemingly opposing forces can seem challenging – and often the balance can easily go astray. If the actor over-releases into the illusion of violence, they can damage their voice at the least and possibly physically harm their acting partner or themselves. Or the fight scene may remain a piece of false and safe choreography that lacks the potential of truly revealing the complexity of human beings in conflict. Or, the fight may become a complex display of athletic prowess but one that is divorced from the overall human context of the story.

The dichotomy is clear: an actor must remain relaxed within choreographed violence to allow the breath and the body to respond viscerally and authentically within the theatrical crafting of creating the illusion of wanting to kill someone or saving oneself from being killed. However, relaxation can also be taken too far. A relaxed body is of no use if, within this state, the actor does not have enough muscular control to maintain the grip on a sword in the midst of the fight. An *energized relaxation* is the quality that is needed. The professional athlete, dancer, or musician are appropriately engaged in specific areas of their bodies and are able to release other areas to enable themselves to be more open to heightened use. The same is true for the actor. The energy expenditure required is specific and focused.

Connecting breath and movement allows the actor to communicate with a greater facility of both skill and craft while enhancing the ability to reveal the complications, ambiguities, and fullness of human nature within dramatic conflict. In addition, the actor's source of physical energy is more fully realized when the breath and body are connected through the building blocks of energized relaxation rather than by physical over-exertion, in which unhelpful breath-holding patterns can develop. Tensions surrounding the breath result in narrowing the use of the voice to the point of inauthentic, damaging, or affected vocal use. The primary physical injury sustained in moments of theatrical violence is overwhelmingly in the area of vocal injury.

Many students practicing stage combat have the tendency to hold the breath and thereby reduce the artistic choices available. This tendency to hold the breath may very well have aided us as a basic survival tactic in human evolution. Remaining silent and still when faced with danger probably came in handy. As human beings *do* hold the breath in ways that sometimes serve us productively, it can be useful to use the breath – either held, actively engaged, or released – as an additional tool for you to explore in your work with stage combat and in the acting process. However, the habitual tendency to hold the breath when confronted with the illusion of violence, a tendency chosen by *default* rather than by *design*, can significantly affect an actor's ability to be authentically present, safe, and effective. Breath-holding as an unconscious and continuous base line develops physical tensions, reduces your availability to respond to impulse, flattens out the ability to reveal something true about the human experience – and in the world of stage combat – greatly increases the risk of accident.

Many martial arts connect their practitioners to an ability to be more accurate and effective through the use of the breath. Aikido teaches a variety of 'breath throws' that depend on the breath being used in ways that are both relaxed and engaged.

(https://vimeo.com/132084603)

(This video is intended for demonstration purposes only and should not be attempted or explored without the guidance of a qualified teacher of Aikido. Serious injury can result from attempting these techniques without proper instruction and training.)

Without this breath connection, the Aikidoist's effectiveness as a martial artist is relegated to muscle energy only. Incorporating Aikido-based drills and warm-ups into actor training can increase the physical skills of balance and coordination, and deepen the actor's connection to the breath. The Aikidoist's training to engage with conflict while effectively engaging the breath's energy is similar to the actor's training to remain in a state of relaxed, yet alert, 'readiness'.

The *Exploration* introduces questions and activities designed to aid your physical engagement. Exercises serve as foundational building blocks that sequentially develop greater skill in the Stage Combat Arts while also increasing your creative availability to impulses with both spontaneity and craft.

Exploration

I   Pay attention to your breath when you are jogging, playing tennis, or playing a favourite athletic sport. Where is it centred? Without forcing or causing anything you may feel is 'correct' to take place, notice the lowest place in your body where you can actually feel the in-breath. Notice for a moment or two what it feels like to breathe less, to override the oxygen your body might be asking for, and yet still remain engaged in the same aerobic activity. Revert to allowing the body to breathe as it needs and notice the difference.

II Take note of your breathing patterns throughout the day. Notice when you breathe and when you hold your breath. In what physical or emotional circumstances is your breath held? In what physical circumstances is your breath released? Is there a pattern? Explore what occurs when your breath is released in situations that are normally characterized by tension. In what ways might this increased breath awareness aid in your work of exploring the physical life of the actor?

III (https://vimeo.com/132084604) Watch this video of Sifu Jerry Gardner in his applications of Wing Chun Kung Fu and Tai Chi. Pay particular attention to his use of both a 'managed breath' and a 'released breath' at different moments throughout his movement. Sifu Gardner is also a practicing Buddhist Rinpoche (spiritual teacher). In what specific ways does the breath inform all of his work?

Exercises

Teaching Tip: The exercises in the chapter are organized under four headings: *Breath, Voice, and Connection*; *Finding Centre*; *Active Listening*, and *Breath and Extension with a Weapon*. Explore the following solo and partnered training exercises to develop an awareness of the breath. The exploration of this chapter focuses on finding a neutral origin of your work to allow for increased freedom of choice and availability to impulse. Within fight choreography, there is no room for physical 'improvisation'; nevertheless the actor must live *internally* with the possibility that the breath and the voice may be open to a degree of flexibility and freedom within a fight scene.

Breath, voice, and connection

The Autonomic Nervous System is the process that controls elements of our physiology that are generally beyond our conscious control, including our heartbeat, digestion, perspiration, and respiration rate. Breathing is also ultimately within the control of this system. We can certainly hold our breath, however, at a certain point of oxygen deprivation the Autonomic Nervous System will kick in, causing unconsciousness to occur so that the body may recalibrate to its natural state of breathing.

The Central Nervous System, where the conscious functioning of behaviour is housed, integrates and coordinates all activity of the body that is within our control. We have learned to control our breath through the central nervous system as protection against emotional and physical harm when we feel threatened. In times of stress, the body tightens and the breath is limited or held. In a very real sense, the more you breathe, the more you feel; and the less you breathe, the less available you are to stimulus and creative choice. When trying to control our feelings, we limit the use of the breath. The lump in the throat, the caught breath, the tight shoulders, the impenetrable militaristic 'toughness' associated with masculinity, and the artificial postural ideal of femininity are all societal responses that can contribute to a restricted breathing pattern. For actors, these patterns of unconscious habits can lead to a limited physical, vocal, and emotional availability as artists.

Through careful and specific explorations, it is possible to recover the ancient wisdom of the body and its connection to a released breath. However, there is an important difference between a 'released breath' and a 'managed breath'. A 'released breath' allows the body to breathe *you*. The breath falls into your body and out on its own accord, without any conscious control and in its own rhythm. This development of an allowance of the breath is the ideal place to start for actors preparing for work within a fight scene. Later, we will explore a 'managed breath' and will discuss ways in which actors can use this breath management as an artistic choice.

Connecting to breath (15–20 minutes)
(https://vimeo.com/132084605)

(I am grateful to Catherine Fitzmaurice for first introducing me to this process.)

Explore the following exercise by engaging only the areas of your body that are being directly engaged and leaving the surrounding musculature, and your breath, to remain free.

1 Lie down on the floor, on your back with a Yoga mat or tumbling mat underneath you. It might be helpful to place a book or a pillow underneath your head to allow your neck to stay aligned. Extend your legs out from your body.

2 Start to be aware of those parts of you that are touching the ground and those parts that are touching the air. Try not to change anything or attempt to achieve a physical ideal. Simply take a few moments to be aware of your body in space.

3 With your legs extended and feet separated by approximately 18″, turn your toes together with your heels apart. As the ribs expand and the diaphragm descends, the breath drops in. Feel the tension at the base of your spine. As the breath falls out, allow that tension at the base of the spine to release your legs and feet outwards to their natural and normal position.

4 Rest and allow yourself to breathe naturally. There is no need to take deep breaths in this position, as clearly your activity of lying on the ground does not require a deep oxygenation of your system.

5 Push the palms of your hands down into the mat. Feel the tension between your shoulder blades. On a breath out, release the tension from between your shoulder blades, allowing your arms and hands to turn upwards towards the ceiling while still remaining on the floor.

6 Place your attention now on the space between the small of your back and the floor. Isolating only those muscles necessary, slowly start to bring the small of your back towards the floor. Feel the tension this creates in your lower back. After a moment or two, allow the breath out to also release your lower back, thereby returning your spine to its natural and normal curvature.

7 Place your attention on the space between the back of your neck and the floor. Allow the back of your neck to move downwards towards the floor. Keep in mind that you will not be successful with placing the back of your neck completely on the floor, and that is not the goal. It is only the experience of mild muscular holding that we are looking to identify and release.

8 As you breathe out, allow your neck to return to its original and relaxed position.

9 Lastly, allow your jaw to release to gravity letting it relax towards your chest and towards the floor. The lips will be *slightly* open. Feel the temperature of the air between your lips.

10 Allow yourself once again to be aware of what parts of you are touching the floor and what is in contact with the air. At this point you might experience a slightly different awareness of your body in space and its connection to gravity.

11 Place your attention on your breath. Notice the nature of your breath without trying to change it or judge it. You are perfectly good at breathing.

12 Notice what parts of you move in response to the breath. Explore by being simply curious about the sensations you experience in relationship to your breath rather than attempting to control the experience.

13 Notice that there is a slight pause after your out-breath, before the next in-breath. And be aware that this slight pause is of a different length for every in-breath. As a reminder, the breath is certainly 'controllable' and we can override the 'pause' telling us when and how much to breathe. However, when we start to tune into the body's natural breath that lies deeper than our conscious control, we begin to bring ourselves into the present and allow ourselves a greater capacity to be responsive to stimulus.

14 Roll over to one side and then onto your knees. Tuck your toes under your feet and rock yourself back into a squatting position, with your feet flat on the ground. Float your tailbone to the ceiling, with your torso and head released to gravity, and gently begin to roll up your spine vertebra by vertebra. Allow yourself to continue breathing, easily, and naturally, as you roll up your spine to a standing position.

15 Check in with how your breath and body feel different having explored this exercise.

As an additional exploration, try visualizing a piece of fight choreography while remaining supine in a lying position, within this state of energized relaxation after completing this exercise. Research has shown that visualizing physical skills prior to performing the action holds great benefits for athletes prior to their competitive events.

Discussion

- Did you experience some energy or increased breath after you stood back up? If you continue to explore in this way, you will soon find that contacting a neutral state prior to any physical work begins to allow you greater energy and potential vitality.

- In what ways is contacting the breath and relaxation prior to a fight rehearsal as important as warming up the muscles for physical engagement?

Partnered release (30 minutes)
(https://vimeo.com/132084606)

(I am grateful to Professor Annie Loui, by whom I have been inspired and have adapted the following two exercises in my own work.)

Physically contacting a partner to aid in their energized relaxation can be a useful warm-up or cool-down. Partners in stage combat scenes are often in close proximity and are frequently asked to engage with each other through physical contact. Exploring safe levels of touch, by directly helping each other contact a more grounded energy through a warm-up, can be a useful practice prior to fight scenes. Stage combat's emphasis on always ensuring your partner's safety is further facilitated by an exploration of the following exercise. In addition, even within scenes that do not require physical violence, engaging within this work potentially increases a deeper connection between you and your acting partner.

Teaching Tip: It can be useful to remind students that the goal of relaxation is not to create a lethargic state. Rather, it is about going deeper into our energy than the 'caffeinated' energy where we often tend to live in various degrees of hyper-engagement. Once the actor begins to explore the nature of engaged relaxation and grounding, he or she is immediately provided with more focus and more useful energy as a foundation for the work to follow. In addition, it is likely that same-sex partnering will often occur within a class. Depending on the maturity level and age of the students, it may be necessary to adjust the pairings to ensure all students are comfortable and able to focus on the work.

---

1   Partner A starts lying on the ground on their back. Partner B sits quietly near the head of Partner A, coordinating their breath pattern with the breath of Partner A.

2   Partner B gently lifts Partner A's head off the floor an inch or two. Partner A should allow the full weight of their head to be

given to Partner B. Partner B is responsible for supporting the full weight of Partner A's head.

3   Partner A can allow their sighs to be vocalized as the head is supported off the floor. Allow the breath to carry the voice (or 'vibration') effortlessly up, through, and out of your empty torso.

4   After a few moments of simply holding the weight of Partner A, Partner B may now start to gently and slowly explore motion of Partner A's head and neck. Bring the chin slowly towards the chest. Turn the head to look gently towards the left and right. The goal is not to 'stretch' Partner A's neck muscles but rather to gently allow Partner A to experience the release of their head and neck. After a few minutes, gently replace Partner A's head back down onto the floor.

5   Partner B moves down to the upper chest of Partner A, standing or kneeling over Partner A's torso. With the palms on the upper chest area below the clavicles, Partner B will extend energy downwards and upwards through their hands and into the upper chest and shoulders of Partner A. Allow this downward-placed energy to initiate on the breath out from Partner A. Repeat four times.

6   Partner B now moves down to the floating ribs of Partner A. Placing his or her hands around the ribs with the fingers spread wide, Partner B will contact Partner A's rib cage area. Partner A will allow the hands of Partner B to spread wide as Partner A expands the ribs outwards on the in-breath. On the breath out, Partner B will help the breath to be gently expelled by adding an inward energy to the ribs as they release back to their relaxed position. Repeat four times.

7   Partner B now moves down to the hip protuberances of the iliac crests, the two hard bones of the pelvis that are in front and near the top of the pelvis. Partner B will place the palms of his or her hands on the two iliac crests with the fingers pointing towards the head of Partner A. Partner B's hands gently provide forward energy throughout Partner A's breath out. This subtle movement will release the lower back towards the ground, both lengthening and relaxing the lower back. Repeat four times.

8   Partner B moves down to place his or her palms on Partner A's knees. With very gentle engagement of energy into the knees – *not a push* – Partner B will apply subtle downwards contact into the knees on the breath out of Partner A. Repeat four times. In the event of any previous knee injury of Partner A, this step may be omitted.

9   Moving down to the legs, Partner B – with a hand under the ankle and a hand under the upper calf, will gently bend the leg of Partner A so that the foot is now flat on the floor. The same procedure will be repeated with the opposite leg. Partner B, by placing the hands on the top of the lower leg (below the knee), will raise both bent legs up towards the belly of Partner A. On Partner A's breath out, Partner B will gently direct the legs of Partner A towards the belly. On the breath back in, the legs will be released back to allow the breath of Partner A to drop back in. Repeat four times. At the conclusion, gently bring the legs, one at a time, back down towards the floor. As the legs are straightened, ensure this action is accomplished slowly and with complete control throughout the return to the ground to avoid any jarring of a sudden straightening to the knee joints.

10   Partner B will now take hold of Partner A's toes. Giving gentle but firm forwards and backwards impulses, the entire body of Partner A can be given an energizing 'bounce' sensation.

11   Once again, Partner B returns to the head of Partner A and supports the weight of the head and neck. Notice any differences in the weight that is now released to Partner B in comparison to the weight given at the beginning of the exercise. As before, explore gentle movement forwards and from side to side as Partner A allows the weight of their head to be given to Partner B. Gently place Partner A's head back onto the mat.

12   Partner A can now start to speak a prepared text while his or her head is being supported. As Partner B supports the head, Partner A can begin adding more intent and volume to the text while still allowing a freedom and energized relaxation of energy to remain present within the body.

13   Complete the exercise by Partner B placing one hand across the forehead of Partner A. The other hand is placed on top, with the fingers pointed in the opposite direction to the hand beneath.

On a breath out, Partner B will extend gentle energy downwards into the 'third eye' area of Partner A. On the breath back in, release the downwards energy of the hands. Repeat four times.

14 Take a few moments to discuss with your partner what was discovered and then switch.

Alignment and release (10 minutes)
(https://vimeo.com/132084660)

As is the case with the previous exercise, this exploration provides an opportunity to further aid the grounding and connection to an acting partner. The goal for both partners is to ensure that the breath remains free and the body centred yet energized and engaged for potential action. This exercise will help facilitate an increased opening and connection to alignment, breath, grounded energy, and energized release.

1 Partner A stands in a neutral position with the feet slightly wider than shoulder-width apart. Partner A will slowly roll down his or her spine to drop over from the waist. Arms are released to gravity from the shoulders. The head drops off the top of the spine towards the floor. The jaw is released.

2 Partner B stands next to Partner A.

3 Partner A – dropped over – should allow the knees to be bent with the torso/groin/belly areas released to gravity between the thighs. Allow the neck to release from between the shoulder blades. Let the feet be in a comfortably wide position apart.

4 With gentle placement of the fingers on the back of Partner A's head, Partner B will easily and softly give subtle and slow impulses to the back of the head to gently remind Partner A to release the head downwards to gravity.

5 Partner B will gently tap Partner A's torso, legs, hands, arms, and feet. As an option, the legs and arms can be 'squeezed out', as if each limb is a large tube of toothpaste, by applying gentle pressure and sliding from the thigh to the ankle and from the shoulder to the wrist.

6 Starting at the base of the spine, using the tips of the fingers, Partner B will gently and slowly 'walk up' the spine of Partner A.

As each vertebra is physically and gently contacted, Partner A will slowly begin to roll up, 'building' one vertebra on top of the other, allowing the knees to remain soft and the breath to stay easy and released.

7   Partner A allows the arms and shoulders to remain released to gravity. Let them hang down in front until the upright position of the torso naturally releases them into their familiar position.

8   The seven cervical vertebrae of the neck extend up and into the base of the skull, rising nearly to the area located between the ears. Continue to build up all of those seven cervical vertebrae until Partner A's head is allowed to gently float on top of the spine. Have Partner A imagine his or her head as a buoy floating on a calm lake.

9   As Partner B releases contact, ask Partner A to visualize – without the effort to 'do' anything – that his or her back is lengthening and widening, his or her chest softening and widening, his or her shoulders releasing to gravity, his or her knees softening and releasing. Without the need to overly 'adjust' their physicality, Partner A can imagine that there is space and fluidity between the bottom of the rib cage and the hips.

10 Partner A should now walk around the room, exploring what it is to be in easy movement. Explore tempo, distance, and sitting/ standing/kneeling/lying-down positions with the movement. Be careful to watch for stiff, robot-like movement in this newfound connection to alignment. Exploring what a flexible instrument feels like is the goal, rather than immobility and stiffness. It is helpful to be reminded that what is *familiar* is not necessarily what is *natural*.

11 Repeat with the other partner dropping over and proceeding through the series of steps listed above.

Discussion

- Take a moment to discuss with your partner in what ways this sense of release and alignment is useful for the actor preparing for a fight scene.

- In what ways does your breath and sense of energized readiness feel different or the same after completing this exercise?

- What makes it challenging for an actor to stay aligned and released when exploring staged violence? In what ways can this gentle warm-up or warm-down help to encourage the habits of breath connection and physical safety within fight rehearsals?

Finding centre

The Stage Combat Arts, including many systems of movement and voice work methods of training, often emphasize the 'centre' of our physicality as being the source of our connection and effectiveness. This physical area is often described as being located approximately two inches below your belly button and about two inches within your abdomen. Engagement to your centre is helpful, in that it increases your access to committed energy in a stage fight and allows you to remain grounded, flexible, connected, and focused within your work on fight scenes. The following exercise begins to explore what this connection to your centre feels like and how to develop an increased sensitivity to moving and engaging from this centre.

We all know what it is to 'jump up'. Explore what it means to 'jump up' several times. Next explore what it means to 'jump down'– gently but with energy and being careful not to put too much pressure on the knees, ankles, and feet. Imagine jumping several inches into the ground. Allow most of your energy to jump downwards with the knees bent. Feel the difference when you connect to a more grounded, energized, and physically lower level of energy. Try to 'jump down' silently – with little to no noise of your feet making contact with the ground.

Many actors tend to be very chest-based or even head-based in their energetic engagement with the world. This exercise of 'jumping down' can serve as a reminder that a more useful connection to an economical use of physical energy is located at the centre, not in the extremities. This awareness that the motor of your energy is in your centre can immeasurably aid your work, helping to sustain both the fight and the text work that often accompanies fight sequences within productions.

Freeze! (10 minutes)

1   As a group, start to walk around the room in a random pattern. After a few moments, begin to pick up the pace. Change

directions. Sit down. Lie down. Sit up. Stand up. Jump up. Walk. Pick up the pace. Jog! Run! Freeze!

2 Explore the possibility that a call to freeze the body does not necessarily require a freezing of the breath. Remember that a controlled and managed physicality does not need to result in excess tensions within the body or a controlled and managed breath.

3 Once again, begin walking around the room. After a few moments, pick up the pace. Change directions. Sit down. Lie down. Sit up. Stand up. Jump up. Walk. Pick up the pace. Jog! Run! Freeze!

4 On this Freeze, start to speak a memorized piece of text, allowing the body to be somewhat physically controlled while the breath and voice are able to be free and released.

5 Continue exploring in this manner, calling for a freeze of movement while exploring a freedom of text within a physically held or even in a possibly somewhat contorted, physically frozen shape.

6 Repeat several more times.

Teaching Tip: The tendency on the call to 'freeze' will be held breaths. Remind students that it is possible for the breath to be free, flexible, and full of potential within a still (or even 'frozen') physicality. In fact, a breath that is open and released allows the student greater success at 'freezing' the body in this exercise.

Discussion

- In what ways was the body more grounded when the breath was engaged and free rather than frozen or held?

- How was it possible to connect with text and breath while your physical movement was 'frozen'?

- Within this exercise, what did you discover that was new or surprising in your text?

Balance warriors (10 minutes)
(https://vimeo.com/132084661)

This exercise further explores the concept of experiencing your centre of gravity and balance. Being able to connect with a partner through grounded energy and a focused sense of physical ease is vital to remaining safe and present with an acting partner in a choreographed fight.

1   Stand facing your partner, centre-to-centre, with feet comfortably placed slightly wider than hip-width apart.

2   Challenge yourself to be silent and focused only on your partner during the exercise.

3   Bend your knees so that the stance resembles what is known in some martial disciplines as the 'horse stance': both feet in parallel, with the toes pointing forwards and the knees bent and aligned over the feet. Imagine the knees as shock absorbers. Allow the breath to be released.

4   Both partners now bring their hands up to face each other, palms to palms but separated by approximately 8″–12″.

5   The goal is to attempt to unbalance your partner with palm-to-palm contact. If a partner steps forwards or back, the other partner 'wins' that round.

6   The contact made between the palms of the hands is characterized as short bursts of energy – 'slapping' your partner's palms with yours to try and unbalance your partner.

7   Both partners can push at the same time or one partner can push and the other may opt to absorb the push.

8   If you feel yourself about to tip over, either forwards or backwards, explore what happens when you allow the breath to deepen even further and allow the knees to bend further to lower your centre of gravity.

9   Find the opportunities to potentially lose. Allow yourself full engagement with your partner and revel in those times you lose.

10 Explore the differences that are experienced when the breath is held and the knees straight and locked. Experience the lack of

physical balance and flexibility that occurs when the breath is even minimally held and the legs slightly straightened.

11 It is very important that both partners understand that no contact can be made with any part of the partner's body other than their palms. To disengage from the game, place your hands by your side.

Centre bounce and twist (10 minutes)
(https://vimeo.com/132084662)

(I am grateful to Sensei Michael Friedl, from whom I initially learned this warm-up.)

This warm-up is borrowed from the practice of many Aikido teachers' in class warm-ups, which encourages the development of a breath connection to your centre. It is a physical exercise that prepares both the mind and body for the energized release of physical engagement that is a significant aspect of stage combat. It is a common misconception that muscle use or force is the source of our power. In reality, there are much more powerful ways to move and respond authentically and with physical commitment by developing a deeper awareness of our centre as the potential origin of all physical and emotional engagement.

1 With your feet a comfortable distance apart, gently bounce up and down – leaving the ground only slightly. Allow the breath to release as you bounce. Allow the shoulders to release.

2 Bounce side to side (eight times). Imagine you are skiing down a mountain and easily, yet energetically, jumping side to side as you navigate the twists and turns of the slope.

3 Bounce on one foot. Then bounce on the other (eight times).

4 Bounce and gently twist your torso and hips in opposite directions (eight times).

5 On the final jump, land with your feet spread slightly wider than shoulder width apart. The knees are softly bent. Allow the breath to release on this final landing.

6 With your knees remaining bent, start to twist from your centre but allow your arms to stay released. Your arms will start to follow the natural movement from your centre. The movement of your hips will begin to bring your arms naturally into a rotation.

7   Imagine your 'motor' being your centre, located two inches below your belly button, and that this motor of your centre is what drives your arm movement. Your arms move solely as a result of your centre moving.

8   Now start to subtly engage your arms and your centre at the same time. Start at 10–20 per cent of engagement with your arms. You are now adding energy to your arms: they are no longer flopping side to side, but their primary motor or source of energy remains at your centre. You should be adding energy to the movement of the arms but not so much that they become rigid and forced. Your arms should feel full of potential power, engagement, and extension within a sense of ease and release.

Discussion

- In what ways does the usefulness of connecting to our physical centre extend beyond stage combat applications for the actor?

- How is the energy of a fight scene usefully explored by subtly engaging with our centre as the origin of our movement?

Active listening

The practice of deeply 'listening' and being connected to an acting partner involves much more than an aural task of 'hearing' what is being said. It is the state we find ourselves in when we are interested in being heard and seen by another and when we are fully present with an acting partner. It is a primary task of the actor to listen holistically with more than our ears and to explore the means to connect with and respond to stimulus from our acting partner. It is possible to look at someone, to establish eye contact, and to not particularly 'see' or be in a true connection with that person. The goal is to develop the capacity to not only look but also to truly see and respond to your acting partner.

Walk, see, breathe (10 minutes)

(I am grateful to Master Fitzmaurice Voicework Teacher, Saul Kotzubei, for first introducing me to this exercise and work.)

Frequently making eye contact with a partner is a primary tool of ensuring safety and effectiveness within a fight. In real-life situations, we rarely look at each other to the extent that we are required to as actors. At times it may be tempting to think that the harder we 'look' at our acting partner, the better our performance will be!

An exploration of what it is to be present with another human being is vital for the safe performance of a fight. This exercise will help you engage and connect with your partner prior to your scene work or in the heightened physical and emotional demands of controlling a fist or a stage combat weapon with safe energy and extension.

1 As a class, start walking in the space. As you walk, be in your own bubble of energy without connecting with anyone else in the class, physically, vocally, or visually.

2 After a minute or so, start to check in via eye contact with other members of the class as you continue mixing and milling throughout the space. Do not stop to look at a partner: only start to briefly 'take in' the fact that other people share the room.

3 Continue to explore making eye contact with others in the space, but now start to spend a few moments in stillness with eye contact with a partner. After these few moments have passed, continue on to another partner.

4 In these moments of stillness, face your partner squarely, with your hips in line with your partner's hips.

5 As you continue to explore connecting silently with other members of the class, remind yourself that it is possible to look and see someone and still breathe. Simply notice when your breath becomes inhibited and remind yourself that it is possible to see someone and breathe at the same time.

6 Allow your breath to be free and natural. There is no need to enforce a particular pattern on your breath.

7   After a few rounds, explore the opposite: what is it to make eye contact and not breathe much or at all? Allow this energy to be present. In what ways might it feel familiar?

8   Once again, return to making eye contact with breath and allow this energy to inform your connections.

9   Start to make slow, gentle, and connected physical contact with other members of the class. Examples may include a hand on a shoulder, a hand placed against a back, a hand to a leg, etc.

10 Once you have made contact with someone with your hand to a body part of your partner's, stay in that moment for a few beats, and then move on to another partner.

11 After a few moments, start to make physical contact with other members of the class without using the hands. Examples may include gently touching a shoulder to a back, placing an elbow softly on a leg, contacting a shoulder with a forearm, etc.

12 Explore the differences between making physical connection with eye contact and without eye contact. Proceed slowly. Enjoy the process of connecting with an acting partner partly through your ability to breathe together.

13 After a few rounds, without talking or pre-planning, give 20 per cent of your weight to a partner in the class. Give the weight of only a single arm, a leg, or a percentage of your torso weight, for instance. After the weight has been received, return to neutral and continue walking to receive or once again give your weight.

14 Repeat this several times with different partners, and simply notice your breath as you do so.

15 As you meet a new partner, start with establishing eye contact and then proceed to give 20 per cent of your weight or receive 20 per cent of the weight of your partner.

16 Now give 50 per cent of your weight to a partner in the class.

17 Continue walking.

18 Now give 90 per cent of your weight to a partner in the class.

19 Repeat with other partners. Notice how your breath is affected.

Be curious about the possibility of giving or receiving weight and still allowing yourself to breathe easily and naturally.

Within choreographed fights, it can happen that even though a partner has 'looked' at their fighting partner, the technique proceeds without the proper safety precautions. Under stress, with the breath held, the 'eye contact' cues of stage combat can be established but without partners truly 'seeing' each other. This can lead to unsafe actions within a fight scene. Within fight rehearsals, it can be valuable to help actors establish a baseline of when they are connecting with a partner and when they are simply looking blindly through space.

Discussion

- In what ways is it natural or unnatural to look at someone and truly 'see' the person?
- How frequently are you in specific contact through the breath with others in your life?
- In what situations do you avoid making much visual contact? In what situations do you make frequent eye contact?

Guardian circle (20 minutes)

(I am grateful to the Education Department at the Oregon Shakespeare Festival, from whom this exercise has been borrowed for the purposes of stage combat training.)

Both partners engaged in a staged fight must be fully committed to ensuring the safety of their partner. *Safety first, safety last, safety always.* And similarly, good acting is often described as the actor being outwardly connected with an acting partner. Romeo must be focused on Juliet and engaged with what he wants in the scene and not thinking if he looks good in his costume. The same is true in a fight scene: the actor is served by being fully engaged in connecting with his or her partner. Once the safe mechanics of stage combat have been thoroughly incorporated, the actor uses the techniques learned to affect his or her acting partner within the intentionality of acting the scene while also maintaining 100 per cent focus on safety and precision.

This duality of the work can be challenging to acquire. It demands both an acted release of illusory aggression and a total fullness of extreme care. The exercise below will enable you to release fully into the precision of care that is vital for any fight scene to be successful and safe.

Teaching Tip: This exercise is best done with a class of ten to thirty students. It can be a useful exercise, especially for younger students, which can determine how capable the class is of making physical contact and responsibly ensuring each other's physical safety. If doing this exercise on a stage or raised platform, keep students well away from the edge of the stage.

1   As a class, form a large circle.

2   One member of the class will volunteer to slowly walk across the circle (Student A), from one periphery of the circle to another. This student will cross their arms across their chest and close their eyes prior to walking across the circle.

3 Those students on the periphery of the circle will stand with their feet hip-width apart, with their weight equally distributed on both feet, and with their knees softly bent. Their hands will be floating out in front of their bodies, palms forwards facing in towards the middle of the circle, in preparation to gently stop the student who is traversing the space.

4 The responsibility of all the students on the periphery of the circle is to ensure the safety of the one student in the middle. Noises, gestures, and actions that detract from the student walking with their eyes closed are discouraged. The goal of the exercise is to ensure that the student in the middle of the group feels 100 per cent safe and protected.

5 The students on the periphery will gently stop Student A, who has walked across the space, by placing their hands on his or her shoulders as he or she arrives at the periphery of the circle. Student A will be gently turned around to once again face the inside of the circle and provided with a soft and gentle physical impulse to once again walk across the space.

6 Repeat several rounds with different students, exploring the development of this trust within the group.

7 It is possible to protect and care for the student in the middle of the circle and to allow your breath to be free. It is equally possible, if you are one of the students with your eyes closed, to breathe while walking with your eyes closed.

8 Now explore having more than one student with closed eyes traversing in the circle. Students on the periphery of the circle must now be more fully aware of who is in the circle and what their individual trajectories are, prior to sending those who are 'blind' across the space.

9 Depending on class size, two to six students will be walking the space inside the circle performing blind walks while being physically cared for by the students on the periphery of the circle.

10 Remember to breathe, ground yourselves, and connect to the entire space.

11 The students on the periphery are now allowed to enter the space if there is perceived to be an imminent collision. Students

on the periphery will enter the space to stop one 'blind student' while another passes harmlessly by. However, if students on the periphery enter the space, they must do so with complete silence, calmness, and grounding.

12 After several minutes of this variation, remove the 'blind' students – except for one – from the space and reassign all (except the one) to the periphery.

13 This one student (with his or her eyes remaining closed) will remain traversing the space.

14 This student will now begin to pick up the pace.

15 All students on the periphery will maintain soft knees, allow their arms to be soft shock absorbers, breathe, and feel their weight and groundedness in the space.

16 The students in the middle of the circle will continue to release the breath.

17 It is possible that the student in the middle will be able to pick up the pace until he or she is traversing the circle in a light jog.

18 After several rounds, instruct the student to reopen his or her eyes and to rejoin the group.

Discussion

- In what ways is this exercise a foundational skill for actors learning stage combat?

- What are the challenges of being in the middle of the circle and what are the challenges of being on the periphery?

- What happens when the breath is held – either for those students on the periphery or for those in the middle walking blindly?

Push hands 1 (20 minutes)
(https://vimeo.com/132084663)

'Push hands' is a form of training practiced within the internal Chinese martial arts. It is borrowed and adapted here to develop an increased ability to connect with an acting partner at a deeper level of physical listening. Emphasis throughout this exercise is on allowing the breath to be replaced naturally and on its own accord. The shoulders, arms, and torso should remain relaxed with energized engagement.

The ability of actors to connect and listen is of high importance. The following exercise further develops this ability to connect psycho-physically prior to engaging within a staged fight.

1   Stand within hand-shaking distance from your partner. Partners should step forwards with their right leg forwards. Extend right wrists to each other so that the outside of the wrist of Partner A makes contact with the outside of the wrist of Partner B. Gently bend your knees into a soft plié. While maintaining connection and contact with arms gently extended – though not stiff – begin to shift weight forwards and back with your partner while maintaining a connection between your wrists. Make sure your arms do not collapse or become loose in the movement of your weight shift. Remain in a neutral and extended connection to your partner, with your knees bent.

2   Notice if you are breathing while you engage with this exercise. If not, gently remind yourself that you can move and breathe at the same time. Your breath can be released and available without any special 'breathing technique' – simply allow yourself to release the breath in whatever way feels most comfortable.

3   Allow the breath to lead the movement and imagine your body is following the action of the breath.

4   As a variation, repeat the exercise, but this time allow your breath to be somewhat held and shallow. After a few moments, return to breathing within the exercise with more fullness and release. Experience the differences. As before, remind yourself to breathe naturally without effort or excess management.

5   Repeat and switch sides.

Discussion

• How do these variations in your breathing (free and released vs. short and shallow) affect you differently?

- In which version do you feel more connected with your partner?
- What differences in connection do you sense with different partners?

Unbendable arm (20 minutes)

This next exercise will continue the investigation of connecting your breath to your physicality. Keep in mind the potential of the breath to increase your capacity to engage with full release and relaxed energy in connection with your partner.

Teaching Tip: For this exercise, it can be helpful to pair up students of a similar size and build. Care should be taken that all students work with gentleness and physical sensitivity to their partner.

---

1   With a partner, stand facing each other squarely, with the right feet of both partners placed slightly forwards. Decide upon a Partner A and a Partner B.

2   Partner A will place their right forearm over the left shoulder on the trapezius muscle of Partner B (avoiding the collarbone, shoulder joint, and neck of Partner B). The hand of Partner A is in a tight fist and the arm is straight but not locked. The fist is held in the 'neutral' position, with the thumb on top (i.e., as if grasping a hammer).

3   Partner A should hold their breath tightly, keep their fist firm and held, and use muscle energy to try and prevent their arm from being bent by their partner.

4   Partner B will place both of their hands on top of Partner A's bicep (*not* the elbow joint) and gently apply downwards pressure to try to make Partner A bend their arm at the elbow.

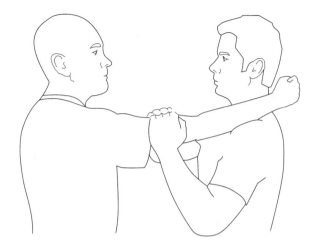

5   The goal for Partner A is to keep their arm straight, and the goal for Partner B is to bend Partner A's arm at the elbow. It is important for Partner A to allow the bend at the elbow to occur but to experience the muscle tension of trying to keep it straight.

6   Release contact and shake it out.

7   This time, Partner A will place their arm on Partner B's shoulder but will allow the fingers of the arms to be energetically extended out and behind Partner B (rather than held in a fist). Partner A will imagine that the centre of the earth holds their power. Imagine that this energy from the earth comes up through the feet, up the legs, through the spine, and out the extended arm of Partner A. The energy extends out the fingers of the extended arm, and imagine that the energy easily travels – like a tremendously long unbendable fire hose fueled by fast-coursing water – for 1,000 miles in the direction that the fingers are pointing.

8   Partner A will now continue breathing in a free manner, while Partner B once again tries to bend Partner A's arm. The more energy that Partner B expends on trying to bend the arm, the more Partner A's breath and energy from the centre of the earth extends through the arm and out beyond.

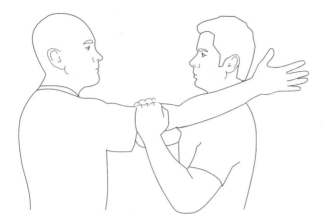

9 Partner A can continue to allow the breath to fuel and be energized by the focus line of this 'unbendable arm'.

10 Release, shake out and reverse the exercise for Partner B.

Teaching Tip: Throughout this book, terms and ideas related to 'Chi' (or 'Ki'), 'energy', 'connection', 'empty torso', and other similar images and metaphors will be used when exploring specific voice and movement work. The purpose is to further aid the students' experiential understanding as they process new ways of coordinating the mind and body. For some students, this way of working is very helpful. For others, anatomic and literal understandings of the processes involved can be more helpful. Regardless, it is important to recognize that there are various methods of introducing these concepts and that the realities of how the body works are an important additional investigation for students to explore.

Discussion

- What did you discover about extension and breath?
- Was the breath able to help you explore an increased sense of power and extension without an excessive use of tension?

- In what ways can you see the breath and its relationship to extension as a powerful, productive, and also subtle source of physical energy?

- In what ways does this exercise develop an ability to extend with energy and commitment but without excess tension?

The arm in this exercise is a line of focus – flexible, supple, relaxed, and yet tremendously strong. It can serve as an example for your entire physical instrument's expression, focus, and ability to be both highly directed and freely released.

One of the aspects that this exercise explores is that of 'extension' – a valuable concept for actors to explore, both from a practical standpoint of extending a weapon within stage combat but also from the mind/spirit/body application of what it is to work from the concept of 'extension'. Excess tension is not helpful for an actor, and the exercises below can be explored from a physical standpoint of releasing the holding patterns that can creep into the work. Particularly with the art of stage combat, it can be tempting to feel that 'muscling' through a fight is better. Certainly there are characters that need to *appear* desperate, effortful, or under great physical distress; however, the actor cannot afford to assume all of the character's tensions as his or her own.

Unbendable arm with text (20 minutes)

1 Repeat the exercise, and while connecting to the 'unbendable arm' with a connection to your breath, see if it is possible to also be connected to a piece of memorized text?

2 Allow the breath to *engage* within the exercise. Support the text with your breath, allowing the voice to be connected, open, expressive, and free. Imagine the breath and voice flowing up from your feet, through your centre, and out your 'unbendable arm' – connecting in a physical manner with your partner.

Wrist grasp (20 minutes)
https://vimeo.com/132084664

Fencing Masters teach a practice referred to as 'le sentiment de fer' – a term that means, in essence, 'sensing the blade' or 'feeling the blade'.

By touching blade to blade in an engaged weapon position, master fencers can feel or 'sense' the intention of the opponent and subtly perceive what the attack might be.

As a training tool for actors studying stage combat, 'le sentiment de fer' can also be used to develop sensitivity to the energy of a partner's body. In addition, it is a valuable practice for 'deep listening', a practice of listening beyond mere auditory signals. Your ability to connect in a kinaesthetic manner to nonverbal cues can be quite subtle. Truly 'listening' to a partner, on stage or in life, involves much more than only what your ears hear.

The exercise below is an adapted Aikido training exercise that develops this physical sensitivity of deep listening and can easily be applied to theatrical weapon work as well as investigations within scene work.

In preparation for this exercise it can be helpful to first spend a few moments exploring such exercises as the 'Spine Roll', allowing the body to reconnect to breath, release, alignment, and spatial awareness.

1   Find a partner. Decide who is Partner A and B. Stand facing each other approximately hand-shaking distance apart.

2   Partner A, with the right hand, will firmly grasp just above the right wrist of Partner B. Make sure the grasp is firm and fully connected, without being uncomfortable.

3   Once connection with the wrist is established, both partners close their eyes for the duration of the exercise. It is important that the work takes place in silence without talking.

4   Breathe naturally and easily.

5   As subtly as possible, Partner B will create an initial short impulse of movement with their wrist in one of four directions:

   a   Vertically Up

   b   Vertically Down

   c   Horizontally to the Left

   d   Horizontally to the Right

6   It is important that these initial impulses be subtle, indeed perhaps almost indecipherable to Partner A's grasp. This physical impulse can be explored as being almost 'molecularly' subtle and certainly too small to be perceived by an observer.

7　When Partner A 'senses' the direction of the impulse, they will 'follow through' with that impulse by moving their own arm in the direction that they sense the impulse is taking them.

8　Repeat the exercise with Partner B grasping Partner A's wrist.

Teaching Tip: At times, students might feel discouraged that they did not respond 'correctly' to the impulses they received from their partner. Or it may be that students feel excited and proud of how successful they were. However, it can be helpful to remind the students that the exercise is about simply exploring what it is to respond to subtle stimuli and to have a partner respond to those stimuli with a committed impulse to move the arm. In this way, the students are 100 per cent successful if they are truly physically listening to their partner and commit to following through on the subtle physical cues they receive, regardless of whether they are 'correct' or not.

Discussion

- After a few minutes of the exploration, discuss what you physically sensed from your partner.

- How does this ability to connect and listen through 'touch' alone potentially transfer to the actor's work within scene work?

- How might this awareness of deep listening connection also inform the actor's work in a fight scene?

- In what ways are both safety and theatrical effectiveness served by the ability of the actors to listen in a full-bodied connection?

Connection and extension (20 minutes)
(https://vimeo.com/132084728)

The work of connecting with a partner, through the careful process of deepening our ability to listen with the whole self, is not about working hard with blood and sweat. It is also not a condition of laxness and de-energization with an 'anything goes' mentality. Instead, it is about developing your awareness of how committed connection is brought about more by developing your sense of energized engagement rather than by increasing levels of tension.

This is an example of a subtle exercise that is made clear when observed in the video. Read the description below and then watch the video. Following along with the video with a partner will aid your understanding. After the basic practice has been learned, return again to refresh your memory of the sequence through the written description of the steps provided below.

When the word 'centre' is referred to, it describes that area two inches below the belly button and about two inches inward from the skin. You can imagine that this 'centre' is able to rotate in any direction.

In the following exercise, explore the differences between using overt muscled effort versus using a full-body engagement of energy.

1   With the left hand, Partner A grasps just above Partner B's right wrist.

2   The agreement that must be maintained throughout the exercise is that the person grasping the wrist (in this case Partner A) must maintain full connection with the entire hand on the wrist of their partner. Avoid the tendency to allow the grasp to occur with the fingers only. The entire palm must remain in contact with the wrist throughout the exercise.

3   Both partners should hold their breath.

4   Partner B allows the wrist to be grasped and turns his or her centre away from Partner A in an attempt to drag Partner A around him or her to the opposite side.

5   Partner B resists Partner A's muscled attempts to move him or her.

6   Both partners relax and shake out a bit.

7   Resume the exercise, again with Partner A grasping just above Partner B's wrist.

8   This time, allowing the breath to be free and unrestricted, Partner B allows the essence of the energy found in the 'Unbendable arm' exercise to allow the arm being grasped to

be extended and in connection to Partner A. The arm should not be tense but simply 'alive' and present with energy.

9 Partner B will imagine that the arm and the centre of his or her body (two inches below his or her navel) are connected. Imagine that if the centre pivots to the left, the arm must pivot to the left at the same time.

10 Partner B will imagine that the energy in his or her centre, extending out through the arm, is connecting to the centre of Partner A.

11 Partner B will now start to slowly pivot to the left maintaining his or her right arm in connection with his or her own centre. This should create the result of Partner A being drawn around Partner B's body easily and effortlessly.

12 Avoid any excessive muscle energy that tries to force your partner to move. Allow the energetic *connection*, rather than muscled force, between Partner B and Partner A to effect the movement.

13 What differences do you feel when you connect with your partner to affect the movement rather than dragging him or her around you with muscled force?

14 Switch sides and repeat the exercise.

Carefully observe the video tutorial to see other similar variations to this exercise that you can use in your own training.

Discussion

- What did you discover about centre-to-centre connection in this exercise? How can the lessons learned of the potential power of the centre be applied throughout the actor's work?

- How is it valuable to face your centre directly towards your partner's centre within stage combat?

Partnered quarterstaff connection (20 minutes)

In our daily interactions with friends, family, and colleagues, we do not often face each other squarely. We tend to offset our centres from each other. Notice next time you shake hands with someone that rarely do we face each other in a true centre-to-centre connection. Be aware the next time you are talking to someone and notice what the body positions are and where your centre of engagement is located. It usually is facing away to some degree from whomever you are talking to. Noticing this habit and *choosing* to connect your centre more squarely towards a partner's centre immediately develops a greater connection and ability to listen with the whole self. The physical practices of stage combat place an importance on connecting centre-to-centre when engaging with a partner.

'Cheating out' is a common direction that asks actors to face their partner at a 45-degree angle to be more fully in connection with an audience. As a rule blindly followed, this practice often results in a lack of connection between acting partners. The Stage Combat Arts provide a means by which actors are able to viscerally explore the energy values of centre-to-centre connection. It is certainly not that disconnecting your centre from your partner is a wrong choice, it is simply that if it is the *only* choice that is available to the actor as an unconscious habit, it invariably limits an actor's expressive potential.

There are times when a direct connection of centres is the most powerful choice. The lesson to be gained is that connecting your centre to your partner's centre is a gift of creative generosity. It is often a requirement in the Stage Combat Arts, and it can be an informed physical choice for the actor within scene work that can lead to deeper engagements.

Using a quarterstaff, partners will explore a form of physical listening with subtle body movements of the hips and centre. The challenge in the exercise is to avoid all conversation and to let the potential of dropping the staff be a reminder of practicing deeper levels of physical connection. Explore staying balanced and fluid throughout the exercise.

Teaching Tip: A quarterstaff is a European fighting stick, often made from hardwood, and has been used throughout history. Oak, ash, bamboo, or rattan poles of approximately one inch in diameter and – six to eight foot lengths are ideal. Closed-toe shoes must be worn with all weapon-based exercises.

(https://vimeo.com/132084731)

1   In a pair, Partners A and B will gently hold a quarterstaff between themselves. One end will be placed firmly against the belly of Partner A, and the opposite end will be placed firmly against Partner B's belly.

2   As a team, Partner A will start the exercise as the 'leader'. He or she will start to move forwards or backwards and Partner B will need to respond appropriately to maintain the position of the staff between the two partners. The staff is secured between the two partners, using only the belly as the point of contact.

3   Ensure your movement with your partner is slow and specific and that your knees are softly bent. This will further allow you and your partner to connect to the subtle clues of movement.

4   Allow the breath to be free and fluid throughout the movement. Explore how it is possible to move and maintain connection while still breathing, easily and naturally.

5   After several minutes, switch sides, so that now Partner B is leading the forwards and backwards movement.

6   As the exploration continues, find subtlety within the impulse to move. Connect to the physical clues felt and received by your partner. Rather than strong or sudden thrusts forwards or a sharp stopping action, find a softness and subtlety to the movement.

7   After several minutes, explore the exercise with neither partner leading or following for the entirety. The partner who is leading will switch spontaneously and the partner who is following will react with spontaneity as well.

8   With your partner, start to explore other directions of movement rather than the linear engagement. Circling, traversing widely through the space, and height differences can all be explored.

9   Further explore this connection using the following methods of eye contact:

    a   Explore while looking only at your partner's eyes

    b   Explore while looking at your partner's centre or solar plexus

    c   Explore while looking at the staff between you

    d   Explore with your eyes closed

10 Allow the breath to be free and responsive.

11 With eyes open but soft, start to explore interacting with another pair in the class. Is it possible to pass under and through another pair exploring the same exercise? With how much ease can this be accomplished?

Variation 1:

(I am grateful to SAFD[1] Certified Teacher Brian Evans for discussions with me regarding the variations of this exercise.)

1 Explore holding the quarterstaff between your and your partner's hands, either connected on the palms of both partners or connected by only the fingers of both partners.

2 As you move forwards and back, allow the energy extended to your partner through the staff to remain constant, with ease, and with a connection to a free breath.

Discussion

- What did you discover is an 'appropriate level' of energy and engagement for this exercise? What happens when partners engage with excess energy?

- How did your sense of listening to your partner change with your eyes closed?

- How did a sense of the eyes being 'soft' affect your connection to your partner? Does 'softness' necessarily mean 'weak' or 'collapsed'? In what ways can seemingly less muscle energy actually equate to more usable physical engagement?

Weight underside (10 minutes)
(https://vimeo.com/132084733)

In the martial art of Aikido, there is an importance placed on the practice of 'Weight underside'. This physical practice of exploring your balance releases tension and rigidity while allowing a grounded, stable platform from which effective movement responsiveness can occur. It is not a muscular 'pushing' or an attempt to unbalance a partner with overt muscular energy. Allowing our movement to have a natural weight and heaviness is part of connecting to our own innate gravity.

The word 'heavy' in this context does not mean immobile or sluggish. Moving with 'Weight underside' allows great fluidity and changeability. An awareness of your movement as emanating from your centre is the basis for developing 'Weight underside'. It taps into a vital energy that is fluid, energetically relaxed, and full of potential power. The following exercise explores the basic foundation of this principle and will be applied in later exercises with weapon work and textual explorations.

1 Partner A stands to the side and slightly behind Partner B. Partner A places his or her hands on the shoulders of Partner B.

2 Holding their breath, Partner A will now attempt to bring Partner B downwards forcing Partner B to bend their knees. Use only muscular energy to perform this action. Partner B should resist the attempt.

3 Separate and pause. Discuss what this feels like and whether Partner A was successful at dropping the weight of Partner B.

4 As before, Partner A reconnects with Partner B's shoulders in the same way. This time, however, Partner A connects through a sense of 'Weight underside' to Partner B and allows the breath to be full and deep. Partner A can imagine that he or she is connected both to the ground and to Partner B through a centre-to-centre engagement. Partner A's elbows stay low and relaxed, the shoulders remain released, and the breath is centred low in the body. The physical contact of the hands on the shoulders is imagined as occurring not only with the hands but also with – energetically – the entire body of Partner A being in psycho-physical connection with Partner B.

5 Explore your partner's relationship to balance – using softness and ease – and to their '3rd leg'. This is their balance point from which your partner is no longer able to maintain their balance but *would* be able to, if indeed they had a 3rd leg.

6 When Partner A drops his or her centre by slightly bending the knees, Partner B's centre should similarly drop – not because Partner A is forcing it to happen but because there is a physical connection between the two partners.

The practice of connecting in this exercise is intended to be an exploration of balance and the development of physical ease within energy. The actor needs to respond to their partner with immediacy and focus. Explore what it is to affect a partner through a relaxed but powerful energy rather than muscled over-effort.

Discussion

- In what specific ways might this exercise in 'Weight underside' connectivity be applied to connecting with a partner in a scene?

- In what ways does the internal energy produced from this exercise hold value for working on a fight scene?

Breath and extension with a weapon

It is of no value to explore one's freedom and 'relaxed readiness' in isolated exercises, only to retighten into habitual patterns of tension during stage combat or scene-based work. This is a primary reason that work on stage combat can be so useful, for it serves as a laboratory for the actor. The art of stage combat as an actor-training tool provides a means to work on skilfully remaining in a creative state within the high stakes of conflict found within dramatic literature.

Teaching Tip: The phrase '*allowing* the breath to fall into the body' and '*allowing* the breath to be released out' is used rather than 'breathe in'. The latter tends to introduce a sense of tension and effort into the breathing pattern. As human beings *do* experience effort and tension, holding or managing of one's breath can be quite useful in the course of representing dramatic conflict.

However, in the beginning stages it often proves more beneficial for students to fully explore the habits of breath release. In your students work, encourage that the breath can be held or limited only as a choice, not as an unconscious habit.

Basic parry system (20 minutes)[2]
(https://vimeo.com/132084734)

What follows is a basic parry system that is flexible and adaptable for a variety of weapons. There are many physical variations to all of the described parries below, based on the type of weapon the actor may be using and the instructor's particular stylistic preferences. While the focus is on the theatrically safe position of the weapon as it proceeds from one parry position to another, the student should be encouraged to allow the previous work on breath and partnered connection to inform the physical practice of these basic stage combat techniques.

In this book's exercises, all partnered blade work occurs with the true edge of the defending blade in contact with the true edge of the attacking blade. At no time does the edge of a blade contact the flat of another blade. In addition, the 'foible' (the last third of the blade closest to the point) is the part of the blade that attacks, while the 'forte' (the first part of the blade closest to the guard) is the part of the blade that parries.[3]

This exercise should be explored as a solo drill, without a partner. In addition, within the structure of a stage combat skills class, the techniques of attacks, parries, and footwork are often taught simultaneously. However, in this book the acquisition of stage combat 'technique' is not the primary purpose – but rather the focus lies in the breath, voice, and body integration with the imagination. For simplicity, all weapon-based exercises are described from the standpoint of right-handed students.

Within this exploration, focus on the process of physically engaging with these movements that hold imaginary martial intent while also avoiding an excess of physical, vocal, and breath tension that can accompany these actions. Allow the body and the breath to remain

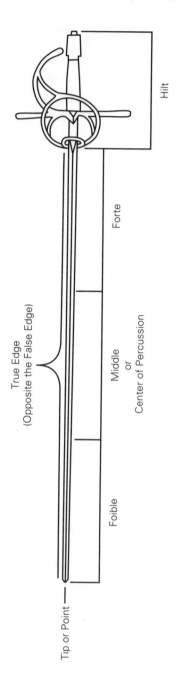

present and use only an *appropriate* amount of effort to perform the basic parry system exercise below.

Teaching Tip: [4] Even in a solo drill, when students are practicing the Stage Combat Arts with 3′ long swords or 6′ long quarterstaffs, this extra length quickly takes up a significant amount of space with a group of students. With training spaces that are too small, this can easily become a serious safety hazard. For this reason, it is highly recommended that at least 200–250 square feet *per student* is allotted for this solo training. In addition, in later exercises in this book when students are partnered with weapons and are moving together, at least 400–500 square feet *per pair* of students is the amount of space that is needed to maintain a safe training environment. For a class of sixteen students, 3,200–4,000 square feet would be an appropriately sized training space. In addition, ceilings must be at least 15′ high with no lights that hang below this level or any other obstructions that would obstruct the action of a sword or staff. Sprung or floating floors designed for movement work are the most safe and appropriate for this training. Avoid cement floors, hard tile, uneven ground, or slippery surfaces.[5] Closed-toe athletic footwear must always be used in stage combat exercises.

---

1 With a Rapier, find a space in the studio with safe clearance of the weapon in all directions. The point of the weapon must *never* cross the face of any other student. All areas of the face, head, neck, groin, and breasts must be avoided.

2 Gently wrap your hand around the handle of the sword. Hold the weapon as if it is a small bird, not so tightly that your grip would crush it and not so loosely that it would fly away. Place your forefinger through the guard, inside the pas d'ane, as shown.[6]

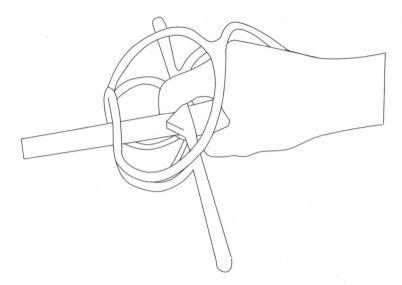

3   Place the position of your feet as if you were water-skiing, at shoulder width apart. Bring one foot (for a right-handed actor, the right foot), further forwards to point directly at your imaginary partner.

4   For your balance, ensure there is both width and depth to your stance.

5   Turn the rear foot on a slight 45-degree angle forwards and bend your knees into an en garde stance.

6   Your hips and centre remain facing towards your imaginary partner rather than being offset to the side, as in the sport of foil fencing. Your body and hips should be in a centre-to-centre orientation with your imaginary partner.

7   Your sword arm gently 'floats' out in front of your centre, palm down, with the elbow of your sword arm approximately a hand's breadth from your torso. The hilt of the weapon floats approximately at the level of your waist. The tip of the sword is directed outside your imaginary partner's body and should be directed below your partner's head, at the level of your partner's left armpit but off-line. Having the point placed no higher than the shoulder ensures that the tip remains below the area of the face.

8   The unarmed hand is floating gently in front of your torso with
the shoulders released.

9   Imagine space between your floating ribs and hip girdle.
Float your ears upwards. Imagine your back lengthening and
widening. Imagine your chest softening. Feel your breath low in
your abdomen and your feet firmly grounded on the floor. You are
grounded not only downwards but also aligned vertically as well.

10   Weight shift forwards and back, using your legs to smoothly
carry your torso through space. Throughout all the weight
shifting actions, keep your knees softly bent. Your head and
torso are able to remain stationary and physically silent in
the forwards and backwards rocking motion. The sword arm
remains still in the activity.

11   Check in with your breath in this rocking action. Are you
breathing? Where do you feel tension creeping in? Is it possible
to allow yourself to breathe freely within this movement?

12 Weight shift back, dropping the point of the weapon to your right (palm down) with the point *outside* the imaginary line of your partner. From this position, bring your right arm towards the left as if you were looking at a watch on your right wrist. The angle of your elbow should be at approximately a 90-degree angle. The true edge of the weapon is now facing towards your left. The wrist is not bent but remains in a strong alignment with your forearm in this parry. You are protecting the target of your left hip at upper thigh height. This is Parry 1, protecting the mid to low inside line, with the point down.

13 Allow your body to breathe and weight shift forwards.

14 Allow the breath to release and weight shift back as you bring your weapon to the right, just off of your right hip with the palm down. The hilt is slightly above waist height. The true edge is now facing to your right. The wrist is in alignment with the forearm. The point is directed below the knees. Allow the angle of the weapon to be a similar angle to your leading thigh (at approximately a 45-degree angle forwards). This is Parry #2, protecting the upper thigh (the low outside line) with the point down.

Teaching Tip: It can be helpful to instruct students that all of these parries are executed with an elbow that is bent. The ending position of the attacks in the following exercise is performed with a straight (but not locked or hyper-extended) arm. The neutral base-line defines that a straight physical line tends to be perceived as an 'attack' and a line that is bent is most often perceived as a parry or as a non-committed attack. The elbow in these parries should be approximately a hand's breadth from the body. This serves to help students refrain from reaching out with a straight arm to parry, an action of over-committed effort.

15 Allow the breath to be replaced and weight shift forwards.

16 On a weight shift back, with a release of the breath, bring the weapon out to your right and upwards in a semi-circular manner to protect your left arm, specifically at a location between the elbow and the shoulder. This target area is also defined as being approximately at the lowest point of the deltoid muscle. The blade of your parry travels across your own body vertically, and at no time does the point ever cross your imaginary partner's body. The point is now directed above the head. The hilt and hand should remain low and emanating from your centre, at approximately waist height on the left side of your body. This is Parry #4, protecting the high inside line. Ensure that your hand, wrist, and forearm maintain a strong alignment. The true edge is facing towards your left.

17 As explored in the 'Weight underside' exercise, allow your body's energy to be settled and grounded. The weapon and arm itself are simply extensions of your centre being grounded.

18 Allow the breath to be replaced and weight shift forwards.

19 Allow the breath to release and weight shift back. Bring the hilt to your right, turning the true edge to face the right, to protect your right arm. The blade remains in its vertical orientation, with the point directed upwards. As before, the point of the weapon never crosses your imaginary partner's body. This is Parry #3, protecting the high outside line, with the point remaining directed upwards. The hilt remains approximately at waist height. As before, maintain a strong alignment of the hand, wrist, and forearm in the parry – with the true edge facing towards the right.

20 Weight shift forwards and allow the breath to fall into your torso.

21 On the weight shift backwards and the breath out, you will protect your head in a Parry of 5. To safely perform this action, from the Parry of 3, start by dropping the point of the rapier outside your partner's body-line (to your right with the palm down), downwards towards the floor. Bring the sword point in close to your centre, making sure to avoid crossing the bodyline of your partner. The point should be directed now to your left, and the weapon is held in a horizontal angle to the ground. Raise your weapon horizontally to end in a position above and in front of your head. At no time does the tip of the weapon cross the body or face of your imaginary partner. Ensure the blade ends up perfectly horizontal to the floor and the forte (the strong part of the blade) is above and in front of the centreline of your head. The true edge is facing upwards towards the direction from which a vertical cut would make contact. Release the tension from your shoulders with your breath. This is Parry 5, protecting the head.

As you learn the physical patterns above, allow the breath to become an integrated part of the physical specificity. It is very easy to practice these physical techniques in isolation and unknowingly begin to introduce tensions surrounding the breath that can limit our eventual potential in a choreographed fight. The daily application of integrating movement with the breath is at the foundation of the actor's craft within the exploration of the stage combat.

Teaching Tip: Though the above exercise is a solo drill of parries, it would be a good reminder for students to be informed at this point that in stage combat, the Recipient (or 'Volunteer' or 'Defender') is ultimately in control of the illusion. The partner who is parrying, for instance, by shifting the weight to the rear, creates the permission for the 'Attacker' to enter the space with a safely controlled extension of the weapon and a weight shift forwards. In partnered stage combat, the Recipient's physical response to a technique must be initiated *prior* to the Attacker's follow-through of the choreographed action. This common safety procedure, known as the Action – Reaction – Action Principle, ensures that the choreography is always a coordinated dance of partners moving together with precision, safety, harmony, and control. In addition, it is often advised that these parries and the accompanying attacks (in addition to footwork techniques) are learned simultaneously within the structure of a stage combat class. For the purposes of this book, in which the focus is less on the skill-building processes of teaching stage combat and more on the connection of movement to the breath, the exercises are isolated. Partnered stage combat should only be undertaken within the structure of a stage combat class and lead by a qualified teacher.

Explore the above exercise with the variations below:

1   Imagine that on each weight shift forwards, you are looking for an opportunity to counterattack. Imagine, however, that your imaginary 'opponent' is quicker on his or her attacks than you are, thereby forcing you to parry in between your attempts to counterattack.

2   Explore reversing the breath pattern: breathing out on the weight shift forwards and allowing the breath to be replaced on the arrival of the final parry position. Explore the breath as being silent on both the inhale and exhale.

3   Explore variations in which the breath is audible – either an audible intake of breath or an audible exhalation – or both. It is recommended that you are well hydrated for this variation.

4   Explore variations in which you breathe little, or not at all, during several of the parries. How does this variation affect your experience?

Discussion

- In what ways does connecting the breath to the movement aid in the performance of the technique?

- How do breath characteristics inform the quality of your physical coordination and balance?

- How does the breath coordinated with your physicality specifically affect your imagination?

- How can informing a fight with choices of the breath viscerally connect the actor to scene work involving violence?

- In what ways might the breath be a major component of stage combat, aiding the illusion of acted aggression?

Basic single rapier cutting drill (30 minutes)[7]
(https://vimeo.com/132084735)

As before, this Basic Cutting Drill is performed as a solo exercise. This time, however, the exploration is 'on the attack' – placing focus on a slow-motion release into the acted aggression and desperation that is often required to create an effective illusion of violence.

Once the basic drill is physically learned without speed, the reminder is to allow the emotional fullness of an attack to be lived through without excess physical tightness that often accompanies acted aggression. Even when engaged within heightened vocal and physical extremes, the actor is served by maintaining an inner ease. The outward appearance may be one of emotionally charged physical destructiveness, and yet you will always be best served when such outward release is accompanied by an inner state of centred and grounded readiness.

Teaching Tip: Speed is unnecessary at this point in the training. It is natural for students to want to go fast. However, many unhelpful habits can form in the process. It is much more effective to remain in slow motion throughout the training exercises in this book. Other terms to aid this careful and slow engagement may include:

'Tai Chi Speed'
'Underwater Speed'
'Matrix Speed'
'Jell-O Speed'
'Don't move faster or harder. Do what you have been doing but with more acting. Act big, move slowly. Turn the acting knob up to 11, but keep the speed knob at 1.'[8]

A 'Fishing Line cut' mimics the energy of the physical extension of a fishing line being cast out and extended into the water.[9] The energy of the cut sends its energy *past* your partner rather than *into* a partner. In the case of the partnered version of this exercise, partners would remain at the safe distance of 6″–10″ from the furthest extension of the weapon. In addition, it is important to note that the actual targets of cutting to the 'hip' and 'arm' are, in reality, never attacked. In this exercise, the target is at a point in space about 6″ off of the hips or arms. Ensure that you and your partner create only the *illusion* of attacks to these targets. As will be frequently reminded in this book, *at no time does the action of the blade ever cross the area of the face, head, neck, groin, or breasts.*

1 As before, find your en garde position with the Rapier. The point of the weapon would be directed off-line, no higher than the shoulder, and outside of your imaginary partner's bodyline. (A right-handed partner facing another right-handed partner would have the point directed off-line of the left armpit of their partner.)

Refer back to the instructions found in the Basic Parry System exercise, if needed.

2 Allowing your breath to drop in, weight shift back. At the same time, bring the hilt to waist level with the blade directed upwards, at your right side. At no time does the point of the weapon cross in front of your partner's bodyline. This action serves as a clear cue to your imaginary partner for a cut to their left hip.

3 Now imagine placing the sword flat on a tabletop. Allowing the breath to release, weight shift forwards as you slide the blade along this imaginary table, horizontal to the ground. Perform a 'fishing line cut' that extends the energy of the attack *past* your imaginary partner's left hip, with the palm upwards. The height of the attack is at the level of the upper thigh. Carefully refer to the video tutorials to see a visual demonstration of safe targeting. All cutting attacks within this exercise are made with the 'true edge' of the blade.

4 Allowing the breath to be replaced, weight shift back and bring the weapon around your head, with the weapon staying close to your body throughout this preparatory action. Perform this action with slow care and exact physical specificity to ensure you do not make contact of any part of the blade or hilt to your head. As you perform this action, allow the wrist to relax slightly so that the blade does not 'helicopter' in a line straight out from your body as it travels around your head. Rather, in this action of bringing the weapon around your head, release the point down to the floor as it travels around your body. (The video tutorial demonstrates both 'Around the Body Cuts' and 'In Front of the Body Cuts'. Explore both options as possible choices.)

5 Following this action, imagine placing the blade again on a flat tabletop to prepare for the next fishing line cut. Allowing the breath to release, weight shift forwards as you slide the weapon flat on the imaginary table, extending the energy of the cut *past* your imaginary partner's right hip, at the height of the upper thigh. The palm faces downwards on the execution of this attack.

6 Allowing the breath to be replaced, weight shift back and bring the weapon around your head, with the weapon again maintaining a close proximity – point down – to your own body. Ensure you practice slowly and smoothly as you breathe through this movement. While the sword is being brought around your body, keep the weapon close, but be mindful of ensuring you also avoid making any contact with the top or sides of your head with any part of the hilt or blade of the weapon.

7 As before, imagine placing the blade on a flat tabletop. With an ease of breath release, weight shift forwards as you slide the weapon flat on the table, extending the energy of the cut *past* your partner's left arm with the palm upwards (at a target between the shoulder and elbow) and imagine yourself always remaining at correct and safe distance.

8 While the body breathes in on its own accord, weight shift back and bring the weapon around your head to your left.

9 Breathe out on an easy vocalized sigh – an 'AH' sound – and extend the energy of the cut *past* your imaginary partner's right arm with the palm downwards, again directed at what would be the mid-point between the elbow and shoulder.

10 Allowing the breath to be replaced, weight shift back and lower the point of the weapon, by releasing the elbow, to your left as you bring the weapon vertically down and by your left shoulder in a circular manner. This action is called a 'moulinet'.

11 On the weight shift forwards, bring the weapon past your left shoulder cutting vertically *past* your imaginary partner's head. Imagine sending the energy again past and above the centre of your imaginary partner's head.

12 As always, the weapon throughout this exercise is at a safe distance of 6″–10″ away from your partner at its furthest extension.

13 Other variations can include the introduction of gentle humming through the exercise, in a manner that helps to sustain continuous and fluid engagement with the breath and the voice.

Allow yourself to simply 'touch' on vibration within the exercise.
Use a gentle hum with the lips closed or an open vowel sound
of /AH/. Imagine the voice as simply travelling on the breath.
It can be helpful to release the voice on this easy flow of the
breath, before adding the release of sound that is intended to
be violent or desperate in nature.

14 Return to neutral with your weapon floating easily out from your
centre, your breath released, your body grounded and energized.

Even within highly charged theatrical moments, skilled actors possess
a sense of ease that permeates the work. The energy of a tornado or
of a violent sea can often be metaphors that aid this understanding:
the tornado rages with its destructive power, yet the centre remains
unchanged and calm. The surface of the sea can devour whole ships,
yet the ocean bottom always remains calm and still, regardless of the
violence on the surface. The actor and the martial artist – operating at
their prime – need to release with energy and heightened engagement,
yet there can be the development of an inner calm (relaxed readiness)
through this release of energy.

Connecting breath with footwork (40 minutes)
(https://vimeo.com/132084943)

A grounding in footwork serves as a primary foundation for the art of
stage combat. The diversity of the physical movement patterns that are
possible adds excitement to a fight sequence and, properly executed,
ensures you and your partner remain balanced and a safe distance
away from each other. When first learning stage combat, it is sometimes
challenging to combine the actions of the blade work with the actions of
moving the body through space. In addition, when you learn footwork
techniques, it is tempting to allow the breath to become held as you
explore the specifics of how the body is moved in space. With this basic
footwork exercise, explore allowing your breath to be released and free
while you gain confident precision with your footwork.

Refer to the basic en garde stance with a Rapier as learned in
the previous exercise of the 'Basic Parry System'. An 'advance' is a
movement of the legs and feet that carries the body forwards in a linear
manner, by stepping forwards with the leading foot followed by the rear

foot. A 'retreat' is the exact opposite of an advance, in that the rear foot steps backwards first, followed by the leading foot. In neither case do the feet pass each other. A 'pass forwards', however, passes the rear foot past the front foot in a linear manner. And a 'pass backwards' passes the leading foot, past the rear foot.

With these explorations of connecting footwork to an energized engagement of the breath, allow your centre and your hips to remain directed at your imaginary partner rather than offsetting your centre to the side or swivelling your hips from side to side on each step. It can be helpful to imagine car head-lights attached to your hips and that these lights are always directed forwards to your imaginary partner. Also, do not slide or drag your feet. Practice a specificity of the footwork while at the same time allowing yourself to experience a freedom of the breath and body within the physical precision.

Explore the following exercise by integrating these basic footwork drills with your breath. Use only an appropriate engagement of necessary energy.

1   As a solo exercise, with knees bent in an en garde stance, move forwards with an advance.

2   Ensure the head and torso remain neutral during the footwork rather than rocking backwards, forwards, to the sides, or up and down. The forwards foot remains pointed directly forwards and the rear foot remains pointing at a 45-degree angle forwards. Allow the knees to stay bent throughout the course of the action.

3   Move forwards with two sequential advances.

4   Allow the breath to be easily free and flexible throughout the footwork. Release your shoulders.

5   Move to the rear with a retreat.

6   Move to the rear with two sequential retreats.

7   Move forwards with a single pass forwards.

8   Move forwards with a second single pass forwards.

9   Move to the rear with a single pass backwards.

10 Move to the rear with second single pass backwards.

11 Move forwards with a double pass forwards. Allow the hips to remain silent.

12 Move to the rear with a double pass back. Allow the hips to remain silent.

After this basic pattern has been learned, now consider how any movement forwards is an attempt to get closer to an opponent to attack. And consider how any movement to the rear is an attempt to move away from an attack. With this in mind, re-explore the exercise with your imagination focused on the fact that when you advance or pass forwards in stage combat, you are likely moving towards an imaginary opponent with a strong intention. And conversely, when you retreat or pass back, you are likely moving away from an imaginary opponent to save yourself from harm. However, at the same time as you start to engage your footwork within the context of a heightened use of your imagination, allow your body to remain energized but available to the breath.

Connecting with a partner through footwork (20 minutes)
(https://vimeo.com/132084944)

A useful further exercise that continues to develop connections between partners is to have each pair of partners move together as one, using the footwork previously explored.

1 With your partner, decide on a Partner A and a Partner B. Explore this exercise without weapons. There should be approximately five feet of distance between you and your partner. Focus only on maintaining this exact distance with your partner.

2 Partner A moves forwards in an advance, while Partner B will maintain distance by moving backwards in a retreat at the same time.

3 Alternatively, when Partner A moves to the rear in a retreat, Partner B moves forwards in an advance to again maintain the distance with which they originally started. This movement should occur in nearly a simultaneous manner.

4 Partner A continues to slowly 'lead' the movement, while Partner B continues to 'follow'.

5 After a few minutes, switch sides so that Partner B now leads the movement, advancing and retreating while Partner A responds in time and maintains the distance.

6 Now, explore a variation in which Partner A begins to 'lead' the movement. However, at some point (and without verbal communication between partners) Partner B will take over as the 'leader'. The goal is to ensure that both partners are moving slowly, so that distance is learned as a skill that can always be maintained. If it is obvious that a partner is clearly moving forwards or backwards prior to their partner having the time to respond, this is an indication that the connection between the partners is not yet established.

Teaching Tip: Distance and connection between partners moving in unison is most helpfully accomplished when the breath of both partners is allowed to be released and free. Help students explore this exercise while maintaining a level of energized relaxation, which can more fully support a deep connection to the breath. Watch for tight shoulders, clenched jaws, a locked gaze in the eyes, and shallow breathing patterns.

Follow-up

Reflective practice questions:

- When do you hold your breath in life? Can you identify situations during the day or in your work, in which the breath is limited?

- In what ways is it possible for us to 'look' at our acting partner but not be in connection with him or her? What are the differences in the breath when we are in connection with another human being rather than only 'looking' at someone?

- What happens to your sense of gravity and connection to the ground when you allow the breath to be free and low in your body?

- Explore times in your life when you are truly connected to another – a close friend, a spouse, a child – in what specific ways do you connect and 'listen' in these relationships? How is this intimate connection of potential benefit for an actor?

- In your process of working on a fight in a class or in a production, explore the difference between a 'released breath' and a breath that is managed. How do both affect your stage combat work?

- Within a choreographed fight (refer to Chapter 3 for examples of choreography that can be used), explore how the centre-to-centre connection is applied.

Additional exercises

Having worked through Chapter 1, repeat the Push hands 1 exercise. It is likely that through your experience of releasing excess tensions and connecting with the breath, you will have a greater awareness of useful physical energy when you return to this exercise.

Allow yourself to find a sense of curiosity in the process of discovery and within your explorations of the micro-moments of each physical exercise within this chapter. This interest in the subtlety of the art is what will drive your growth rather than ambition to achieve mastery. Exercises from Chapter 1 serve as helpful warm-ups for your fight rehearsals on preparing the body and activating its connection to the vitality of the breath.

Notes

1   'SAFD' throughout the book refers to the Society of American Fight Directors.
2   Refer to the twenty-three-hour video series published by Dueling Arts International: *And They Fight*, by Dueling Arts International Founder and Master Teacher, Gregory Hoffman. This series offers a helpful set of video tutorials for the safe and effective performance of armed stage combat. See the Bibliography for more information.
3   Refer to the video demonstration of this exercise, as well as the recommended reading section at the end of the chapter, for more in-depth instruction for safe blade contact.

4   I am grateful for discussions with Dueling Arts International Master
Teacher/Society of American Fight Directors Certified Teacher and Fight
Director – Paul Dennhardt – regarding this 'Teaching Tip'.

5   Refer to the National Association of Schools of Dance 'Standards/
Handbook' for more recommendations regarding appropriate floor and
training spaces for movement. (www.nasd.arts-accredit.org/)

6   For a thorough text on technique with this weapon, refer to SAFD Fight
Master Dale Girard's excellent text, *Actors On Guard*. Chapter 4 of
Fight Master Girard's book ('Getting the Feel of Steel') contains in-depth
instruction in this weapon. See the Bibliography for more information.

7   The Swept Hilt Rapier in the video is the artistic craftsmanship of SAFD
Certified Teacher, Neil Massey. His work can be found at www.roguesteel
.com.

8   As advised in workshops by SAFD Certified Teacher DC Wright.

9   I am grateful to Gregory Hoffman for first introducing me to the term
'fishing line cut'.

Further reading

Carey, David; Carey, Rebecca, *Vocal Arts Workbook and DVD*, Methuen
Drama, London, 2008. Chapter 1: Relaxation, Release, Alignment, pp. 1–38.

Fitzmaurice, Catherine, *Breathing Is Meaning*. http://www.fitzmauricevoice
.com/products.html

Girard, Dale, *Actors On Guard: A Practical Guide for the Use of Rapier and
Dagger for Stage and Screen*, Routledge, New York, 1997. Chapter 1:
Safety First!, pp. 1–8. Chapter 2: The Sword and the Stage, pp. 9–26.
Chapter 3: Stance and Footwork, pp. 27–69. Chapter 6: The Parries of the
Single Rapier, pp. 123–156.

Hoffman, Gregory, *And They Fight*, DVD Series. http://www.trueedgepictures
.com/dvds/

Houseman, Barbara, *Finding Your Voice*, Nick Hern Books, London, 2002.
Chapter 2: Body Work, pp. 15–57.

Kotzubei, Saul, *To Breathe or Not to Breathe*. http://www.voicecoachla.com
/writing

Lane, Richard, *Swashbuckling*, Proscenium Publishers, New York, 1999. Part
II: Stretching and Warming Up, pp. 77–108, and Sword Fighting Footwork,
pp. 131–146.

Loui, Annie, *The Physical Actor*, Routledge, New York, 2009. Chapter 1:
Warm-up and Alignment, pp. 5–31.

Marshall, Lorna, *The Body Speaks*, Palgrave Macmillan, New York, 2001. Part
One: Discovery and Preparation, pp. 3–51.

Rodenburg, Patsy, *The Second Circle*, Norton & Company, New York, 2008.
Part One: Finding Your Presence, pp. 3–75.

2
INTENTION AND FOCUS

Framework

In a well-played fight scene, the movement is the result of thought, intention, and specifically placed goals. Instructors of stage combat teach that the choreography is often learned as a connected series of openings, tactics and intentions rather than choreographic patterns divorced from the text or story. Choreographed violence in a production is physical dialogue. If the fight is a series of moves focusing on heightened athleticism but disconnected from character thought, feeling, and action, it may be interesting to watch for the pure physical energy of the event but it may also disconnect the audience from the story.

'Play one action at a time' is advice offered by teachers of acting to encourage students to develop clear, strong choices and to follow through fully with those interactive choices. It is the collective set of individual 'choices' that define the work of the actor rather than performances characterized by a wash of generalized behaviour without focus and clarity.

All action, all text, and all physical behaviour on stage are essentially 'heightened' actions, not the everyday and mundane but life as compressed and highlighted. It is the placement of artistic choices that allows the audience to connect and follow the story of these heightened circumstances. For this reason, the choices the actor makes can be made by design rather than by default. If the actor is limited to accidental choices – choices that can only be made when inspiration strikes or only based on the actor's personal habits, the actor may be limiting his or her artistry to a narrowly defined palette. This is not to imply, however, that inspiration and spontaneity are enemies of artistic work. Rather, the task is to explore the marriage of well-developed skill in connection with an available responsiveness to impulse. The study of the Stage Combat Arts allows you to explore how to fully 'play one action at a time' with energy and with the high stakes inherent within moments of physical conflict.

Exploration

1   Take the time to explore your 'purpose' or 'intent' and how your behaviour – vocally, physically, and emotionally – changes as a result of particular environments. In what ways do you employ a variety of tactics when engaging with your peers, colleagues, friends, and family? In what ways is this awareness of basic human behaviour helpful for the actor in training?

2   Be observant of those around you – colleagues, students, friends, family – and the specific ways in which behaviour changes based on the environment and relationship. We all wear figurative masks to hide certain aspects of ourselves and reveal other elements of our personality. How do these masks change, or remain constant, based on changing situations, environments, and relationships?

3   Think back on a particular theatrical memory you have in which you were particularly moved, inspired, or impressed as an audience member. What were the essential qualities and memories of that experience? In what ways is your remembrance of the event visual? In what ways is your memory of the event aural? Think of an actor that seemed powerful or remarkable in that moment. How did the actor physically engage with authenticity and focused energy?

Exercises

Teaching Tip: The exercises in the chapter are organized under three headings: *Movement and Intention; Connecting with Images;* and *Connecting with a Partner.* The development of Focus and Intention in the actor's work is highly informed by the exploration of the Stage Combat Arts. The physical exploration of these exercises promotes a deeper understanding of the benefits of playing one action at a time. It develops in the actor the important ability to focus the images, thoughts, emotions, and intentions through specifically playable actions. And it provides the actor with physical exercises that develop deeper connections between scene partners and an increase in active listening skills. The actor's ability to work with flexibility, freedom, and expressivity is largely dependent on the development of these principles of physical connection.

Movement and intention

(I am grateful to Sensei Michael Friedl for first introducing me to the exercises in this section.)

Without intention and focus, movement lacks purpose and meaning. You will soon find, through your work in the Stage Combat Arts as a training tool, that an ability to live fully in each and every moment is honed. The Stage Combat Arts support your facility to be fully engaged in the physical, textual, vocal, and emotional events that comprise an effective fight scene. For instance, the action of a swipe with an evasion has a beginning, a middle, and an end. A thrust to the torso, a roundhouse punch to the jaw, a push – all have moments within the techniques that are open to potential choice and playable action. What specific physical, vocal, and emotional responses may occur when the thrust 'hits home' or when the punch makes contact? What happens physically and emotionally when the choreographed swipe to the head 'unexpectedly' does not make contact and is instead 'evaded' choreographically by the other character? It is this attention to detail that allows your work to develop with greater freedom of artistic expression.

Push hands 2 (10 minutes)
(https://vimeo.com/132084945)

This exercise is a follow-up of the Push hands exercise from Chapter 1. However, this variation includes connecting the movement more fully to intention. Emphasis throughout this exercise is on allowing the breath to be replaced naturally and on its own accord. The breath should fall in and out rather than be forced, pushed, or managed. The shoulders, arms, and torso can remain relaxed with energized engagement.

Teaching Tip: The focus of the work is on a careful and slow exploration of the process. The tendency will be for students to speed up. Encourage students to find an ability to connect and extend without speed. An increase in speed can be developed much later, once the basic building blocks of connection and intention have been fully experienced.

---

1   Stand within hand-shaking distance from your partner. Partners should step forward with their left foot into an en garde stance, with knees bent. Extend left wrists to each other so that the outside of the wrist of Partner A makes contact with the outside of the wrist of Partner B. Gently bend your knees into a soft plié. While maintaining contact with arms gently extended, begin to shift your weight forwards and backwards while maintaining a connection between your wrists. All weight shifts occur as a result of the leg movement gently rocking you forwards and backwards rather than the upper torso leaning forwards or backwards. Avoid excessive leaning with the head and torso or vertical displacement. Make sure your arms don't collapse or become loose in the movement of your weight shift but remain in a neutral and extended connection to your partner.

2   As explored in Chapter 1, notice if you are allowing the breath to be replaced naturally while you do this exercise. If not, remind yourself that you can move and breathe freely at the same time.

3   Now, on the weight shift forwards, Partner A will extend their fingers of their left hand to the sternum of Partner B. The intent is to touch Partner B on the sternum. Partner B will weight shift back.

> **Teaching Tip:** For women, the target of the 'sternum' may need to be adjusted slightly higher to avoid the breasts. In all of this work, however, avoid any contact or proximity to the neck and larynx.

4 At the moment that Partner B has weight shifted fully backwards, and Partner A has weight shifted fully forwards with the intent to touch Partner B's sternum, Partner B then gently turns their hips to the left. Allow the arm to remain in connection with the movement of the hips, to effectively displace the forward-moving intention of Partner A.

5 The entire sequence is now repeated in the opposite direction, with Partner B extending towards the sternum of Partner A, with a mutual weight shift backwards (for Partner A) and forwards (for Partner B).

6 It is important that the forward-bending knee of the 'Attacker' (or the partner extending forwards) stays over the front foot and does not extend further out over the toes. This is to ensure the health of the complicated structures within the knee joint, which can suffer strain and stress if over extended out beyond the toe area.

> **Teaching Tip:** It is easy within this exercise to allow the breath to freeze or to be overly managed in controlled out-breaths. If this occurs, repeat the exercise with a curiosity about what happens when the breath is allowed to be free within this exploration of physicalized intention and focus.

Discussion

- Discuss what it is to offer the 'gift' of being an obstacle to your partner. How is being an effective obstacle as a partner within a scene an act of creative generosity?

- What are the differences between a released breath and a breath that is managed in this exercise? How do both variations affect your internal energy and physical engagements within this exercise?

Push hands variation (10 minutes)

Within scene work, which character is leading and which is following can be explored within this exercise. This exercise can start to explore who is leading and how far intentions can be played out and perhaps interrupted by secondary intentions and unusual tactics. Explore this exercise with text to engage the inner dynamics of a scene.

1 Using a partner with whom you are working on an already memorized scene, re-establish the basic physical pattern learned in 'Push hands 2'.

2 When you are ready, start to speak your text while you weight shift with intention.

3 Explore possibilities of increased or decreased speed of the exercise within the scene and also of potential physical pauses that may spontaneously occur.

4 Maintain your balance with your partner but also find a selected moment or two when your partner has weight shifted forwards, in which you may gently pull them further forward in an attempt to carefully unbalance your partner. Be careful not to unbalance your partner too regularly, but explore how this physical element starts to inform the internal nature of your scene.

5 After several minutes, stop, shake out, and discuss with your partner what you discovered.

Teaching Tip: Ensure students are both breathing and speaking through the scene while exploring this exercise. It is important that the subtle physical engagement of this exercise does not devolve into a tug of war or wrestling match. It can be easy for students to disengage the voice and only focus on the physical element.

This exploration is about connecting the body, the voice, and the text. With groups that have the maturity to explore in this manner, students may find interesting and new elements in their scene work through such physical exploration.

Cut and turn (10 minutes)
(https://vimeo.com/132084946)

This basic cutting exercise is adapted and borrowed from many martial disciplines that employ the use of the sword. It explores focus, physical extension, and precision of movement, as well as balance, and the development of an appropriate expenditure of effort.

As actors it can be tempting to 'slide' into creative choices and into the next acted moment, before the present moment has fully played out. When this occurs, the specificity of the story becomes generalized, and a full and visceral connection within each playable action of a fight or a scene is muddied. Within this exercise explore what it is to play one action at a time, fully and completely.

As this footwork movement is characterized by 'sliding' forwards – largely maintaining connection with the ground – it is recommended that bare feet or socks be worn on an appropriately safe and smooth surface. A dance or movement studio is ideal.

Teaching Tip: Ensure you use a training room with at least a 15´ high ceiling. For safety of all students, refer to the space requirements listed the Teaching Tip for the exercise, 'Basic Parry System' in Chapter 1. Strict care must be used to ensure no weapon is dropped or comes into proximity of the students' feet. Ensure the floor is free of all debris, that the surface is smooth and appropriate for movement work without shoes. This footwork style is specific to the Aikido exercises in this book and is *not* intended to be used for stage combat techniques or drills.

1 Assume the basic en garde footwork stance – refer back to the 'Solo Basic Cutting Drill' from Chapter 1 for a reminder of this stance.

2 Using a bokken, a wooden training sword used in martial disciplines, lightly but firmly grasp the handle with both hands. Place your right foot forward and lightly bend the knees. The right hand should be placed forward next to the handguard (or 'tsuba') of the weapon with the left hand closer to the end of the bokken's handle. Allow the point of the bokken to be directed at the centre of your imaginary partner's sternum.

3 Breathe normally and fluidly. Release your shoulders and allow your belly to be responsive to the breath. Neither hold the breath nor control it but simply allow yourself to breathe naturally.

4 Bring the sword up vertically past your head, slide with your right foot forwards, followed up with your left foot, and cut down with the sword to the height of the midline of an imaginary partner, with your sword ending in a horizontal relationship to the ground. The right foot should remain the leading foot.

5 Bring the sword around the right side of your head and turn – by pivoting on your feet – a full 180 degrees – to your left. The bokken should now be placed behind your back and head with the point facing behind you. Your left foot should now be facing forward in the exact opposite direction from which you initially started.

6 As before, prepare the vertical cut behind your head and slide forwards with your left foot, allowing the right foot to gently slide forwards as well into a comfortable en garde stance. As you finish the footwork, follow through with the cut, bringing the sword down to midline height.

7 Let the breath fall in to your torso on the preparation and release out on the extension of the cut.

8 Repeat the entire sequence three or four times.

Discussion

- In this exercise, explore the basic principle of committing 100 per cent to the cut forwards and 100 per cent to the cut to the rear.

- Is it possible to take in an awareness of the entire room while focusing on cutting down to both directions?

- Be aware that the tendency will be to short-change the full commitment to cutting in both directions by not quite turning a full 90 degrees and by looking down at your feet (trust yourself that they are there) or by creating unnecessary tension and a diminished awareness of your space by holding your breath.

Eight-ways footwork (20 minutes)
(https://vimeo.com/132084947)

As a variation of the exercise above, explore the following exercise that demands that 100 per cent of your focus be placed on moving to eight different directions sequentially. As before, this exercise is much more than a drill that practices physical control and awareness. Its purpose here is to further aid actors in their *experiential* understanding and ability to implement what it is to play one action at a time. Understanding these principles on a basic physical level, you will set the foundation for being more able to implement the principles of fully playing one action at a time when working with a partner on text.

In this exercise, explore the footwork pattern without a bokken to become familiar with the movement. Each time you slide forwards with either your right or left foot, assume your rear foot is sliding forward as well. The movement is a basic fencer's 'advance', except that your feet lightly glide in a sliding manner on the ground and maintain connection with the ground at all times. It is important to note that this sliding of the feet is not the recommended footwork pattern used in stage combat. Again, it is required that an appropriately safe, smoothly finished surface (i.e., dance or movement studio) is used for safety.

1 Imagine that there is a large clock on the floor and that you are standing at the centre. 12:00 is directly in front of you.

2 Stand in a neutral en garde stance, with your left foot forward.

3   Slide forward with your left foot to the front, at 12:00 on the clock.

4   Pivot to your right 180 degrees and slide forward with your right foot to the rear 6:00 on the clock.

5   Your body breathes in naturally on its own on each pivot and breathes out when you slide.

6   Now step with your left foot to your left (what would be 3:00 on the clock) and slide with your left foot 100 per cent towards your left.

7   Pivot 180 degrees (to 9:00 on the clock) and slide to your right with your right foot 100 per cent.

8   Now step with your left foot to approximately 7:30 on the clock and slide with your left foot 100 per cent in that direction.

9   Pivot a full 90 degrees (to 1:30 on the clock) and slide with your right foot 100 per cent in this direction

10 Now step with your left foot to approximately 11:30 on the clock and slide with your left foot 100 per cent in this direction.

11 Pivot 90 degrees (to 4:30 on the clock) and slide with your right foot 100 per cent in this direction.

Carefully refer to the video demonstration and practice the footwork until the sequence is learned. The goal is to develop physical specificity and build an understanding of the effectiveness of fully playing one action at a time within a fight scene or when engaging with a text and with a partner.

Eight-ways bladework (20 minutes)
(https://vimeo.com/132084996)

As before, the sequence of the footwork remains the same. However, now the cutting actions of the bokken are introduced. The task is finding your ability to fully commit to the beginning, middle, and end of each cut while allowing your breath to be engaged and released. Fully complete each action prior to moving on to the next action.

As actors, the tendency in a choreographed fight sequence or in a rehearsal of a scene is to want to go fast. To get to the product of 'fight performance' and to feel like a 'sword fighter' is indeed exciting and enjoyable. However, this exercise is an opportunity to slow down and place value on the specific moment-to-moment playing of each cutting action. The eventual development of a quicker performance pace, after working specifically and slowly, will ultimately allow you more freedom, fullness, and safety within a choreographed fight.

1   Stand in a neutral en garde stance, with your left foot forward.

2   Slide forward with your left foot to the front at 12:00 on the clock. At the same time, prepare the bokken behind your head and on the slide forward cut down to an imaginary partner's midline.

3   Pivot to the rear. Release the bokken to circle to the left behind your head and slide forward with your right foot to the rear 6:00 on the clock. At the same time, cut down with the bokken to an imaginary partner's midline.

4   Pivot 45 degrees to the left (what would be 3:00 on the clock). Bring the bokken vertically up behind your head and slide with your left foot 100 per cent. On the slide forward, cut down with the bokken to an imaginary partner's midline.

5   Pivot 90 degrees (to 9:00 on the clock). Let the bokken circle to the left behind your head and slide with your right foot 100 per cent. As you slide forward, bring the cut down to your imaginary partner's midline.

6   Pivot approximately to the 45-degree angle (to 7:30 on the clock) and bring the bokken vertically up behind your head. Slide with your left foot forward 100 per cent and cut down with the bokken to your imaginary partner's midline.

7   Pivot a full 90 degrees (to 1:30 on the clock) – bringing the bokken in a circular manner to the left behind your head. Slide with your right foot 100 per cent forward and bring the cut down to your imaginary partner's midline.

8   Pivot approximately 45 degrees (to 11:30 on the clock) – bringing the bokken up for preparation vertically behind your head – and slide with your left foot 100 per cent, completing the cut downwards.

9 Pivot 90 degrees (to 4:30 on the clock) – allowing the bokken
   to circle around your head to the left. Slide with your right foot
   100 per cent forward and finish the cut.

Connecting with images

Dramatic literature is rich with characters that are required to place images
in physical space. With Shakespeare's works alone, you might be asked
to fully imagine a plethora of images, sights, sounds, and remembrances.
Sebastian in *Twelfth Night* must imagine the experience of meeting Olivia
and try to reason out his own sanity while he 'sees' the sun and Olivia's
beauty in his imagination. Macbeth is tortured by his own sanity by seeing
visions of a dagger, while Lady Macbeth is equally tortured by her spiralling
bloody imaginations. Juliet clearly imagines the galloping steeds that will
bring Romeo to her bedchamber. Caliban and Ariel envision a world in
which their lives are marked by freedom rather than by enslavement.
The Stage Combat Arts are a powerful tool in developing the actor's
imagination. The application of learning unarmed and weapon-based
drills further refines the actor's confidence in the power of engaging with
the imagination and an ability to place images with specificity and clarity.

Solo single rapier phrase (20 minutes)
(https://vimeo.com/132084998)

This cutting drill is performed as a solo basic training drill. Refer to the
'Basic Cutting Drill' in Chapter 2 for a reminder of how to hold the sword
and of the basic techniques involved.

Explore the following exercise with a focus on the specific connections
between the breath, the body, and the imagination.

1 As a reminder of the basic stance, refer to the directions found
   in the 'Basic Parry System' exercise of Chapter 1.

2 Your sword arm 'floats' out in front of your chest, palm down,
   with the elbow of your sword arm approximately a hand's
   breadth from your torso. The tip of the sword is directed outside
   your imaginary partner's body. For safety, the point remains
   below the level of your imaginary partner's head at armpit level,

no higher than the shoulder of your imaginary partner. At no time is the sword ever brought into proximity of your imaginary partner's head or face area.

3 Weight shift backwards, bringing your weapon's hilt back to your right at waist level, with the weapon's point directed upwards in a cue. At no time would the tip of your weapon pass in front of your imaginary partner's face, head, groin, breasts, or neck.

4 Imagine placing the weapon flat on a table. Weight shift forward and as you do so, slide the blade along this imaginary flat table and perform a fishing line cut to your imaginary partner's left hip, at the level of their upper thigh. Keep your hand palm up throughout the action of cutting to your imaginary partner's left hip. Imagine your partner protecting their left upper thigh, in a parry of 1. Allow the breath to release on the extension of the cut. Remember that this is called a 'fishing line cut' as the action is similar to casting a fishing line out and beyond your imaginary partner's body. The action with a partner would extend the energy of the sword cut *past* your partner's body.

5 Weight shift back as the breath enters your body; bring your Rapier around your body to prepare a fishing line cut to your imaginary partner's right arm. Remember to keep the weapon close to you as it travels around your body, with the point low. Don't 'helicopter' the point up and out to the side in this action. As before, practice slowly and with physical precision to ensure the weapon never comes into contact with your head as it travels around your body.

6 Following this action, imagine placing the weapon on an imaginary flat table and – as you rock forward – slide the blade along this horizontal table surface towards your imaginary partner's right arm, with the palm down. Remember that the imaginary target would be at the mid-point between the elbow and the shoulder, and at a safe distance of 6″–10″ from the furthest extension of the weapon (refer to Chapter 1 as a review of 'safe distance'). Imagine your partner protecting their right arm by parrying this attack with their Rapier, in a parry of 3. The breath releases freely on this physical extension.

7   Weight shift backwards, breathe, and imagine establishing an eye contact cue with a partner.

8   Bring your weapon up high to a cued position, with the hilt just outside of your left shoulder, with the point of the weapon directed upwards. The point of the weapon on this cue should go nowhere near the face of your partner, and at no time does your sword point cross in front of your partner's body-line.

9   Imagine your partner ducking horizontally downwards. After you imagine your partner has evaded, spot the target of where your imaginary partner's head *used to be*. With an easy release of an out-breath, slowly swipe horizontally across the area where your imaginary partner's ear-line used to be on a weight shift forward. Keep your hand in pronation (with the palm facing downwards to the floor) throughout the action of this swipe. The sword travels perfectly horizontally to the ground, without any angle, curve, or wobble in this action.

10 Weight shift back again as your body naturally breathes in, and imagine re-establishing eye contact with your partner. Cue your Rapier, palm down, to your right waist with the point facing your imaginary partner's belly while shifting your weight to the rear. Ensure your point would never cross your imaginary partner's face. With your palm remaining facing downwards towards the floor (i.e., pronation), extend the point of the weapon towards your imaginary opponent's belly. After your arm is safely extended, step your leading foot forward the length of one or two foot lengths into a lunge as you allow your breath to release. Straighten your rear leg and ensure your forward knee does not extend further forward than your ankle within the lunge. Keep the rear foot firmly planted on the ground rather than allowing the rear foot to roll forward. The little toe of the rear foot stays connected to the ground. Allow the extension of the sword to *precede* your action of the lunge.

11 Imagine your Rapier thrusting into your partner's belly. Feel the heavy impact of steel puncturing flesh. Move slowly and with

fluidity. Breathe. Look into your imaginary partner's eyes as he or she realizes that your skill has driven the point of the weapon deep into their belly.

12 On a breath in, turn your palm upwards, which causes the pain to increase in your imaginary acting partner, adding insult to injury. Ensure this twisting action of the sword does not bring the point of the weapon upwards. Always maintain balance, complete control, and *exact* precision on the placement and action of your entire body and weapon while allowing yourself to breathe freely. Proceed slowly and with specific awareness of the actions of your body and breath.

13 Pull the sword out, down, and pointing away from your imaginary partner as you breathe out.

Repeat the exercise and continue to explore with curiosity about your breath – when you hold it and when it is released, as well as when you breathe in and when you breathe out. The exploration is about a freedom of the breath, not the control of a 'calming' and managed breath pattern. Allow the unarmed hand to stay actively engaged by allowing that arm to stay fluid – extending outwards to your left for counterbalance on the attack and coming closer to the body on the weight shifts to the rear.

Solo basic cutting drill with imagery and sound (20 minutes)

1 Close your eyes and imagine yourself preparing for combat – the desperation, the rage of trying to kill another human being, and the fear of not wanting to die at the end of a razor sharp weapon. What are the sounds you hear? The smells? The sights? The taste in your mouth? What do your eyes feel like? What is the temperature of the air between your lips?

2 The tendency might be to hold the breath and tighten the chest while engaging with these images. Is it possible to breathe and imagine violence at the same time? Move at half-speed, as if you are mirroring a speed similar to many Tai Chi forms. Imagine it is your breath that moves your body.

3   Imagine yourself in 1650 preparing for a duel; perform the basic
    cutting drill described in the previous exercise. Fully commit
    to the action of weight shifting back and forward during the
    cutting action. Image the sights and sounds of what you hope
    to accomplish by cutting your imaginary opponent's arm and
    visualize his or her parry that arrived only a moment before your
    cut landed on their flesh.

Discussion

* Where in your physical exploration do you feel the most
  expressive? Where do you feel the most release? In what ways
  do you feel an increased connection and engagement with your
  breath and body?

* Is it possible to maintain an inner sense of ease and release
  throughout the exercise, even within an imaginative connection
  to the life-and-death nature of violence, by being in connection
  with your breath?

31 Jo-Count Kata (2–3 hours)
(https://vimeo.com/132085004)

The Jo is a wooden staff that is defined as a weapon made of hardwood,
of approximately 5´–7´ in length, and the diameter of about an inch.
The '31 Jo-Count Kata' is one of Aikido's most familiar weapon training
drills. It is performed with two variations: without a partner and a slightly
different physical pattern that occurs with a partner. For the actor, it is a
valuable physical sequence to learn. It connects the body, the breath,
the imagination, and the voice with focus, energy, and integrated
ease. This drill is traditionally performed with the martial artist verbally
counting off the numbers as the techniques with the Jo are executed.
This vocal commitment allows you to integrate the breath and the body
throughout the physical pattern of movement.

Due to the nature and variety of the footwork and specific hand
placements on the staff, this exercise requires a close observation of
the video tutorial. Refer to the video segment that specifically leads you
through this exercise.

Start with left foot forwards and with the Jo in the left hand with the end resting on the floor by the left foot.

1   Lift the Jo by bringing the right hand over the top of the end facing the ceiling to grasp the weapon. Bring it upwards to thrust towards your partner's centre.

2   Slide back and slightly towards your right while you bring the Jo upwards into a rising block above your head.

3   Slide forward and thrust towards the centre of your imaginary partner.

4   Slide back and slightly towards your right while you bring the Jo upwards into a rising block above your head.

5   Rotate the Jo in a circular motion above the head, carefully observing the hand change in the video, and strike vertically downwards as you step forwards with your right leg.

6   Slide forwards with the left leg, and strike vertically down.

7   Turn 180 degrees to the rear and slide forwards with your right leg as you strike vertically down.

8   Slide forwards with your left leg and strike vertically down.

9   Place the Jo vertically by your left ear and swing the weapon diagonally downwards and to the right as you circularly step back with your right leg. This is a strike that proceeds diagonally downwards and would be intended to strike your opponent's knee. The Jo ends with it pointing towards the rear and the left leg forwards.

10 Step forwards with the right leg raising the Jo to a high block on your left side.

11 Perform a circular action of the weapon horizontal to your body, (a 'moulinet') on the right side and strike down vertically as you step forwards with the left leg.

12 Switch hands so that the left hand is now forwards.

13 Slide forwards with the left leg and thrust centre.

14 Slide back and slightly to the right. Raise the Jo to the right with a rising block.

15 Circle the Jo above your head, switching the grip, and step forwards on your right leg as you strike vertically down.

16 Thrust behind you to an imaginary partner's knee.

17 Step forwards with your left leg as you swing the back end of the Jo forwards, attacking an imaginary partner's knee.

18 Flip your Jo in your left hand.

19 Thrust towards your imaginary partner's kneecap.

20 Pivot the Jo in front of you as you gently kneel down onto your left knee and strike towards your imaginary partner's knee.

21 On your left knee, thrust behind you to an imaginary opponent.

22 Stand and thrust to your imaginary partner's sternum.

23 Flip the Jo in your left hand.

24 Thrust to your imaginary partner's sternum.

25 Thrust again to your imaginary partner's sternum.

26 Thrust behind you.

27 Block the left leg with the rear end of the Jo as you step back with your left foot.

28 Raise the Jo and strike to your imaginary opponent's face.

29 Flip the Jo in your right hand.

30 Thrust towards your imaginary opponent's centre.

31 Perform a moulinet on the right side, step off-line slightly to your left and strike down at your imaginary opponent's head.

A related Aikido drill – the 13 Jo Count Kata – accomplishes a similar training goal as the previous exercise. Carefully watch the video tutorial (https://vimeo.com/132085005) to explore how this additional training drill continues to reinforce your connection to movement in relationship to your breath and voice.

Connecting with a partner

As discussed in Chapter 1, listening to a partner and finding those connections that reside deeper than our aural listening skills are primary tools for the actor to develop. The Stage Combat Arts provide those physical possibilities of how to more fully listen and connect on stage. The actor who is able to engage with the individual micro-moments of the craft will ultimately develop greater freedom and resonance in their work.

Arm and centre connection (20 minutes)

This exercise is an Aikido warm-up partnering drill that is designed to develop a sense of connection between partners. Three basic principles of Aikido – Connect, Blend, and Extend – are incorporated into this exercise. Its connections for you as an actor are: 1) it further develops a sensitivity to how it physically feels to connect with purpose to a partner and 2) it promotes a facility of an appropriate expenditure of effort in the performance of a fight scene.

A common tendency in scene work is to play an intention-based action *despite* your partner's presence, unconsciously disregarding a partner's co-engagement in the scene. The strict playing of blindly driven objectives can, at times, prevent partners in a scene from responding and being truly present to each other. How to play an intention fully and completely and yet equally allow for the possibility of active listening is the area of investigation for these exercises. This Aikido warm-up explores how focus and intention are possible while also listening and remaining fully available to the possibility of being affected by your acting partner.

- Partner A Intention: To firmly grasp the arm, just above the wrist, of Partner B to prevent movement and immobilize the arm of Partner B.

- Partner B Intention: To develop a connection with Partner A and diffuse the attack by either:
  - Variation 1: Partner B blending with Partner A, turning to face the same direction as Partner A.

○ Variation 2: Partner B redirecting the energy and entering into Partner A's space.[1]

Variation 1
(https://vimeo.com/132085006)

1 Partner A firmly grabs Partner B's right arm with their left hand, just above the wrist. Partner A's left foot is forward, right foot back. Partner B's right foot is forward and the left foot is back.

2 The intention of Partner A is to stop Partner B from moving his or her arm. Partner B's arm being grabbed by Partner A, remains relaxed but connected. The arm being grasped is fully extended but relaxed, engaged but also free of excess tension.

3 Partner A should be grasping with a firm energy – not pushing or pulling B's arm in any way but only firmly grasping with full focus on Partner B's arm, just above the wrist.

4 Partner B should now turn his or her fingers of the arm being grasped towards their own centre. Partner B can now freely turn around his or her own hand by swinging the left leg back to a position directly beside and next to Partner A. Partner B should now be facing the same direction as Partner A.

5 As this turn happens, the hands of Partner B extend forwards 100 per cent into a similar posture described in the 'Unbendable arm' exercise of Chapter 1.

6 Repeat on the other side, reverse the feet, and reverse the wrist grasps. Repeat until the basic physical pattern is learned and capable of being repeated.

Teaching Tip: Refer your students to the 'Unbendable arm' exercise of Chapter 1 for a review of the concept of extension being full but free of tension.

Variation 2
(https://vimeo.com/132085082)

1 As before, repeat steps 1–6 above. As before, face your partner and grasp your partner's right arm just above the wrist with your left hand.

2 Partner A, with the right arm being grasped, should raise it from his or her centre.

3 Partner A – stepping forwards with his or her left foot while bringing the left hand underneath the right arm – can now safely remove the grasp of Partner B.

4 Partner A can now place his or her right hand on the right shoulder of Partner B while gently grasping the left wrist of Partner B.

5 Partner A should now have been effectively turned away from Partner B.

Spontaneous response (10 minutes)

Practice the two variations above until the partners can perform them with ease. Then start to explore this exercise in relationship to engaging with intention, allowing yourself to respond *in the moment* to your partner's energy. Try not to pre-plan which variation you will perform. Allow your energy to settle and your breath to drop in low as you physically listen to the subtle variations of your partner's grasp.

1 The partner performing the technique should allow the variation (Variation 1 or 2 from above) to occur. The variation that is performed should be a direct response to the energy given by the 'Attacker'. If the partner is grasping the wrist with the slightest pull or twist, Variation 2 might be appropriate. However, if the Attacker grasps with the subtlest push, Variation 1 might be applied.

2 Remind the 'Attacker' (i.e., the 'wrist grasper') that he or she should grasp the wrist without any intention of pulling or pushing but only of grasping firmly and solidly. However, each arm grasp will be minutely different based on body size and slight variations of physical commitment that are inevitable as the exercise progresses.

3 It is the physically based listening to these variations that allows a response, which is an 'in-the-moment' reaction to the impulse that was given. Move slowly, breathe freely without excessive control, and explore a fully committed intention of grasping the arm or in moving in response to the grasp.

Keep in mind that the focus of this exercise is not to develop a martial facility to respond to a real attack. Its purpose here is to further support your exploration of what it means to connect and listen to a partner physically. For this reason, it is important to stay fluid and slow in your movement, with a curiosity about how this exploration connects to your text-based work as well as to your physical engagement as an artist.

In this exercise, explore what it is to feel the connection without the need to visually check in with your partner. Partner B can be free to have 100 per cent of his or her attention forward into space, since Partner B can literally 'feel' the connection. To look at your hands and see if the connection is still there is unnecessary.

This exercise explores what it means to commit fully to an action with intention while allowing flow and a possibility of change based on the impulses that are received. It develops an awareness of what it feels like to remain present with the breath and body to what is actually happening with an acting partner rather than what an actor wishes would be happening or hoped would be happening, in a scene. It is this connection to being responsibly and safely 'in the present moment' that lies at the heart of good acting and effective stage combat. This exercise highlights, in a safe but physically direct manner, the basic principles of developing your relationship to an acting partner through the process of physically 'listening' to your partner.

Aikido breath stretch (30 minutes)

In these stretching and connection exercises with a partner, you will explore ways of preparing the body with Aikido-based flexibility exercises. In addition, these exercises will continue your exploration of developing your connection with a partner through the breath. Find those areas that require physical engagement while allowing other areas of your body to be free, relaxed, and yet energized.

(https://vimeo.com/132085083) The movement of the legs and feet provide the foundation for the exercises to follow. Start by watching this video of Aikido-based footwork to develop a physical foundation for the exploration below.

> **Teaching Tip:** Students with back injuries or tightness may be advised to sit this exercise out. In addition, it is important for students and teachers to recognize that these exercises are not intended to be martially oriented in the context of this book. Explore them with the intention of continuing your development of what it means to be in connection with a partner with the breath, through gentle stretches of a martial origin.

Variation 1: Backwards stretch 1 (Soyendo)
(https://vimeo.com/132085084)

(The 'Applied Practice' in this video is intended for demonstration purposes only and should not be attempted or explored without the guidance of a qualified teacher of Aikido. Serious injury can result from attempting these techniques without proper instruction and training.)

1   Partner A, stand facing your partner with your right foot forward and right arm extended towards your partner.

2   Partner B, stand facing your partner with your right foot forward. Partner B now grasps Partner A's arm, just above the wrist, with your right hand.

3   Partner A now slides forwards directly to the right side of Partner B.

4   At this point, Partner A brings his or her left arm up and towards Partner B's sternum and allows the arm and hand to 'blossom' up towards the ceiling. The palm will end up 'supinated', or palm upwards.

5   Partner A will easily and gently and only as far as he or she feels comfortable, gently extend backwards.

6   Partner B may bring their hands to Partner A's left arm to help support their own weight in this backward-directed stretch.

7   After a few moments, Partner A will assist Partner B back into a neutral, standing position.

8   Switch partners and repeat.

Variation 2: Forward stretch (Kaiten Nage)
(https://vimeo.com/132085085)

(The 'Applied Practice' in this video is intended for demonstration purposes only and should not be attempted or explored without the guidance of a qualified teacher of Aikido. Serious injury can result from attempting these techniques without proper instruction and training.)

1 Partner A stands facing Partner B with his or her left foot forward. The left arm is extended to Partner B to grasp.

2 Partner B faces Partner B with the right foot forward and grasps Partner A's left arm, just above the wrist, with his or her right hand.

3 Partner A lifts his or her left arm and steps underneath Partner B's arm to face the same direction Partner B is facing.

4 At this point, Partner A slowly 'cuts down' all the way to the ground while taking a step back with his or her left leg. While this action takes place, Partner B will also take a step back with his or her right leg.

5 As Partner B is now in a bent over position, Partner A will be able to easily and gently place his or her left hand on the top of Partner B's head.

6 Partner A will extend Partner B's right arm upwards and, being careful to move slowly and in gentle connection with taking care of Partner B, will extend the arm towards Partner B's back in a slow stretch.

7 After a moment or two, Partner A will help bring Partner B's arm down to the floor in a neutral position and carefully assist Partner B back up to a standing position.

Teaching Tip: Two additional Aikido stretches are listed in the video section. Refer to the video for in-depth exploration of these related exercises. (https://vimeo.com/132085086)

(The 'Applied Practice' in this video is intended for demonstration purposes only and should not be attempted or explored without the guidance of a qualified teacher of Aikido. Serious injury can result from attempting these techniques without proper instruction and training.)

Discussion

- Where and when was your breath limited? Where and when was your breath released?
- How did the breath affect your physical relationship of being in connection with your partner?

Knife focus and text (30 minutes)

We all have personal knowledge of injury as the result of a knife. Hopefully, we have not been involved in back-alley knife fights, but most of us know the sharp sudden shock and surprising pain of accidentally cutting ourselves with a kitchen knife while preparing food. It is this universal knowledge of a weapon so personal as the knife – a weapon that forces a close proximity between partners – that allows its safe prop usage to be an excellent tool for the student studying acting and voice work.

A primary goal of these exercises is to allow you to utilize the Stage Combat Arts to find deeper layers of meaning within text work. Our interpretation of texts – finding exact definitions of words, precise relationships, clear intentions, and choosing visceral tactics – are vital rehearsal practices. However, if the work starts and ends solely as an intellectual analysis, the discoveries that are possible and the deeper sub-textual meanings that are available can never be fully realized. Allow yourself to discover deeper sensitivity, awareness, and connection to your voice and text through the body's physical connection to intention and the imagination.

> **Teaching Tip:** It is highly recommended that the instructor, prior to the group engaging with the exercise, should first physically demonstrate the safe distance of 18″–24″ between partners. All students must know exactly where and how far away the knife will be placed from their bodies so that the benefits of the relationship to acting and voice can be fully incorporated without fear of injury. Always avoid crossing the areas of the face, head, neck, breasts, or groin. Each partner's primary requirement is to ensure the safety of their fight partner 100 per cent of the time.

Throughout this exercise it is imperative and vital that only safe (extremely dull, non-edged, non-pointed) theatrical props are employed. All weapons onstage must be safe theatrical versions. A list of stage combat weapon suppliers is supplied in the Appendix. Once safe theatrical weapons are acquired, all weapons must still be treated as potentially dangerous.

Variation 1

Divide the class into two groups – A and B. Let Group A form a line on one side of the room with Group B on the opposite side. Each line of students should be at least 15′–20′ apart. Each line of students faces the opposite line across the room, with each student having a corresponding partner in the opposing group.

Group A will have a safe theatrical knife in their hands by their side. At the instructor's 'go', all partners (A's and B's) will walk slowly towards each other stopping and facing each other in the centre of the room.

1   After all partners have stopped in their walk towards each other, Partner As slowly raise their knives – palm down (i.e., pronation) – with a straight arm with the knife pointed *outside the body-line of their partner. It is imperative that the knife points are raised no higher than the middle of the sternum and not near the throat or face area.*

2 Once the knife is raised outside Partner B's body-line, only then can the knife be slowly brought in to be directed at the partner's sternum. The knife point must be at a safe distance of 18″–24″ from Partner B.

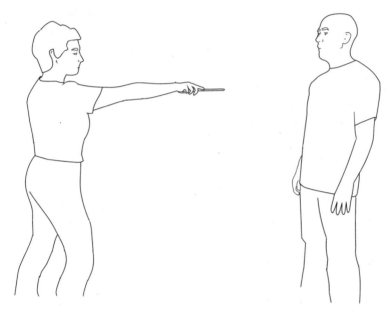

3 Remain in this position for 10–15 seconds, allowing the breath to be affected by this physicality.

4 During this pause for exploration, ensure that your arm holding the knife is not locked and that the breath is released and free. Keep the knife at a safe distance and height (i.e., away from necks and heads).

5 After a few moments, lower the knife to your side without turning your back to your partner and slowly back towards your starting position.

6 Repeat the exercise with the opposite partner.

After Partner A has tried the exercise above, follow the directions to further explore this added variation:

1 Group A will walk towards Group B. As before, bring the knife up slowly and again raised *outside* of the body-line and at a safe distance. The hand holding the knife will now be held palm up (i.e., supination) and brought slowly to be directed at Group B's sternums and remaining at a safe out of distance measure.

2   After this position has been experienced for a few moments, Group A should slowly lower the knives. Group A should now give the knives to their partners in Group B.

3   As before, without turning around and walking back, each group moves slowly back to their original starting positions by walking backwards, remaining facing their partners.

4   The entire sequence is repeated with Group B extending the knives, first with the palm down (pronation) and then with the palm up (supination). The focus wants to be an exploration of how the physical subtleties influence the breath and the imagination of the actor.

Discussion

- Which variation felt the most intentional?
- What variation felt the most emotionally available?
- In what ways did the variations affect the actors holding the knives?
- In what ways did the variations affect the actors that were being 'threatened'?
- In what ways was the breath affected?
- Were there any 'breath holdings' and why? If so, discuss how holding the breath as an option might be useful as an actor.

Variation 2
(I am grateful to Catherine Fitzmaurice for her work and teachings of a practice termed the 'Focus Line', from which this exercise has been adapted.)

Students will explore the energy present with a knife being held during the speaking of a prepared monologue.

Teaching Tip: A helpful warm-up to this exercise is the 'Unbendable arm' exercise of Chapter 1.

1   In pairs scattered in the room, each group will have a knife. (As always, ensure that this prop is a theatrically safe and completely blunt weapon that has been manufactured by a recognized supplier of theatrical weaponry. Refer to the Appendix for a listing of recommended suppliers.) Partner A will once again slowly extend his or her knife – palm down – *at correct and safe distance* to Partner B's sternum. Ensure the knife never crosses the face.

2   With the arm extended, Partner A will begin to deliver their memorized monologue to Partner B.

3   Allow the arm/knife extension to be an extension from your 'centre'. Imagine that your breath and voice originates from low in your abdomen, travels down and around your pelvis, rises up through your spine, up through your neck, up through your head and extends out from your forehead. In this way, you can imagine that your breath and voice can be influenced by the fullness of what it means to be a human being, in that it connects with your entire physicality. At the same time as you explore this 'focus line' of energy of your voice travelling up and out your forehead, imagine that the energy of this line extends out through your arm holding the knife and towards your partner.

4   Allow this exploration to be both a flexible and a focused line of energy and physical engagement, directed to Partner B. It can also be helpful to imagine this line of energy as potentially being a 'spiral' in nature rather than a direct line of engagement between you and your partner. In addition, this line of energy is not only directed at or towards Partner B, but it also allows you to be equally *influenced* and *affected* by Partner B.

5 After several moments, allow the knife arm to slowly release back down to the side.

6 Repeat the exercise, with the arm and knife extended towards the partner's sternum. However, this time allow the arm/hand/knife to be placed in supination (palm towards the ceiling).

7 As before, engage with the same piece of text allowing the position of the arm/knife relationship to affect the text.

8 After a few minutes, lower the knife and repeat the entire sequence with Partner B now holding the knife and speaking prepared text.

9 Lastly, speak your text to your partner without the knives present. In what ways can you feel the effects of this 'focus line' exploration on your breath, voice, and body having engaged in this variation?

Variation 3

1 Assign groups of three, with one knife assigned per group.

2 Partner A will speak a memorized monologue to Partner B, with the knife arm extended in pronation (again, always safely at a measure).

3 At intervals within the text, Partner C, standing next to Partner A, will facilitate a variety of actions with the knife arm of Partner A. Partner A allows Partner C to physically take control of his or her knife arm. The following variations can be employed.

a Partner C will turn the arm/hand of Partner A into supination.

b Partner C will turn the arm/hand of Partner A into pronation.

c Partner C will lower the arm/hand of Partner A to point the knife towards the belly of Partner B.

d Partner C will slowly and carefully bend the knife arm of Partner A at the elbow.

    e Partner C will gently and slowly straighten the knife arm of Partner A.

    f Partner C will slowly bring the knife arm of Partner A down to A's own side.

Teaching Tip: Ensure Partner C is moving the arm slowly in space. The possibility of moving the arm too quickly, or too frequently, adds unhelpful confusion to the exercise. Instead, encourage all acting partners to fully listen to the memorized piece and to always move the arm with the intention of aiding the speaker to find deeper connections to their text work. The possibility exists that partners will find additional meanings and subtleties in the text.

Discussion

- Have each group discuss the effects that the knife variations had on their text. How did pronation affect the text?

- How was it different (or similar) to speak the text while the knife was in supination?

- How did the partner holding the knife receive energy from their text partner?

- Catherine Fitzmaurice, a master teacher of voice and text work, speaks of how it is a possibility for actors to 'become' the text with a full authentic presence rather than simply 'doing' the text well. In what ways might this exercise have aided the 'becoming' of the text rather than only a skilful interpretation of the text?

As an added variation to all of the above knife exercises, an exploration of adding a second knife to a pair of two students adds to the possibilities and resonances that are possible. Add the second knife to the partner who is not speaking, but ensure the knife is only held beside the body. The simple act of both partners possessing a knife, though only one partner may be actively using it, holds additional potential for the development of an actor's connection to his or her text.

Basic knife cuts and text (40 minutes)
(https://vimeo.com/132085635)

Finding the layers of emotional meaning within a text, beyond and deeper than the literal meanings, can be helpful when exploring your text work. It is a particularly useful engagement when working on Shakespeare or other heightened piece of text to suppose that an understanding of the literal meanings of the text is sufficient. As actors exploring a scene or a monologue, it can be tempting to decide upon an initial reading of the text as being the final result and to make artistic choices prior to a more full exploration is undertaken. For this reason, it is useful to employ the Stage Combat Arts to discover surprising connections or deeper choices you have access to within your scene or monologue work.

Teaching Tip: As is reminded in the previous exercise, it is extremely important that only specifically constructed, completely blunt training knives designed for the purpose of stage combat work are used. Any weapon that is even slightly sharp, or has burrs on the blade, is very dangerous and should not be used under any circumstances.

---

1 Partner A (the partner holding the knife in their right hand) will stand opposite Partner B (without a knife). Partner A, holding the knife in their right hand, places his or her left foot forward with the right foot behind. Allow the knees to soften and bend into a gentle plié. In the case of a left-handed student, simply reverse the hand and feet positions. Partner B stands facing Partner A squarely.

2   As Partner A, ensure you are at a safe distance of 6″–10″ away
    from Partner B, at the furthest extension of the knife from your
    partner.

3   Establish eye contact with your partner and then look at the
    target of your partner's belly, at or near the level of their belly
    button. Slowly, at ¼ speed (or 'Tai Chi Speed'), and maintaining
    6″–10″ of safe distance, cut perfectly horizontally across the
    belly of Partner B. The cut should travel from the attacker's
    viewpoint from the right to the left, with the palm upwards.

4   Now Partner A should cut from the left to the right, with the
    palm downward. As before, this cut remains at correct and safe
    distance.

5   Explore allowing the breath to fall into the body on the
    preparation for the cut and to release easily from the body on
    the execution of the action.

6   Repeat the pattern of these two cuts several times to ensure
    accuracy, a connection to the breath, and an awareness of the
    connection between you and your partner.

7   Explore a piece of text – a monologue or a scene – in which
    one partner has the knife and is exploring this exercise while
    performing the cutting action and the other is receiving.
    Continue to move slowly, but allow the possibility that the
    movement itself starts to affect potential resonance and change
    within the acting possibilities.

8   Repeat the process with Partner B exploring the process.

Variation 1

1   After both you and your partner have explored this series of
    two cuts, now Partner A will check their distance by gently and
    carefully placing the very dull knife edge (again, stage combat
    constructed weapons only!) on the side of the belly, avoiding
    the rib cage and hip bones of Partner B. Do not place the
    dulled point of the knife on your partner's body, only the dulled
    edge. Partner B will help Partner A specifically locate the exact
    placement of the knife that feels comfortable. The area of the

ribs and pelvis cannot be made contact with but rather only the soft area of the abdomen.

2 Partner A will once again cut across Partner B's belly; however, Partner A's actions will specifically proceed through the following steps prior to each cut:

a Eye Contact

b Prepare

c Spot the Target

d Gently Place the Knife on the Target

e Gently Follow Through

Teaching Tip: As a reminder, it is vital to remember that the weapon being used in this exercise has been specifically designed by a professional for stage combat use only. The prop weapon must be very dull, with no point, and be completely free of any burrs, guards, or decorative items that could potentially snag or in any way harm your partner.

3 It is very important to place the knife edge on the target first and then *gently* follow through rather than performing the cut in all one action.

4 Proceed through these cuts, following these five steps on each cut.

5 Partner B, throughout the action of having the knife placed on his or her belly and then drawn across, will not react to the action but rather neutrally receive and present a clear target for Partner A.

6 Though the knife is now making gentle contact, allow the breath to remain released and free.

7 As before, add text to this action, as the knife is being placed and drawn across. Explore how the text, in conjunction and integration with the physical action, might change or develop in new and unexpected ways.

Variation 2

1 As before, Partner A will cut across Partner B's safely placed and targeted area of the belly. However, at this point, Partner B will allow his or her torso to slightly turn in the direction that the cut proceeds. Partner B will ensure that the turn of his or her body occurs slightly *after* the cut has occurred. In addition, after the first cut and reaction has occurred, Partner B will return his or her torso and belly target to neutral to re-establish eye contact and to clearly present the belly target for Partner A to safely place the next cut.

2 After this pattern has been explored, Partner A can now imagine that the knife can also be transformed into a cauterizing medical device that 'heals' wounds. Partner A will explore both the action of 'cutting' and the action of 'healing' Partner B within these two actions of the knife across Partner B's belly.

3 Start to add text to the physical exercise and explore how the physical actions of both cutting and healing inform your authentic connections to the language of your text.

4 Explore other possibilities that the 'knife' can not only Cut and Heal but also Tickle, Stroke, and Comfort or Rip, Tear, and Slice.

5 Ensure you remain in control and proceed slowly. Avoid any overt pressure on your partner's belly and allow the knife action to be 100 per cent safe, controlled, and imaginatively engaged through your physical precision.

6 Continue to add your text to the physical exploration, and allow the physical action to inform, influence, and deepen your connections to the text as the primary investigation.

7 Explore the possibility that you, as the character, can 'see' and 'take in' what damage you have done to the person you are speaking to. In the moment of your speaking and moving, imagine creating *more* damage (and how this affects your text) or imagine that the wounds you have created in your partner need to be 'healed'. Throughout this exercise in connecting to text, allow the movement to occur with your text at the same time you are speaking rather than placing your movement before or after your text.

Discussion

- What did you discover about your text and the relationship to your partner that was surprising or new?

- In what ways were you surprised by what you found, connecting movement to language?

- How were your breath, voice, and text naturally affected by the physical actions in ways that were embodied and open to impulse but yet physically safe, precise, and with the utmost care for your partner?

Follow-up

Reflective practice questions:

- Eye contact is a large part of intention. Where and when the eyes focus their gaze can reveal a great deal about intention, emotional outlook, and character relationships. In conversation, human beings rarely maintain eye contact focus for 100 per cent of the time. We often search out images, remember memories, and form thoughts. In stage combat, frequently checking in with eye contact is of vital importance for cueing and ensuring safety protocols. For actors it is beneficial to explore eye contact variations within scene work as well as within dramatic physical conflict:

  o Explore a scene with constant eye contact. Try never looking away from your partner's eyes and allow this intimacy of contact to influence your responsiveness and connection to your partner.

  o Explore the same scene with the same level of intimate connection that constant eye contact developed, but this time rarely make direct eye contact. Be aware of how these differences affect the work.[2]

Notes

1　As an option, this variation can also be explored by Partner B turning
　　Partner A more fully. In this alternate version, Partner A is turned
　　completely to face the same direction as Partner B.
2　I have been inspired by David Hlavsa's book, *An Actor Rehearses*. For
　　additional helpful exercises to explore within rehearsals, this book is
　　recommended. See the Bibliography for more information.

Further reading

Carey, Rebecca; Carey, David, *The Verbal Arts Workbook*, Methuen, London,
　　2010. Chapter 2: Image, pp. 33–58.

Lane, Richard, *Swashbuckling: A Step-by-Step Guide to the Art of Stage
　　Combat and Theatrical Swordplay*, Limelight Editions, New York, 1999.
　　Chapter 8: Defensive Rapier Forms, pp. 147–175, Chapter 9: Attack Rapier
　　Forms, pp. 177–198.

Loui, Annie, *The Physical Actor*, Routledge, New York, 2009. Chapter 4:
　　Partnering, pp. 92–132.

Nachmanovitch, Stephen, *Free Play*, Penguin Putnam, New York, 1990.
　　Chapter 3: Obstacles and Openings, pp. 115–160.

Oida, Yoshi, *The Invisible Actor*, Methuen Drama, London, 1997. Chapter 2:
　　Moving, pp. 14–29.

Thong Dang, Phong, *Advanced Aikido*, Tuttle Martial Arts, Vermont, 2006.
　　Chapter 4: Understanding and Using Ki, pp. 38–42.

3

STAGE COMBAT ARTS AND VOICE

Framework

(The work of Catherine Fitzmaurice has significantly informed this chapter. In addition, I have been inspired by the excellent articles written by Bonnie Rafael. Refer to the Bibliography for more information.)

The voice and the breath are deeply connected with the acts of both real and illusionary violence. The grunts of effort, the exhaled breaths of physical collapse, the groans of pain, the screams of terror, the cries of mourning, the breaths of effort, and the blood-curdling yells of impending battle are all part of the body's natural responses to violence. However, in theatrical fight scenes, the voice can become constricted, held, or monotone when the actor is challenged with the heightened physical, emotional, and vocal demands that these scenes require. The task is to be able to release the vocal energy that is often needed and, at the same time, to maintain responsible control of the body and voice. It is a bit like tapping your head while you rub your belly. At first the actions seem to be incompatible, but after some time working on the physical and vocal skills, the task can become achievable and even simple.

The fight director needs to be an advocate for the actor, in collaboration with the director and the text/voice director. Problems can arise when the fight becomes too complicated for the actors to perform safely with confidence and, thereby, disconnects the physicality from the story. The actor then is set the difficult task of re-engaging with the story without letting the text and acting elements become victims of the physical action that preceded it. Fights need to be designed in ways that serve the story, the context, and the needs of the production while at the same time ensuring that they do not sacrifice the actors to actions that cannot be performed safely (physically or vocally) or with effective credibility (physically or vocally). As has been mentioned, within a dramatic text, the fight is the evolution of physical dialogue when the verbal dialogue between characters no longer suffices.

If the actor has waited until the start of rehearsals to begin work on the heightened demands of the voice within violence, the voice will not be able to accommodate the needs of the tasks at hand. The actor in a fight scene needs to allow the breath to remain low and centred, ensure the jaw remains free of excess tension, release the root of the tongue from excess tension, and allow the throat to be open and released. This energized but relaxed state reduces throat tightening that is a result of an over-effortful use of the breath and frees the voice to more fully respond healthily and truthfully to the heightened circumstances of theatrical violence. The work of this chapter is designed to help you develop a greater freedom and fullness of the voice as an instrument capable of both extreme and subtle expressivity. As explored in Chapters 1 and 2, your connection to the breath is the foundation of healthy and effective vocal work required within moments of heightened physical engagement.

It can be helpful to identify four basic elements to pay attention to within fight scenes and which the following exercises in this chapter will address:

1 **Care of the Vocal Instrument:** The voice's challenges often occur before the rehearsal process of a fight has begun. Simple preventative choices can greatly support the actor's vocal health in a fight scene.

2 **Body Alignment and Isolation of Effort:** An understanding of an appropriate expenditure of effort and the alignment of the body is vital for the fully engaged, flexible, and healthy support of the voice.

3 **Use of the Breath:** The actor is well served by being able to breathe with release and flexibility. To choose to not breathe (or to limit your breathing) can be a valid artistic choice; however, it is less helpful to have a reduced capacity for breath as an unconscious habit. Over-exertion often begins with the in-breath. This over-exertion – when it is a regular habitual

response, not an occasion of artistic choice – sets the stage for vocal folds drying on the in-breath and over-engagement on the out-breath, which in turn can create strain on the voice.

4   **Resonance and Pitch:** Different individuals experience their vocal vibrations in different areas of the body when engaged in the illusions of physical confrontation. Developing the flexibility to allow vocal resonance and placement into and through areas of the body can be helpful within scenes of violence.

Exploration

1   Be aware during your day what your voice *feels* like rather than what it sounds like. Is there a sense of vibration and of resonance that can be felt during your everyday speech?

2   Where do you feel your voice specifically? Is it felt in your chest, your face, your nose, or some other part of your body? It requires quite a subtle awareness to feel the vibration in your own voice. And it is a productive exercise to become aware of how your voice feels in your body rather than overly focusing on how it sounds.

Exercises

Teaching Tip: The exercises in the chapter are organized under seven headings: *Vocal Care; Alignment and Isolation of Effort; Breath Energy; Vocal Expression in Fight Scenes; Voice and Body; Vocal Choice;* and *Vocal Extremes.* The exercises focus on developing a vocal instrument capable of revealing a fullness of humanity during physical conflict, without damaging the vocal instrument for the sake of expression. The focus is on exploring ways to balance releasing into the heightened energy required for fight scenes and developing the control necessary to connect with the theatrical requirements of text and story.

Vocal care

There are lifestyles and activities that contribute to vocal health and others that potentially weaken the voice, contributing to vocal strain when engaged in the demanding use of the voice in fight scenes. The following is a summary of the primary preventative choices that can reduce or eliminate vocal strain.

1 **Stay well hydrated:** The vocal folds require moisture. It is recommended to drink small amounts of water frequently throughout the day rather than two or three large drinks at widely separated intervals. Though the vocal folds are sturdy and strong, they can nevertheless be subject to a loss of function and flexibility through the drying effects of not drinking enough water. In addition, cool-mist and warm-mist vaporizers are valuable for ensuring that the throat stays moist during the night. It is important that the artist engaged with stage combat stays well hydrated throughout the work. Do not wait until you are thirsty to drink water. By the time you are thirsty, your body is already dehydrated. It takes approximately four hours for the water you drink to hydrate your vocal folds.

2 **Get enough rest:** As actors, it can be difficult to get enough sleep as rehearsals can cause us to stay up late, and afterwards we can feel tempted to relax by hitting the smoky bars with our colleagues. Sleep deprivation can accumulate and diminish the overall health of the voice.

3 **Avoid irritants:** Smoking and drinking alcohol are both ill-advised when the voice is required to engage with a heightened fullness. Both greatly contribute to loss of hydration, a primary requirement for the voice to operate effectively. Medications, allergies, and certain foods (i.e., coffee, cola, sugary foods) can all contribute to acid reflux and dehydration. As much as possible, avoid frequent throat clearing and coughing.

4 **Warm-Up:** Warming-up the voice is just as important as warming-up the muscles for physical engagement prior to an athletic activity. An actor who has physically warmed up but has not spent an equal time vocally warming up their instrument

might damage the voice when engaged in stage combat. Vocal injury is the most frequent tissue damage experienced by actors performing scenes of violence. Taking the time to warm up your voice prepares you for the performance of effective and safely performed fight scenes.

5   **Warm-Down:** Just as the body should be allowed a time to warm-down after physically strenuous exercise, to better prepare the instrument for demanding work at the next rehearsal, so too should the voice be allowed an opportunity to gently reneutralize after the demands of a vocally demanding rehearsal or performance.

Physical and vocal warm-up for fights (30 minutes)

> *Teaching Tip:* Immediately stretching muscles before physical activity is potentially damaging for the muscles. Always begin a class warm-up with movement that begins to engage the muscles with cardio-based energy and movement freedom rather than 'cold-stretching'.

Throughout this physical warm-up, begin to connect the body to the breath. Allow yourself to breathe and gently vocalize within the stretch. Feel your voice's vibrations and your breath within the physical engagement. It is helpful to introduce the following elements within this warm-up:

1   Gently trill through the lips by blowing through them, causing them to vibrate.

2   Begin to explore a gentle hum in the middle of your range.

3   Feel the vibrations in your lips during the hum.

4   Awaken and allow your body to experience the vibrations resulting from open vowel sounds of AH, AY, EE, EYE, OH, OO.

5 Bring your feet together and bounce vertically without leaving the ground, and let your arms release up into vertical circles by your side. Let the 'motor' driving the movement of your arms be located at your centre rather than simply circling your arms at the shoulders.

6 Allow your breath to release and flow naturally in and out on the bouncing action.

7 Repeat the bounce, but this time let your arms go for the circular ride in the opposite direction.

8 Start with your feet together and gently bounce on your feet, leaving the ground only slightly.

9 Allow your shoulders and arms to hang loosely by your side as you continue bouncing.

10 Start to bounce forward and back. Repeat six to ten times. Breathe.

11 Bounce side to side. Repeat six to ten times. Breathe.

12 Bounce on only one foot and then the other. Repeat. Breathe.

13 Bounce and twist by allowing the upper half of your body (from the waist up) to gently turn to the right on a bounce and then to the left on a bounce. Repeat six to ten times. Breathe.

14 Land with your feet wider than hip width apart in a deep plié. Start to twist to your right and left – with your centre as the motor – and allow the arms to simply go for the ride by gently swinging from one side to the other.

15 Allow your breath to be free and engaged on the twisting action.

16 After several rotations, start to add energy to your arms but maintain your centre as the driving force of the arm movement. All movement of the arms and legs has your physical centre as its source and originator.

17 Now start to reach out and imagine pulling the energy in towards you, as you twist from side to side. As you twist to your left, reach out to your left with your right arm and hand and pull the energy in and towards you. Repeat four to six times.

18 Reach out now to your left with your right arm over your head. Hold for a count of 4 and breathe.

19 Reach out to your right with your left arm over your head. Hold for a count of 4 and breathe.

20 Reach down towards the ground with both arms and breathe.

21 Reach backwards and upwards with both arms (at a 45-degree angle behind you) and breathe.

22 Come back to centre.

23 Starting towards your left, make a circle with your entire torso – allowing the breath to be connected and free – as you circle down and round and back. Repeat in the opposite direction.

24 Place both elbows above your knees on your thighs and rest your torso so that your belly can fall towards the floor.

25 Place your palms of your hands down onto your upper thighs, just above the knee. Shift your weight – with your feet maintaining connection with the floor from side to side. Breathe.

26 Come back to centre. Roll down your spine and grasp your ankles and gently straighten your legs. Do not bounce. Only straighten your legs as much as feels comfortable within the stretch. Breathe.

27 After a few moments, let your hands release the grasp from your ankles and allow your arms to hang loosely from your shoulders.

28 Walk your feet in so that they are directly beside each other: heel toe heel toe heel toe – until your feet are placed together.

29 Start to now build up your spine – vertebra by vertebra – on a count of 10.

30 Once you have built up your entire spine, roll your shoulders backwards four times. Breathe freely.

31 Roll your shoulders forward four times. Breathe freely.

32 Turn your head to the right, to the centre, and to the left. Repeat four times.

33 Look up at a 45-degree angle and down at a 45-degree angle. Repeat four times.

34 Bring your right ear to your right shoulder. Gently place your right hand over your left ear. Do not pull; simply allow the weight of your arm to gently stretch your neck.

35 Lift your left arm straight up to the ceiling and slowly bring it down to your side. Imagine grabbing a pail of sand with that left hand. Allow that imaginary weight to gently stretch your neck.

36 Gently help bring your head back up to centre with your right hand.

37 Bring your left ear to your left shoulder. Place your left hand over your right ear. Do not pull; simply allow the weight of your arm to gently stretch your neck.

38 Lift your right arm straight up to the ceiling and slowly bring it down to your side. Imagine grabbing a pail of sand with that right hand. Allow that imaginary weight to gently stretch your neck.

39 Gently help your head back up to centre with your left hand.

40 With the palms of your hands placed just above your knees, create small circular rotations with your knees. Reverse and repeat. Breathe.

41 Place your hands on your hips and start to create small circles with your hips. Reverse direction.

42 Widen the feet out to hip width apart and create wider circles. Move slowly and breathe. Find those areas in which there might be slight holding or tension and gently 'massage' your movement through those areas.

43 Come back to centre: aligned, neutral, free, and ready to move.

Lunging stretches (10 minutes)
(https://vimeo.com/132085639)

During this exercise, as you complete the arm rotations while counting out loud, allow the action of the physical stretch to be accompanied by a free and released breath. Let the belly release and allow the ribs to remain free to movement from the breath.

1 Lunge out directly to your left with your left foot. Ensure the left knee is directly over your left heel. Circle your right arm forward from the shoulder eight times. Count the arm circles out loud without vocal push or strain.

2 End with your right arm reaching forward, palm up towards the ceiling.

3 Allow the breath to release the stretch.

4 Repeat the arm circles, this time proceeding in the opposite direction. After eight rotations, reach forward with the right arm (palm down)and the left elbow gently resting just above your left knee.

5 Breathe into the ribs.

6 Place your right palm on the floor. Allow the rear right heel to come off the floor in a 'Runner's Lunge'.

7 Feel the breath releasing the stretch.

8 Lift your left hand towards the ceiling and gently turn your head to look up at that left hand.

9 Breathe through the stretch.

10 Bring your left hand down to meet your right hand on the floor.

11 Imagine your entire torso is breathing you.

12 Bring your right knee to the floor.

13 Feel the breath drop in and out on its own timing.

14 Bring your right heel to your right buttock.

15 Breathe.

16 Release the right foot again back to the 'Runner's Lunge'.

17 Breathe through the stretch.

18 Walk your torso to the centre.

19 Breathe.

20 Walk your torso towards the right and repeat the entire sequence of 'Lunging Stretches' on your right.

21 After you have completed the right side, come back to centre; roll up your spine to finish the exercise.

Jaw/tongue release (20 minutes)
(https://vimeo.com/132085641)

Jaw and tongue tension alone can be responsible for the development of unhelpful vocal and physical tensions that can spread throughout the body and breath. Releasing a tight jaw can substantially aid you within the heightened vocal demands of stage combat. Jaw tension can stifle creative inspiration and effectively suppress the free and expressive availability within your work.

1   Find your masseter muscle by gently massaging the sides of your jaw with your fingers. The muscle that is being touched is the 'Clint Eastwood muscle', made famous by his notorious cigar-clenching jaw tension. An easy way to find this muscle is to clench your teeth, which effectively engages and defines this muscle.

2   Gently massage this muscle, allowing the weight of gravity to let your jaw hang comfortably open, without being forced.

3   Place your thumbs behind your ears, in the small indentation that occurs behind the ear lobe where the jaw hinges to the skull.

4   Drawing vertically down the line of the jaw to where it sharply turns towards the chin, follow the jaw line down and out with your hands. 'Throw' the tension out and away four times.

5   With the thumbs placed under the jaw, massage this fleshy area. This is where the root of the tongue is located. Tongue tension helps to contribute to jaw tension and vocal tension. Releasing this area prior to a fight scene can have the effect of increasing freedom within your vocal apparatus.

Resonance warm-up (10 minutes)

The resonance and placement of the voice can have beneficial effects for your vocal engagements within fight scenes. Including a resonance warm-up prior to a fight rehearsal greatly increases the vocal expressivity and authenticity of the voice and text.

1   Start in a standing dropped-over position, with the knees easily bent and the belly released between the thighs.

2 Allow the breath to release, and imagine the throat as being a large empty tube through which an easy, unvoiced sigh can release through an empty torso, out of the empty tube known as your throat. Allow these easy sighs to release into a pool of sighs onto the floor.

3 Start to allow the sighs to touch on voice – and let them continue to remain an easy release of sound that effortlessly releases from your empty torso downwards into the pool of vibrations on the floor.

4 Start to slowly build up your spine, vertebra by vertebra, allowing the shoulders to remain released to gravity until they naturally fall into place.

5 Allow yourself to breathe between those easy sighs as you build up through your seven Cervical Vertebrae.

6 Once you are again standing upright, nod your head four times in easy 'nods' of 'yes's'. Remember to imagine that your neck is an empty tube that provides an unimpeded pathway for the breath and voice to travel with ease and energized relaxation.

7 Turn your head four times in easy 'no's'. Experience your voice effortlessly travelling on your breath with easy released sighs.

8 Bring your left ear gently towards your left shoulder followed by the right ear towards the right shoulder – four times – in gentle MAYBE movements. These movements of the head are not intended to be stretches of the neck muscles, but simply gentle reminders that a sense of movement and freedom of the neck is possible while voicing soft sighs through a spacious, relaxed, energized, and open vocal tract.

9 Allow your knees to be soft with your feet hip-width apart. Allow your shoulders to release to gravity. Imagine your back widening and your chest softening. Imagine that there is space between your floating ribs and your hip girdle. Allow your belly to soften. Imagine your head as a buoy floating gently on still water.

10 Start to hum with your lips closed. Let there be space in your mouth as if there is a hint of a yawn in the back of your mouth.

11 Feel the vibration in your lips and see if you can feel it start to tickle your nose and your ears.

12 Play with pitch. In what pitch of your hum can you feel the most vibration?

13 Explore experiencing the resonance in your nose with vibration and pitch. Allow the volume to be gentle. There might be a tendency to increase the volume to feel more vibration. Instead, explore with ease and allow the vibration of the body to be fully experienced. This is possible when the muscles are energized but released, rather than held by effort and strain.

14 Continue to explore through pitch and vibration on a gentle hum. Explore through the following areas as the focus of your vibration.

  o Roof of the mouth

  o Behind your eyes

  o Nose

  o Lips

  o Behind the upper front teeth

15 Using an NG sound – by raising the back of your tongue up towards your soft palate and allowing your lips to open slightly – explore various pitch patterns that allow you to feel the vibrations in and around your nose. As you sound, explore by touching your nose and feel those vibrations, both externally through touch, and through an internal sensitivity of feeling this vibration.

16 Stick your tongue out and, with your lips enclosing your tongue, once again HUM. Explore gently and easily as you continue to experience your vibrations created through sound.

17 Voice a sequence of 'me, me, me, me, me, me's', experiencing your vibrations in and around your nose.

18 On open AH's with low pitch choices, experience the vibration that is possible within the chest. Place one hand on your sternum, and feel how your voice resonates in your entire torso.

19 With an open AY (as in GREAT), feel your voice in the middle of your mouth. Imagine the breath and its accompanying vibration originating from your centre low in your abdomen, travelling up your empty torso, releasing through your empty tube-like throat, bouncing off the top of your hard palate, and falling out through your mouth.[1]

20 Continue to explore with EE, into OO, once again back into NG.

21 Return to the position with your tongue sticking out, with your lips tightly enclosing your tongue, and voicing on a hum.

22 Conclude by experiencing vibration in your lips, hard palate, and chest – in that order – with vocalized MMMM-AAAHHH's. Allow the sound to bypass your throat as a large empty tube through which breath and its accompanying vibration can pass without impediment.

Teaching Tip: A useful example of the body's effect on resonance and vibration can be demonstrated to the class by holding an empty plastic water bottle or a tuning fork. When the body is open to impulse through energized relaxation, the body is open to vibration and increased resonance. To demonstrate this principle, hold an empty water bottle firmly around the middle of the bottle. Strike the bottle with an object and it will be easily found that the empty plastic water bottle vibrates little, if at all. When our bodies are held with muscular rigidity and over-effort, our capacity to resonate fully is distinctly reduced. Now hold the bottle gently near its top or bottom, placing as little effort into grasping the bottle as possible. Once again, strike the bottle with an object. It will be found that when the bottle is held loosely by its end, the bottle will vibrate a great deal more. It is true for our voices as well that the more we hold on to our physical tensions, the less we are in touch with our own resonance and the less available we are to impulse and emotional availability.

Alignment and isolation of effort

In our everyday lives, we generally only engage the amount of physical effort that is needed and appropriate for any given task. Cooking dinner, driving a car, walking down the street, dressing in the morning – are all tasks in which excessive efforts are clearly unwarranted. In a similar way, actors can train through the Stage Combat Arts to find the *appropriate level* of energy required for the given task of interacting with an acting partner. By learning how to isolate the physical safe actions of stage combat, an acted release is possible within the heightened circumstances of theatrical moments. This allows a freedom of how, when, and where to most specifically engage the body and voice.

The following exercises develop and hone this ability to engage with physical energy appropriate to the task.

Neutral mask (30 minutes)

(I have been inspired by Sears Eldredge's excellent book, 'Mask Improvisation'. See the Bibliography for more information.)

It can be possible to over-rely on the expressiveness of facial gestures and discount the body's expressive potential. Embracing the fullness of physical storytelling is a practice that mask work can help further develop and define. In the theatre, it is more often the body that communicates to an audience a character's thought and feeling, rather than the face.

The neutral mask allows an exploration of alignment and connecting you equally to both verticality and grounding. This mask work allows you to develop a more sensitive awareness of your body in space and can help to develop the healthy and effective use of your voice and body in stage combat.

Teaching Tip: A full-length mirror – preferably full body length – is useful for this exercise.

It is important to clean the inside of the mask after every usage to avoid the spread of disease. Depending on the mask used, a cleaning of the inside of the mask with a soft, dampened cloth with a mild solution will suffice. For a list of mask suppliers, refer to the Appendix.

1 Either in a group or as a solo exercise, quietly contemplate the qualities of the Neutral Mask while holding it in front of you. In what ways is it similar to and different from a male or female face? In what ways is it neither tall nor short, old nor young? Take notice of what defines this mask as 'neutral'. It is full of potential within any direction of movement – physically, vocally, or emotionally.

2 After you have taken the time necessary to make mental notes about the qualities of your mask, make your way to the mirror and with your mask in your hands, one hand gently holding onto the strap and the other on the 'chin' of the mask, close your eyes. With your eyes closed, put on the mask and after it is secure, reopen your eyes and see yourself through the mask for the first time. Back up from the mirror so that you can allow the mask to inform your entire physicality. Start to explore what it means to be a breathing human being within neutrality.

3 Begin to walk in the space within the neutral mask.

4 As you walk in the space, be curious about how the mask affects your vitality, presence, stillness, energized awareness of self, and the freedom of your breath.

5 Be mindful of not looking for any predetermined expected result – simply become aware of what you are experiencing.

6 After a few minutes, become aware of other mask-wearing actors in the room. What is your response to connecting to a partner within the Neutral Mask?

7 After a few moments, return to facing the mirror, close your eyes and gently remove the mask. Take a moment to journal your observations and then share your thoughts with the class.

Discussion

- What have you discovered about your own neutrality and potential energy within a fight scene, based on your time spent in the mask?

- What happened to your sense of alignment and awareness of effort?

- Did you experience some increased vitality, presence, awareness, or freedom in your physicality?

Teaching Tip: In addition to the Neutral Mask work, the incorporation of half and full-faced character masks aids in developing a more full-bodied presence within the art of stage combat. The physicality of fight work can be helpfully deepened by the physical specificity that mask work develops.

Solo cutting drill with neutral mask (30 minutes)

In this neutral mask work, students develop an awareness of a more fully embodied relationship towards physical complicity within a fight, building on the previous exercise.

1 Stand facing a mirror with your sword on the floor in front of you and a neutral mask in hand.

2 Close your eyes and put the neutral mask on. After it is secure, open your eyes to see that your face now is incapable of expression and bring your attention to the fact that your body and breath are the sole source of your artistry.

3 Imagine your head floating upwards to the ceiling, as if it is now a buoy gently resting on the surface of a calm lake. Imagine your shoulders releasing downwards. Imagine your chest softening and widening. Imagine your spine – the length, width, flexibility, and strength that connects your entire self from the

base of your pelvis to the centre of your head. Imagine the space between the bottom of your ribs and your pelvic bowl as being wide and open. Imagine space and a sense of warmth in your hips, your knees, and your ankles. Feel the coolness of the air moving between your lips.

4 While wearing the mask, pick up your sword and once again come en garde and imagine what it is to face an opponent in a duel. Allow your breath to release and allow the tension in your abdomen to gently release. Is it possible to allow a release and engagement of the breath, as well as a 'softness' in your chest/shoulder/back/knees to be present – even while imagining your impending violent actions?

5 Notice that all focus is now on your body and the expressive potential of your physicality.

6 Practice the 'Basic single rapier cutting drill' in Chapter 1 (in the 'Breath and Extension with a Weapon' section). Engage with the actions of your sword drill, focusing the awareness on your body. Be aware of your weight-shifting actions, the engagement of your unarmed hand, the relationship of your torso to your hip girdle, and the angle of your head and neck, while imagining your opponent.

7 Remember to stay engaged with a freedom of your breath. Simply allow your body to *breathe you*, without attempting to engage your breath in any perception of what a 'correct breath' in this exercise looks like.

8 After completion of the drill, place the sword gently down in front of you and, closing your eyes, remove the mask. Reopen your eyes, and discuss what you discovered.

Discussion

- What differences did you notice in your physicality?
- What differences did you notice in your breath?
- Was there an increased development of physical exploration and expressiveness?
- How was your imagery more specifically placed and realized?

Breath energy

As we have explored in detail, the breath is a vital component of the flexible and revealing capacity of the voice. The fight director and the actor can skilfully add realism to a fight by scoring the breath within the choreography. The illusion of impulsivity and unpredictability of the breath and of the voice greatly aids a fight's appearance of spontaneity. Learning to support the breath and being able to control your breath allows the possibility of greater expressive choice within a fight.

Freeing the ribs to the breath (20 minutes)
(https://vimeo.com/132085642)

(I am grateful to have learned this exercise from Catherine Fitzmaurice.)

On the impulse to in-breath, the ribs expand out and up to allow more oxygen to enter into the lungs. The pattern that increases the possibility of vocal injury in fight scenes, is one in which the ribs then squeeze inwards on the out-breath, creating excess pressure through the throat where the vocal folds, and other sensitive tissues responsible for vocal production, are located. This creates a tightening within the larynx and potentially strains the voice. It is for this reason that the development of a greater release and freedom of the ribs can be very useful within fight scenes.

First, warm up the torso and rib cage in relationship to the breath:

1   Find a comfortable place in the room to lie down on a Yoga mat or a padded surface on your back. Lie with your legs outstretched and your arms gently resting on the floor 6″–10″ from your body.

2   It can be helpful to place a firm pillow under your head to allow a full alignment through the neck.

3   Allow the breath to find its own rhythm and explore what it is to wait for the impulse to breathe, on its own timing. Let your belly be soft.

4   Bring your feet towards your buttocks so that your feet are flat on the floor with your knees pointed towards the ceiling.

5   Place your arms a little further out to either side as you allow both your knees to slowly lower to the right. Depending on your

level of flexibility, it can be useful to place a small pillow under your knees, or between your knees in this resting position.

6 Let your head turn to the left as your knees lower gently to the right.

7 Feel the opening in your ribs within this stretch. Allow yourself to breathe. Wait for your body's impulse to breathe.

8 Return your legs and knees to neutral, and repeat on the other side. Pay particular attention to the free movement of the ribs in relationship to your breathing.

9 Roll over to one side. Slowly make your way to a standing position. Notice the difference in your breath and the increased freedom that may be felt in the movement of your ribs.

With a partner, use the following exercise to further your awareness that the ribs can be responsive to the breath:

10 Partner A, on a Yoga mat or a padded surface, will crouch face down into the Yoga position known as the 'Child's Pose'. (Specific directions for this position are found below.) Allow the arms to be gently stretched forward, opening the back and the ribs.

11 Partner B will gently contact areas of Partner A's back with his or her fingers, or with the palms of the hands. Any location on the back can be touched – from between the shoulder blades to the base of the spine.

12 When Partner A feels the location of the contact, he or she will imagine allowing the breath to be released into the area that is being touched. Allow the possibility that the entire back and the ribs can be responsive to the breath.

13 To avoid hyperventilation, allow yourself to *wait* for the impulse to breathe. Listen to the body's natural responses rather than trying to control the breath.

14 Following the completion of the exercise, gently take your time to sit up and discuss what you discovered with your partner.

'Child's Pose' is a resting position borrowed from Yoga practices that allows the breath and the body to experience release and a deeper connection to the breath. The following steps are aids to help you further explore this pose.

1   Using a Yoga mat, kneel gently on the floor.

2   Gently sit back on your heels.

3   Allow yourself to release the breath.

4   With your knees separated, rest your torso between or on your thighs.

5   Your hands may rest gently out in front of you with the arms extended and the palms downwards on the floor. The elbows are in contact with the ground.

6   Rest in this position for several moments.

7   From this position, explore walking your fingers 1″ or 2″ further forward, and then allow your elbows to re-release softly to the ground.

8   Stay in this pose for several minutes or as long as feels pleasant and useful.

Discussion

- What surprised you about your breathing?

- In what areas could you feel gentle movement of your breathing as your partner contacted your back with their hand? Perhaps you felt movement in areas of the body you thought would not be responsive to the breath?

- Explore what it is to engage with a fight scene after this breathing exploration. In what ways does this increase in breath connection affect your work in a choreographed fight?

Finding your breath for fight work (30 minutes)

(I am grateful to Catherine Fitzmaurice, from whom I learned this exercise.)

The specific awareness of breath support is essential for the actor. In fight scenes, the vocal work needs to be specifically placed to avoid injury. Breath is the source and the foundation for all vocal and physical action. As the volume of your voice increases, the level of deep breath support also needs to equally engage, without squeezing the ribs down and in. The following exercise provides a basic foundation for finding the appropriate engagement of the breath support muscles involved in the creation of sound within fight scene work. It can also be a useful exercise to frequently return to and explore during fight rehearsal warm-ups.

1 Start by lying on the floor, with the feet flat on the ground and the knees pointing upwards towards the ceiling.

2 Let your body sink into the floor.

3 Allow your eyes to soften in your head.

4 Allow your jaw to gently release to gravity and your lips to partly open.

5 Wait for the impulse to breathe and remind yourself that the body will breathe *you*. Notice the slight pause between the out-breath and the next impulse of the in-breath. Notice too how this slight pause changes in duration each time your breath is released.

6 Place one hand on your belly.

7 Simply notice, without trying to change anything, how your belly gently releases on the breath in. Allow the out-breath to be a gentle sigh without any control or management of the sound.

8 On the next breath in, imagine a crying child above you near the ceiling.

9 On the out-breath – and with your hand still gently resting on your belly – softly quiet the child with the sound of SH…

10 Repeat this sound several times and be aware of the physical engagement of your belly under your hand.

11 Engage with the following sounds on your out-breaths while taking notice of the action of your belly beneath your hand:

   a   Wuza, wuza, wuza, wuza…

   b   Willaby, willaby, willaby, willaby

    c Momalapopola, Momalapopola, Momalapopola, Momalapopola…

    d One by one by one by one by one by one by one….

    e One by two by three by four by five by six by seven…

12 On the next breath in, follow these steps in this order:

    a Place one hand on your ribs. The ribs can initiate the movement by gently swinging up and out on the in-breath.

    b Allow the belly to subtly release out during the in-breath. It is not a 'pushing' of the belly out, but a more gentle release that naturally occurs by the action of the descending diaphragm.

    c On the out-breath, allow the engagement to initiate in the lower belly with a gentle voicing on a 'SH' sound.

    d Ensure that the ribs *float* back to their original starting place during your engagement of the sound.

13 Explore the steps above from both a kneeling position and a standing upright position. Feel the new sensations of your breath in your body from these physical positions off of the floor.

When your breath is engaged with the deep muscles of support, the voice is able to respond more fully and freely. It is a good practice to regularly engage with this awareness of breath support while working on choreographed fight sequences. Clearly all this becomes more challenging when the actor comes off the relaxed position on the floor and engages within a choreographed fight. The reason to develop the habits in isolation, however, is that once positive effects are recognized, the actor is more able and ready to apply the work within more demanding physicalizations. The actor must develop a fine-tuned awareness of his or her muscular systems, including the muscles of the breath.

The muscle known as the 'Transversus Abdominis' – a muscle that is largely responsible for effective breath engagement, located deep in our torso – plays an important role in vocal support that is both full and connected. You can find this muscle by exploring the following exercise:

Vocal support for fight work (20 minutes)
(https://vimeo.com/132085643)

(I am grateful to Catherine Fitzmaurice to incorporate this work.)

1 Stand with your weight equally distributed on both feet and your feet spread at a comfortable distance of approximately hip-width apart. Allow your knees to be soft.

2 Imagine yourself – after a long winter of eating fattening foods – trying to squeeze into your more tightly fitting new summer jeans.

3 Perform the action of 'zipping up' the front zipper that is now too tight. The lower belly engages inwards as you perform the action of zipping up your pants.

4 Notice that when this particular muscle is located and activated, the ribs gently release out to the side. The actor is well-served by exploring in detail the isolation of this Transversus Abdominis muscle as the primary source of breath support.

5 Explore saying the words, 'No', 'Go', and 'Stop' from this place of deep support.

The muscles attached to and between the ribs – the Intercostals – are responsible for the movement of the ribs in relationship to the breath. These muscles allow your ribs to expand outwards on the breath in. They are also the muscles that can be trained to *not* squeeze the ribs habitually inwards and downwards when heightened use of the voice is required. It is partly this over-effort of squeezing the ribs inwards during vocalized fight scenes, forcing the air up and out with excess energy, that creates excessive tightening in the larynx and resultant tensions in both the body and the voice.

Fitzmaurice voicework: modified cobra (20 minutes)
(https://vimeo.com/132085703)

Though this exercise is similar to a Yoga position, it is distinctly different in that it asks you to experience a release of control with the breath. The focus is less on maintaining the posture muscularly, and more on finding those areas of muscular engagement while allowing other areas of the body and the breath to experience release. This is precisely what the actor can develop to advance in the work of stage combat.

Every person's body will respond to these breathing exercises differently. The written descriptions and video are meant only as guidelines and not as prescriptive 'forms' for how your individual body must look as you explore. Do the work as your body finds helpful. If you have lower back injuries or excess tightness, this might be a good exercise to sit out or observe the first time, to determine what is most comfortable and helpful. What is important is the isolation of engagement and the potential of breath release, rather than copying the exact image of the model described or in the video tutorial.

Explore the next two exercises prior to fight rehearsals, and notice the effect it has on your vocal, physical, and emotional availability within your fight scene work.

1 Complete 2–3 minutes of gentle activity to allow the muscles to begin moving and warming up:

   a With feet wider than shoulder width apart, gently lean and stretch to your left.

   b Gently lean and stretch to your right.

   c Gently extend and stretch down to the floor.

   d Roll up your spine, vertebra by vertebra, into an upright and aligned position.

   e With your arms out in front of you, gently turn to your right and look over your right shoulder. Be aware of where you are looking and what specifically you are looking at.

   f Gently turn your arms and torso to your left, and look over your left shoulder. Again, take note of where you are looking and specifically what you are looking at.

   g Now turn your arms and torso to the left again, but look over your right shoulder with your head. Ensure you are using some energy to look over your right shoulder. Stay in this position for a count of 5.

   h Turn your torso and arms again to your right but make a gentle but concerted engagement to look over your left shoulder. Stay in this position for a count of 5.

i Return again to turning your arms and torso to look over your left shoulder. Notice now where you are looking.

j Turn again with your arms and torso to look over your right shoulder. As before, notice where you are looking.

2 Lie on the floor on your belly. Place your hands, palms down, flat on the floor near your shoulders.

3 Notice what parts of you are touching the ground and what parts of you are touching the air.

4 Tighten your buttocks and thighs, and with a out-breath allow the tightening to release. Feel your pelvis releasing more fully towards the floor.

5 With your hands still remaining flat on the floor under and near your shoulders, and without tightening your buttocks, start to push up through your hands so that your upper chest and torso are lifted off the floor slightly.

6 Your head and neck are released at a point in your spine between your shoulder blades. Allow the head to drop towards the floor as you push upwards, while you are engaging with your arms only. Ensure that your arms remain bent and that the elbows remain pointed towards your hips.

7 This position is intended to be somewhat challenging. However, allow the effort of it to be focused only within your bent arms. Your torso, head, neck, belly, buttocks, thighs, and your breathing are relaxed and released.

8 As the effort increases in your arms, allow the breath to respond. You may find that the arms begin to tremble slightly. This 'tremor' is normal and has a potentially valuable effect on releasing the breath more fully as the physical position becomes somewhat challenging.

9 In this position, the ribs and upper chest are more open to the breath and it may be possible for you to allow these areas to release a little further on each in-breath.

10 On each out-breath, let the breath simply fall out of your torso – with either voiced or unvoiced sighs – without any control or any need to sustain vocally.

11 Wait for your body's impulse to breathe, and explore the possibility that the ribs can be subtly responsive to movement with the breath.

12 Whenever you feel ready, gently start to release your arms and bring your chest once again towards the ground so that you are again lying prone on the floor. Bring yourself immediately back into the Yoga position of the Child's Pose, to allow the lower back to release.

13 In the Child's Pose, it can be helpful to have a partner gently give some pressure on both sides of your lower back, not on the spine.

14 Tuck your toes under your feet and rock yourself back into a crouching position with your feet flat on the floor. Let your torso and belly fall between your thighs and allow your head to remain heavy and released to the floor.

15 Float your tailbone upwards to the ceiling while allowing the torso to remain in a drop-over.

16 Start to slowly roll up your spine, vertebra by vertebra, letting your arms and shoulders remain released to gravity until they naturally fall into place.

Discussion

- After coming to a standing position, in what ways does your breath feel different?

- In what ways might you feel more vitality, energy, and availability?

Fitzmaurice voicework: the healthy cow (20 minutes)
(https://vimeo.com/132085704)

Often when actors are told to 'breathe' in a fight, they do so with slow, controlled, and managed breaths that can tend to maintain tensions in the body, emotions, and voice. While breathing, in and of itself, is much better than the opposite, it can also be helpful to explore the freedom of a natural *release* of the breath rather than controlling it. A breath that is effectively free and engaged, increases the actor's energy, aliveness, spontaneity, and availability and thus provides a wider range of full vocal freedom.

The video demonstration is only one example of this exercise. Do not feel like you must rigorously copy this exact form but rather explore this work in a way that is most useful for you.

1 Start by lying on the ground on your back in a comfortable position with your legs outstretched.

2 Stretch everything out – arms, legs, tongue, and eyes.

3 Scrunch everything very tight into a small, round ball. Add sound to this scrunch.

4 Stretch everything out, as if you are a large starfish. Add sound.

5 Then shake it all out.

6 Add sound to the shaking out.

7 Repeat the scrunch, stretch, and shake.

8 Allow yourself to now lie comfortably on the floor, again with your legs outstretched.

9 Imagine that you are lying on a warm, sandy beach and that your body is filled with warm sand.

10 Feel your gravity on the sand. Notice those parts of you that are touching the warm sand and those parts of you that are touching the warm summer air.

11 Allow your body to breathe with its own natural rhythms – gently releasing the air, pausing, and then gently allowing your body to breathe *you*.

12 Let your jaw fall gently to gravity towards your chest and towards the floor. Feel the temperature of the air between your lips and in your mouth.

13 Without changing anything or forcing yourself to breathe in any particular way, notice the areas of actual movement with your breath. Allow yourself to internally sense the movement of the breath. Can you feel it in your belly? Ribs? Lower abdomen? Pelvic floor? Groin? Small of your back?

14 While you continue to allow your breath to be present, roll over onto your belly.

15 Bring yourself to all fours, with your hands placed directly under your shoulders and your elbows pointed towards your hips.

16 Allow your back and entire spine to droop downwards towards the floor. Allow your belly to release to gravity. Imagine yourself a happy, healthy cow in the field, grazing on warm grass, with your belly fully released.

17 Your head and neck are also released to gravity. Imagine a point between your shoulder blades, and release your neck from this area of the spine.

18 In this position, let your breath release. Allow your voice to simply sigh and fall out without extending the sound in any way.

19 With the points of your elbows still pointing towards your hips and while ensuring your head and neck remain released, start to bend your elbows as you take some of the weight of your torso into your arms.

20 It is possible at this point that your arms will start to 'tremor' – a kind of unintentional muscular response. It is quite a natural, normal, and healthy response in this position. If you do not experience this tremor, that is not a problem. Allow the belly to stay released to the floor, with the ribs free and the head and neck released.

21 Within the somewhat effortful nature of this position, explore what it is to allow your breath to be affected and easy sighs to simply fall out of your mouth onto the ground below.

22 After 30 seconds or so (or whenever you feel it is necessary), relax by bringing the torso and hips backwards into the Child's Pose. Let your thighs be separated enough to allow the belly to release to gravity between your legs.

23 Explore what it is to make this transition into the resting pose while you still allow the breath to be present.

24 Take a moment to feel the new energy of your breath and the vitality that the exploration may have developed.

25 Tuck your toes under your feet and rock yourself back onto the soles of your feet while still allowing your head and neck to be released.

26 Gently straightening your legs and floating your hips towards the ceiling, continue to breathe easily and naturally. Start to slowly build up your spine – vertebra by vertebra. Allow at least 30–60 seconds to build up into a standing position while you continue to breathe.

Discussion

- After you stand up, discuss with a partner how these two exercises affected you.

- In what ways did you feel more aware your surroundings and in touch with your own impulses?

- How might this type of exploration be valuable for an actor preparing to train or to perform scenes of physical violence and confrontation?

Teaching Tip: Training opportunities in Fitzmaurice Voicework® are offered worldwide. Visit www.fitzmauricevoice.com to learn more about this type of training and to find teachers near you. In addition, Saul Kotzubei – a Master Fitzmaurice Voicework Teacher and the Co-Director of the Fitzmaurice Institute – has a helpful website with articles and training opportunities, found at www .voicecoachla.com.

Vocal expression in fight scenes

It is tempting to create the sounds of violence – screaming, sounds of injury, shock, fright, rage, and dying groans – through vocal strain. While there are methods that can be employed to aid the actor's vocal release of harsh sounds while also maintaining vocal health, it is very important for actor's to first experience release and openness within the vocal tract.

Sound itself is composed of vibrations in the airwaves that originate as vibrations from the vocal folds. These vibrations travel and make actual, physical contact with the tympanic membrane and with the miniscule bones within the inner ear (the malleus, incus, and stapes). The vibrations contacting these small structures in the ear are what we perceive as 'sound'. In this way, any sound we make directly contacts and physically connects with another human being. The act of sounding and speaking can essentially be seen as an act of physically touching whom we are speaking to and claiming one's right to be heard. Our first sounds at birth were a result of a need and of discomfort. Only later in life does the voice become associated with intellectual processing rather than immediate responses from impulse. Our work will be building the capacity to use the voice as a potential weapon that can not only hit its target with precision but can also be used with a variety of tactical combative variations.

The first step is finding and deepening areas of focus and placement by experiencing your voice in specific resonators in the body to develop released sounds. You can imagine the throat as a big empty tube through which the supported breath and voice can pass unimpeded, without tensions.

Hey you, get away from my car! (20 minutes)

In a fight scene, the throat and jaw are best served by remaining free and released at the same time as other parts of the body are engaged with a degree of muscular energy. This can be a challenging mixture to find, particularly when confronted with the heightened physical needs of a demanding fight. It is important to hone this ability, however, as the allowance of freedom within energy is a large part of the process of engaging the voice within scenes of dramatic physical conflict.

The exercise below is a good practice to engage with, as text work begins to be introduced into a choreographed fight. The goal of the exercise is to find the balance between engaged support of the voice and energized relaxation.

1   Speak the phrase: '*Hey you, get away from my car!*' to a
    partner standing 2–3 feet away. Only reach to your partner in
    front of you with your voice, not beyond your partner. Be aware

of the possibility that the aggressive quality of the phrase might create unneeded vocal tension by tightening of the breath or of the muscles within the chest, jaw, or neck. If so, allow that excess tension to release on the breath.

2 Ensure that you are breathing and connecting your sound to thought and impulse. It can be helpful to imagine your partner is next to a specific brand of car and is about to scrape its shiny new paint with a set of keys.

3 Allow the vibration of your voice to travel unimpeded up and out of your throat and mouth. If you feel any tension, grabbing, or vocal grinding, reduce the volume of your sound, and imagine spaciousness and freedom in your throat. Remind yourself that the vibration can travel with unimpeded flow on your breath. Imagine that your voice is simply the vibration of sound travelling effortlessly on the breath.

4 Slowly start to add more volume as you speak the phrase. Allow your connection to deep abdominal support to engage your breath.

5 Now place more distance between yourself and your partner. As you gradually increase the distance, start to also increase your deep breath support and subsequent vocal volume. As you are further away and as the intensity of your impulse or inspiration to speak increases, the in-breath will also get larger. In addition, the ribs will expand more to give you the air and energy you need, to say what needs to be said.

6 Allow the focus of your sound to be forward-placed, and feel your voice connecting with the roof of your mouth.

7 As you sequentially add greater and greater intention, volume, and energy, be aware of the possibility of any additional vocal strain that may occur. If you feel any throat-tightening, return again to a softer volume. Remind yourself that the vibration of your voice can travel on the breath with ease and flow, even in vocal extremes.

8 Start to place your body into postures of aggression and speak the line. Bend your knees, clench your fists, and point

threateningly at your imagined transgressor. Allow the throat
and the voice to remain free while engaging the deep muscles
of breath support.

9　Explore other words in place of 'car'. Allow the vowels their
full support and engagement as you speak the following
variations:

a　*'Hey you, get away from my Mazda Miati!'*

b　*'Hey you, get away from my Range Rover!'*

c　*'Hey you, get away from my Porsche!'*

d　*'Hey you, get away from my Ferrari!'*

e　*'Hey you, get away from my Audi!'*

Consonant and vowel violence (2–3 hours)

*(I have been inspired by the writings of Cicely Berry and Barbara
Houseman. See the Bibliography for more information.)*

A balance of both consonant and vowel energy is vital for the full textual
engagement of fight scenes to be released and fully realized. In a fight
sequence, the vowels carry the emotional content. The consonants
allow the structure of the vowels their full form, meaning, and potential
explosive content.

It is when the verbal attacks and counterattacks of the spoken text
no longer suffice, that physical violence must then occur. Exploring an
authentic expressivity in the verbal muscularity of the fight scene is a
vital prerequisite to fully engaging, with a seamless transition, into the
physical dialogue of the fight choreography. The specific nature and
quality of the language sounds within a scene can act as helpful clues
to the building of the physical confrontation that evolves out of the
dialogue.

A basic experiential understanding of the sounds of spoken English
can be helpful in developing a fuller awareness of the possibilities that
exist within language. Use the following chart as a point for beginning
your exploration of verbal dexterity within fight scenes. Explore the
words provided – words that are often used within fight scenes – and

allow the consonants and vowels to live fully in the body. Allow the full vibrations, explosiveness, and potential visceral danger of the sounds themselves to be felt and experienced while at the same time ensuring that the throat, jaw, and shoulders remain within an energized relaxation. Always work from deep vocal support.

The system used below provides an introduction to the sounds we make when speaking English. However, for a more complete analysis of the sounds possible, and their more exact definitions using the International Phonetic Alphabet, please refer to the available resources listed in the *Suggested Readings* at the end of this chapter.

1   Stand in a neutral stance, with your weight equally distributed on both feet.

2   First explore the sounds themselves in isolation. Experience the specific actions of the lips, teeth, jaw, and tongue that are involved in sounding each vowel or consonant.

3   Now, speak each of the words listed below – allowing the consonant and vowel energy to be both full and authentic.

4   Next, as each word is spoken, find a physical gesture or whole-body integration that can occur on the word. Allow that physical energy to influence the sounds and images within the word.

5   Ensure that while speaking and physicalizing each word, the vocal tract remains free and open. Allow your vocal resonance and placement to be placed forwards in the facial mask rather than focused in the throat. As is reminded in the previous exercise, always work from vocal support.

Consonants

- *Voiced Stop-Plosives:*
    - B (*Battle*)
    - D (*Die*)
    - G (*Dog*)

- **_Unvoiced Stop-Plosives:_**
  - P (*P*rick)
  - T (*T*rick)
  - K (*K*ick)

- **_Nasals:_**
  - M (*M*urder)
  - N (Spur*n*)
  - NG (Killi*ng*)

- **_Affricates_:**
  - CH (*Ch*arge)
  - J (*J*u*dg*e)

- **_Voiced Fricatives:_**
  - V (*V*iolent)
  - TH (I will kill *Th*ee)
  - Z (Dies)
  - ZH (Lie*g*e)

- **_Voiceless Fricatives:_**
  - F (*F*ate)
  - TH (*Th*row)
  - S (*S*word)
  - SH (*Sh*ut)
  - H (*H*ell)

- **_Voiced Continuants:_**
  - W (*W*ar)
  - R (*R*ip)
  - Y (*Y*ell)

Vowels

- **Long Vowels:**
  - OO (Fool)
  - AH (Father)
  - ER (Murder)
  - EE (Feel)

- **Diphthong Vowels:**
  - OH (Go)
  - OW (Foul)
  - AY (Rake)
  - EYE (Die)
  - OY (Foible)
  - EAR (Fear)
  - AIR (Scare)
  - URE (Fury)

- **Short Vowels:**
  - U (Foot)
  - UH (Gun)
  - A (Smack)
  - EH (Dead)
  - I (Hit)

Once an awareness of these sounds has been developed and you have been sensitized to a variety of consonant and vowel sounds that are possible, read aloud the following scene from *Romeo and Juliet* with an acting partner. As you continue to explore fight scene work, it is important to be sensitive to the hidden clues of how the language informs your emotional connections that affect your physicality. The internal dynamics of sound within language greatly aids the emotional propelling of the conflict of the scene into physical confrontation. How characters specifically use sounds within language is a form of behaviour affecting both how they move and how they fight.

Romeo and Juliet (Act III Scene I)

Scene summary: In Act III scene I, Tybalt insults and challenges Romeo to fight. Mercutio intervenes and fights with Tybalt. Through the physical interference of Romeo, Mercutio suffers a fatal wound from a thrust by Tybalt.

TYBALT:
Romeo, the love I bear thee can afford
No better term than this: thou art a villain.

ROMEO:
Tybalt, the reason that I have to love thee
Doth much excuse the appertaining rage
To such a greeting. Villain am I none;
Therefore farewell, I see thou knowest me not.

TYBALT:
Boy, this shall not excuse the injuries
Thou hast done me, therefore turn and draw.

ROMEO:
I do protest I never injured thee,
But love thee better than thou canst devise,
Till thou shalt know the reason of my love,
And so, good Capulet – which name I tender
As dearly as mine own – be satisfied.

MERCUTIO:
O calm, dishonourable, vile submission!
Alla stoccata carries it away.
[Draws]
Tybalt, you rat-catcher, will you walk?

TYBALT:
What wouldst thou have with me?

MERCUTIO:
Good King of Cats, nothing but one of your nine lives; that I mean to make bold withal, and as you shall use me hereafter, dry-beat the

rest of the eight. Will you pluck your sword out of his pilcher by the ears? Make haste, lest mine be about your ears ere it be out.

TYBALT:

I am for you.

ROMEO:

Gentle Mercutio, put thy rapier up.

MERCUTIO:

Come, sir, your passado.

[*They fight.*]

ROMEO:

Draw, Benvolio, beat down their weapons.

Gentlemen, for shame, forbear this outrage!

Tybalt, Mercutio, the Prince expressly hath

Forbid this bandying in Verona streets.

[*Romeo steps between them.*]

Hold, Tybalt! Good Mercutio!

[*Tybalt under Romeo's arms thrusts Mercutio in. Away Tybalt.*]

1. Focus first on the vowel sounds of the scene as you read through the text. Allow the vowels to be elongated, stretched, experienced, and fully sounded. Do not try to only speak the vowels but rather allow the vowels to lead the way as you speak through the text.

2. Ensure that you approach this exercise with a connection to how the sounds affect your 'internal geography'[2] rather than simply going through the motions of speaking the vowels. The 'internal geography' is the state of the emotions, thoughts, and images that result from outside stimuli. Just as real landscapes contain unique 'geographies' that determine the hills and valleys of the land, in a similar manner the actor has access to the quality of the inner geography of the mind and emotions. Allow the focus on the vowels to affect your thoughts, feelings, and images as you progress through the exploration.

3. What images, thoughts, and associations occur?

4. Now focus on the consonants as the primary driving force of the scene. Allow the Stop-Plosives to fully explode. Engage with the Fricative Consonants as sounds that indeed have a quality of 'friction'.

5. As before, rather than focusing solely on the technical aspects of the exercise, allow the consonant action to once again inform

your thoughts, images, intentions, and emotional availability within the sounds of the language itself.

6. Focusing on the consonants, did you experience a sense of violence in the movement of the language? A vitality inherent in the verbal confrontation? How might the consonant action of a text inform the seamless transition into physical violence?

7. Return again to reading the scene with your partner, allowing the focus on the vowels and consonants to naturally exist without placing overt focus on the sounds.

Discussion

1   Discuss how the vowel and consonant energy of the scene has changed. In what ways might this specificity of sound placement influence your vocal connection within fight scenes?

2   In what ways do the vowel and consonant sounds themselves affect the specificity of imagery?

3   What sounds or images particularly affected you?

4   What sounds and images did you hear differently?

5   In what ways did the complexity and flexibility of the sounds and images influence the physical engagement?

6   In what ways did the physicalization become a natural extension of the sounds and words?

Pitch, pace, and volume (60 minutes)

(I am grateful to Fitzmaurice Associate Teacher Jeff Morrison for first introducing me to this approach, as well as to Roberta Carerri of the Odin Teatret.)

To aid the connections between scene work and fight work, the following exercise exploring the vocal qualities of Pitch, Pace, and Volume helps to develop connections within the text work that encompasses fight scenes. The vocal and textual choices that are in the text leading up to a fight can directly influence the vocal choices within a fight. If a scene is played at a high level of intensity with little variation in Pitch,

Pace, and Volume and with overly tense physical choices, the fight's vocalizations will tend towards a similar level of simplified and monotone vocal responses. There is a tendency within scenes of violence, to only explore high levels of volume and at regular rhythms. The goal of this work is to explore the vocal and textual differentiations that are possible before, during, and after a choreographed fight.

Below is a suggested text for practice in gaining familiarity and flexibility with the process. Choose a piece of your own or memorize the text of Henry V below. Explore the monologue by speaking it to one acting partner. Engage pitch choices, volume differentiations, and pace variations that can further develop the seamless transition of your scene work into a choreographed fight that incorporates specific vocal responsiveness.

Henry V (Act III Scene III)

HENRY:
How yet resolves the governor of this town?
This is the latest parle we will admit;
Therefore to our best mercy give yourselves;
Or like men proud of destruction
Defy us to our worst: for, as I am a soldier,
A name that in my thoughts becomes me best,
If I begin the battery once again,
I will not leave the half-achieved Harfleur
Till in her ashes she lie buried.
The gates of mercy shall be all shut up,
And the flesh'd soldier, rough and hard of heart,
In liberty of bloody hand shall range
With conscience wide as well, mowing like grass
Your fresh-fair virgins and your flowering infants.
Therefore, you men of Harfleur,
Take pity of your town and of your people,
Whiles yet my soldiers are in my command;
Whiles yet the cool and temperate wind of grace
O'er blows the filthy and contagious clouds
Of heady murder, spoil and villainy.
If not, why, in a moment look to see

The blind and bloody soldier with foul hand
Defile the locks of your shrill-shrieking daughters;
Your fathers taken by the silver beards,
And their most reverend heads dash'd to the walls,
Your naked infants spitted upon pikes,
While the mad mothers with their howls confused
Do break the clouds.
What say you? Will you yield, and this avoid,
Or, guilty in defence, be thus destroyed?

Pitch

1 The partner who is the 'speaker' will speak the speech to their partner who is the 'conductor'.

2 The 'conductor' – listening closely to the content of the language – will place their hand at various heights, indicating the pitch range of which the 'speaker' will respond accordingly.

3 Allow the pitch changes to vary from both subtle to dramatic builds and cutbacks. The 'conductor' will explore with a sensitivity to deeply listening and responding to the natural changes in pitch that can aid the 'speaker's' text.

Pace

4 Again, the partner who is the 'speaker' will stand and speak the text to his or her partner who is the 'conductor'.

5 The 'conductor', using their hand to make circular movements towards themselves, will determine the 'speaker's' rate of speech. Quick circular movements will require a quicker rate of speech and a slower circular movement will signify a slower rate of speech.

6 The 'conductor' also has the option of placing their hand forwards in a 'stop' gesture, at which point the 'speaker' must pause. When the 'conductor' is ready for the 'speaker' to continue, the circular hand gestures resume.

7 Explore a variety of changes with rhythm – not for their own sake but for the purpose of aiding the 'speaker' in more deeply exploring the possibilities of intention and the specificity of images within the text.

Volume

1 This time the 'conductor' places their hand at various distances from the 'speaker'.

2 The 'speaker's' volume increases or decreases based on the distance the 'conductor' places him or herself. Either the hand can move in isolation or the 'conductor' may also walk towards or away from the speaker to conduct the 'speaker' into various volumes.

3 The 'speaker' should ensure that full vocal breath support is engaged. Refer to 'Finding your Breath for Fight Work' exercise from earlier in this chapter to reconnect with the practice of vocal support.

Discussion

1   How does the applications of a specific connection to pitch, pace, and volume transfer to work within the sounds of a fight?

2   How does this work aid you in connecting more fully to the language with a fight scene?

Voice and body

Your emotional availability as an actor is experienced through the body; thus finding your body's connection to your breath and to your voice is a primary investigation. This breath-body-emotion availability encourages greater artistic physical flexibility, interpersonal connection, and responsiveness. This section explores a variety of warm-ups for the body and the voice that promotes this flexibility and development of both skill and your availability to moment-to-moment responsiveness to an acting partner even within the highly choreographed nature of fight scenes.

Shakespeare's insults (30 minutes)

Explore the possibility that as you speak the insult to a partner, that your breath can be full and deep, your jaw released, your belly and chest soft, and your ribs available to *floating* downwards on the out-breath rather than squeezing in. Any vocal strain present indicates excess tension in the breath and within the throat. Ensure that your voice and throat remain free and open and that the primary muscular engagement occurs only in the deep muscles of breath support.

1   Choose an insult from the list below and practice speaking it alone several times. Allow yourself to fully commit to the sounds within the insult. Bite into the consonants and allow the vowels their full space.

2   Using the insults listed below, explore fully voicing the insult to a partner.

3   Allow the image of a smile in the back of your throat to provide a freedom of passage of breath and voice.

4 It can also be helpful to imagine only a *hint* of a yawn as you speak your insult to your partner.

5 Be aware of your vibrations and resonances. In what ways does your voice *feel* differently to you? It can be tempting to *listen* to your sound, which is deceptive due to the fact that we can never truly hear ourselves accurately, as others do. It can be very valuable to develop the capacity to feel the vibration and resonance differences that occur within your voice and body rather than to primarily listen to your own sound.

Teaching Tip: It can be tempting to revert to previously held vocal habits when reconnecting with aggressive text. If this is the case, gently remind the students that full vocal energy can occur without vocal tension. Encourage in your students that the voice can be felt and experienced rather than evaluated through hearing only.

---

1 ***Henry IV Part 2 (2.1.38-39)***

   {You} arrant, malmsey-nose knave!

2 ***Henry V (4.4.19)***

   Thou damned and luxurious mountain goat.

3 ***Julius Caesar (1.1.35)***

   You blocks, you stones, you worse than senseless things!

4 **King Lear (2.2.64)**

   Thou whoreson zed! Thou unnecessary letter!

5 **Love's Labour's Lost (4.1.67)**

   You pernicious and indubitate beggar!

6 **Measure for Measure (5.1.125)**

   [You] have a blasting and a scandalous breath.

7 **All's Well That Ends Well (1.1.119-20)**

   [Your] virginity breeds mites, much like a cheese.

8 **Antony and Cleopatra (2.5.42)**

   I have a mind to strike thee ere thou speak'st.

9 **As You Like It (5.1.55-57)**

   I will kill thee a hundred and fifty ways. Therefore tremble and depart.

10 **Coriolanus (4.5.191-192)**

   [I'll] scotch [you] and notch [you] like a carbonado.

11 **Cymbeline (4.2.85-86)**

   Thou art some fool, I am loath to beat thee.

12 **Hamlet (5.2.113-14)**

   [You are] spacious in the possession of dirt.

13 **Henry IV Part I (2.2.23-24)**

   [You] are the veriest varlet that ever chewed with a tooth.

14 **Richard II (2.1.156-57)**

   [You] rough rug-headed kerns, which live like venom!

15 **Richard II (5.5.107)**

   Go thou and fill another room in hell.

16 **Taming of the Shrew (2.1.397)**

   A vengeance on your crafty wither'd hide!

17 **Taming of the Shrew (4.1.144)**

   [You] whoreson beetle-headed, flap-ear'd knave!

18 **Taking of the Shrew (2.1 204)**

   If I be waspish, best beware my sting.

19 **The Tempest (1.1.40-41)**

   A pox o' your throat, you bawling, blasphemous, incharitable dog!

20 **The Tempest (1.1.43-44)**

   Hang, cur! Hang, you whoreson, insolent noise-maker!

21 **The Tempest (1.1.47-48)**

   [You are] as leaky as an unstanched wench.

22 Richard III (1. 3. 680)

Stay, dog, for thou shalt hear me.

23 Henry VI Part I (5. 4. 2677)

Decrepit miser! Base ignoble wretch!

24 Comedy of Errors (4. 4. 24)

Thou whoreson, senseless villain!

25 A Midsummer Night's Dream (3. 2. 293)

You juggler! You canker-blossom!

Head swipe and evasion with voice (20 minutes)
(https://vimeo.com/132085708)

(I am grateful to Gregory Hoffman, the Founder and Master Teacher of Dueling Arts International, for first introducing me to this evasion process, from which this exercise has been inspire and adapted.)

Once you have explored the support, engagement and release that occurs through an open passage of the throat, start to learn the basic technique of a head swipe with an evasion of a ducking action.

1. Memorize the following process of cues necessary for the safe execution of a swipe to the head that is ducked by a partner using an epee-bladed sabre-hilted single sword. With this weapon, gently but firmly place the palm of your hand on the grip, with the thumb placed on the flat part of the grip.

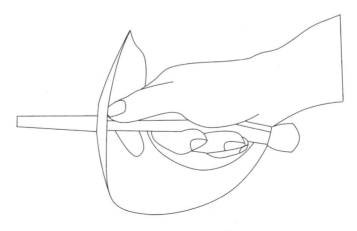

Teaching Tip: Alternatively, depending on class size, maturity, or age of the group, use only a pool noodle cut down to approximately 3 feet in length for this exercise.

---

a *Eye Contact:* Stand in a basic en garde stance. Refer to the exercise of the 'Basic Parry System' in Chapter 1 for a reminder of this stance. Establish eye contact with your partner. Take the time to ensure your partner is ready.

b *Preparation*: For right-handed students, the weapon is held in the right hand and the right foot is forwards. Lower the point of your weapon towards your right and towards the floor, before bringing it across your body to the left. At no time does the point of your sword cross the face or any part of your partner's body. After you have cleared your partner's body with the point down, raise the point of your weapon towards the ceiling and bring the hilt to just outside your left shoulder. The arm has crossed your body in this position and the blade is vertical. Allow the breath to drop in on the preparation. Be aware that at the same time as the action of this cue occurs, you should be continuing to look at the target area your sword will travel *after* your partner has initiated the correct response of evading.

c *Evasion*: See your partner evade by vertically lowering themselves downwards, however, make sure you continue looking at where their head *used to be* as they begin their action of evading. (Refer to #2, Step C, for a more detailed description of this movement.)

d *Attack:* Imagine sliding your sword slowly across a high table and cutting straight across where your partner's ears used to be. Ensure that you are looking at the target of where your partner's head *used to be*. Do not continue looking in your partner's eyes as they perform the duck. The body tends to go where it is looking. If you continue looking *at* your partner, you run the risk of bringing your sword down *into* your partner. The action of the swipe needs to be safely, slowly, and be very precisely placed. Do not bring your sword close to your partner's head by 'tracking' their movement downwards. Ensure your hand throughout this swiping action remains palm down rather than wobbling, twisting, or arcing your arm or hand during the swipe.[3] The swipe ends to your right, where the weapon can still be seen with your peripheral vision. Make sure the weapon does not twist behind you. During the action of the swipe, weight shift forwards. (Alternatively, explore this swipe with a small lunging action forwards. The video tutorial demonstrates both variations. Explore both options under the guidance of a stage combat teacher.) Ensure your leading foot remains pointed forwards and that your rear foot remains grounded. Keep the forward knee over the ankle of the foot rather than the knee extending out over or beyond the toes. Allow the breath to be easily released out on the execution of the swipe.

e *Recovery*: After your sword swipe has safely been performed and the technique has been completed, ensure the point of your weapon stays well away from your partner and never crosses their face as you both recover into an en garde stance.

2 Practice the safe evasion process that the partner who is evading must follow:

a *Eye Contact:* Stand neutrally with your right foot forwards. Establish eye contact with your imaginary partner. Breathe.

b *Preparation:* Watch your imaginary partner prepare their sword to their left shoulder. See that sword preparation land cleanly and precisely near their left shoulder. Allow the breath to fall in to your empty torso as you see the cue.

c *Evasion:* Imagine that there is a plumb line, with a weight attached to your tailbone that can vertically lower your hips towards the ground. During the action, allow your torso to remain in vertical alignment. Do not lean forwards or bend from the waist. With your legs well separated, bend at your knees as you vertically lower your torso downwards. Ensure your knees do not make contact with the ground. Keep your eyes on your partner and their sword, to ensure you remain aware of the placement of their weapon and the relative placement of their body throughout the technique. You must be able to maintain your vision on your partner so that you can see their swipe of the sword as it passes harmlessly over where your head used to be. Breathe out on your evasion. While you evade, it is important that your sword does not in any way threaten your partner nor does it raise upwards into the pathway of the swiping blade.

d *Attack:* Imagine seeing your partner's sword harmlessly pass overhead where your head used to be.

e *Recovery:* Having imagined that your partner's sword has now safely cleared, stand back up and prepare to repeat the exercise.

With your partner, speak aloud these five steps as you practice this exercise. Proceed slowly and precisely to learn the precision needed to perform this technique safely and effectively.

Teaching Tip: Both 'out of distance' and 'in distance' head swipes can be employed. However, if performed out of distance, it is recommended that at least 24" of distance is maintained between the furthest extension of the weapon and the partner who is ducking. As a reminder, explore this partnered technique only under the guidance of a stage combat teacher, as there are many considerations of distance, targeting, and audience/performer angles that are very specific features of safely and effectively performing this technique. As always, safety must be the #1 priority in all stage combat techniques.

Begin to find the variations in which sound, text and the physical actions are connected. Use the following as a foundation for starting to connect text to violence:

1   Speak the text *before the physical action occurs*.

2   Speak the text *after the physical action has occurred*.

As a general rule, avoid speaking the text and performing the action at the same time. Speaking text and performing stage combat techniques simultaneously often results in a loss of clarity – vocally, physically, and emotionally. The actor can only play one action at a time. Allowing yourself to engage fully in the insult verbally, followed by the insult physically – or vice versa – often more clearly defines the intentions for the audience and heightens the released intentional engagement for the actor.

Proceeding first with slow-motion, explore this basic swipe and evasion drill with breath, open sound, consonants, and finally text in the following order:

Version 1

Proceeding at 1/4 speed, perform the process listed above with a partner.

1   For both partners, allow your body to silently breathe in on the preparation of the attack.

2   For both partners, allow your breath to release silently on the follow-through of the attack and the evasion.

3   Switch partners.

Variation 2

Explore variations of *when* the breathing impulse – either inhaling or exhaling – occurs. Holding or delaying when the breath-in or breath-out occurs adds depth of dimension and the illusion of spontaneity within a fight.

Variation 3

Explore audible intakes of breath as options throughout the fight sequence. Possible placement of an audible intake might be:

1   On the preparation of the attack from the partner who evades.

2   On the action of evading.

3   On the preparation of the attack.

Version 4

Start to add voiced sounds to the sequence of the head swipe:

1 Allow yourself to silently breathe-in on the preparation of the attack.

2 Allow a vocalized vowel to release out on the follow-through of the attack and the evasion. Ensure that the release of the vocalized vowel is preceded with a gentle silent /h/ to avoid a hard Glottal Attack (or 'strong glottal stop') on the vowel.

3 Switch partners.

Teaching Tip: What is a 'Hard-Glottal Attack'? Saying 'Uh OH!' can be used to feel how the folds can forcefully be brought together. This type of vocal attack can create possibilities for muscular tensions in the jaw, tongue, shoulders, and neck. It is very useful to start a committed sound within a fight with an openly breathed, unvoiced /h/ prior to the vowel sound that is released. This allows the vocal folds to come together with more gentleness and effectiveness in a way that allows a fullness of sound to occur but does not create as much literal violence within the structures of the vocal apparatus. It can be helpful to recognize that each vocal fold is approximately only the size of your pinky fingernail and the two structures vibrate near the rate of a bee's wings.

Version 5

(I am grateful to Brian Evans – SAFD Certified Teacher and Associate Instructor of Fitzmaurice Voicework – for our discussions regarding connecting the voice to violence within this exercise.)

1 Allow your breath to be silent on the preparation of the attack

2 On the evasion, release a short sound of the start of a curse word. However, limit yourself to only the first consonant sounds. A 'fffu' or a 'shhhi' – and other variations – can be used.

3 On the attack, explore adding vowel sounds, but do not limit yourself to the most commonly used vowel sounds within fight scenes, characterized as repeated grunts of 'AH', 'ARGH', and 'OOPH'. Instead, explore what happens when short, staccato – or longer sounds – of various vowels are released on the attack and or the evasion. Try 'ee!', 'oh!', 'uh!', 'i!' (as in 'hit'), 'eye!', and 'oo!', and 'aye!'

4 Allow the sounds to always connect to an emotional and imaginative authenticity within your physicality.

Version 6

1 Allow your bodies to silently allow the breath in on the preparation of the attack.

2 Release a vocalized consonant/vowel cluster on the follow-through of the attack. Examples can include:

   a BOEZT!

   b VAPT!

   c CROHPT!

   d TRAYPT!

3 Check in to ensure that your breath is free, supported placement is forwards, jaw is soft, and that the neck is released. Knees should remain soft and pliable rather than locked. If you find that you are starting to experience vocal tensions, re-explore releasing only on a completely silent breath and slowly build your way up to adding vocalized sound.

Teaching Tip: Ensure that students are allowing the knees to be soft throughout their work in the Stage Combat Arts. Locked knees can result in tensions that proceed all the way up through the body, including within the vocal tract. When the knees are even slightly softened, the breath can have a tendency to deepen and a grounding of both the voice and the body develops.

At the first sign of vocal strain or excess effort in the voice with any of these variations, take the time to coordinate the physicality with the breath. Build the habit that the voice in stage combat can be free and released instead of tight and strained.

Variation 7

1 Allow yourself to silently allow the breath to drop in on the preparation of the attack.

2 Use one of the words from the list below to release on both the attack and the evasion:

Attacker	Defender
Die!	Help!
Yes!	No!
Now!	Never!
Away!	Stop!

3 Allow the ribs to remain free and flexible to the breath. As you engage with the committed expression of these words, avoid the temptation to squeeze the ribs inwards on your out-breath. Instead, imagine the ribs continuing to expand outwards when there is increased vocal demand.

4 Find an opportunity to repeat words ('Die Die *DIE* Die Die' or 'no no *NO*') before or after the head swipe occurs. Find variations of rising tempo, decreasing tempo, and regular tempos within the repetition of these words or sounds. Allow tempo alone to begin influencing character thought and feeling. When adding language, be sure to proceed in slow-motion and communicate with your partner exactly when – vocally – the action of cueing the swipe will occur within the physicality.

5 Add pitch, pace, and volume differentiations to these words.

6 Watch for the tendency to allow the added element of vocal commitment to degrade the physical safety practices that have been previously practiced.

Variation 8

1   Silently allow the breath in on the preparation of the attack and evasion.

2   As might be found in contemporary plays, use one of the heightened pieces of text below to speak to your partner. Explore placing emphasis on speaking only before or after your choreographed head swipe sequence.

3   Allow the deep muscles of breath support to be engaged, leaving the ribs and muscles within the throat to be free and open.

4   As before, if vocal strain starts to become a part of the work, re-explore the head swipe with only a released breath. Take note of how this action of the body and breath feels. Take your time to work your way back up to using text within the movement while still maintaining an element of freedom within the breath and voice.

5   Find your unique 'take' on the phrase by finding the most important word within each sentence. Allow that word its full expression – using pitch, pace, and volume to communicate your specific and creative choice.

- 'Please, just shut up!'
- 'You are screwed!'
- 'Stop talking and listen!'
- 'What is it you want? What?!'
- 'You don't want to mess with me!'
- 'Come with me, now!'
- 'You are lying. I saw what happened!'
- 'Tell me. Now!'

Discussion

- How does it inform the line to be full vocally and physically but without excess vocal or physical tension?
- How does the quality of the breath affect the emotions within the physicality of a head swipe?

- How does an incorporation of the breath and the voice affect the ways in which a character might be either provoked to violence or the ways in which a character may attempt to avoid violence?

Vocal choice

(I have been inspired by the research and writings of Rocco Dal Vera in his article 'The Voice in Heightened Affective States' found in the VASTA journal, 'The Voice in Violence'. See the Bibliography for more information.)

There are many emotional, physical, and tactical variations that can inform the nature of vocal responses during a stage fight. In your work you can discover creative choices that most fully reveal the vocal storytelling events during the course of a fight. For instance, each active verb in the lists of playable tactics (found in the 'Exploring Tactics' exercise of Chapter 4) could uniquely influence the voice within a fight scene. However, as a foundational starting point for your further explorations, below are six basic categories of many common elements that may affect the voice within fight scenes.

1 Breath
    a Held
    b Managed
    c Free
2 Anger/Aggression
3 Fear
4 Pain
    a Emotional
    b Physical
5 Effort
6 Process of Dying

Within a fight, the truthful variations of your vocal responses begin to add the illusion of spontaneity to a fight, in which the violence appears to be occurring for the first time. The descriptions below are highly subject to a great variety of subtle differences, volumes, rhythms, qualities, resonances, pitches, and durations. While clarity of storytelling, theatricality, intentionality, and theatrical environments ultimately dictate the development of the artistic choices, we will use the following basic descriptions as starting points for the further exploration of vocal response to text.

The emotional responses described must be translated into playable intentions and tactics. Playing 'Anger' or 'Fear' leads to presentational acting habits that are devoid of human authenticity and truth. It needs to be the intentionality of the moment that results in these potential emotions. Nevertheless, this awareness of vocal response to emotional states can be helpful within the process of developing intention-oriented creative choices.

I. Sounds of breath

The breath – either held, managed, or free – offers many choices within fight scenes. The 'held breath' when faced with the fight or flight response is one of many artistic choices that can be a part of your artistic arsenal. This is not the breath-holding pattern that tends to be part of an unconscious habit but rather the conscious exploration of breath-holding (as an artistic choice) that may be the result of fear, aggression, or shock within a scene of violent confrontation.

The Yoga-like 'managed breath' – in which variations of controlled breathing patterns are engaged by the actor – communicates and develops a very specific level of energy and focus.

And the energized relaxation of a 'free breath', a released breathing pattern that allows the actor to breathe with freedom and impulse, develops a third variation that is applicable to many moments within fight scenes.

Actors are sometimes hesitant to engage with a character's experience of exhaustion within the breath. At the end of a long fight, as an artistic choice a character may begin to feel fatigue. The accompanying effort that the breath pattern develops can further deepen the illusion of human beings in physical conflict.

- *Audible Breath Inhalation and Release:* When the throat is relaxed and free, the breath is silent on both the inhalation and exhalation. However, an audible sound of the breath can be a valuable choice for actors to explore, when consciously employed, within a fight scene.

o   Audible inhales of breath occurs when the breath is inhaled through a slight closure or engagement of the vocal folds, creating sound that is unique and potentially disturbing in its quality of sound. It tends to be the sound made when we witness a car accident or when a child nearly stumbles and falls.

o   The stage combat technique of being choked often requires an audible inhalation. At times, actors mistakenly play the illusion of being choked by breathing out or holding the breath during the technique. Instead, the body's natural response would be to attempt to *inhale* and breathe more. Within the theatrical technique of a choke, the illusion is that the throat is being restricted. The sound of the character's need for oxygen will result in sounds that are produced through the effort of the character's breath trying to *enter* the lungs. It is often much more effective to explore breathing options during this technique than to cut off or limit the breath.

•   *Inaudible Breath Inhalation and Release:* In addition to the breath being able to be *audibly* inhaled and exhaled, the breath can also be inhaled and exhaled *inaudibly*. A silent inhalation is created by an open and released vocal tract. Though the inhalation can be without sound, silence does not mean that this breathing pattern does not affect the actor or audience.

II. Anger/Aggression

The energy of this sound is outwardly directed. Imagine a line of focus originating in the centre of your abdomen, travelling down and around your pelvis, up your entire spine, and out your third eye in the middle of your forehead.

•   For men, pitch variations generally occur within the middle of the range. For women, the general pitch range occurs towards the higher end of the range. However, for the actor, be aware of consistently high placed vocal pitches being an indication of excess tension.

- Breath is highly supported and engaged.
- Breath is often centred low in the body. Explore feeling your breath through your nose, as well as potentially through your teeth.
- Articulation is highly engaged.
- Engage only the deep muscles of breath support in the torso while allowing the muscles within the throat to stay open and relaxed. Imagine the ribs expanding outwards (rather than squeezing inwards) in your vocalization of aggressive sound.
- Remember, that the actor cannot afford to assume all of the character's tensions as his or her own.

III. Fear

The energy of this sound is inwardly directed. Imagine the energy of the sound *entering* your body rather than being *expelled* from your body as it is with Anger/Aggression.

The fear of the unknown, fear of what may be, fear of inflicting damage or being the recipient of injury is present in many scenes of violence. Recognizing the possibility of defeat but fighting onwards regardless of the dangers can be a tremendously compelling human experience to witness within the context of a story. Allowing a character to experience fear, and the accompanied vocal and physical manifestations of trying to hide this emotion, further develops the illusion of spontaneity and danger.

- The speech rate tends to be quick.
- The breath tends to be focused high in the chest.
- The breath tends to quicken.
- The average pitch range tends towards the higher registers within this emotive state.

IV. Pain

The effects of pain physically and emotionally, and the evolution of how the sensation of pain evolves after the body suffers a violent action, affect the breath and the voice's connection to pitch, rhythm, quality, resonance, and intensity. In addition, as SAFD Fight Master Dale Girard explains in his book, *Actors On Guard*, it has been found that injuries that occur in or near the centre of the body tend to result in lower vocal pitches. Injuries that occur further from the centre of the body tend to result in higher vocal pitches.

It is also well documented that adrenalin can alter the sensation of pain. There are many reports of individuals sustaining major injuries but not immediately realizing the extent of the injury.

'Emotional Pain' is an important element with the vocalizations of a fight scene. Characters in fight scenes have opportunities – both physically and emotionally – to 'get into trouble'. Find those moments when an emotional pain of your character might be experienced within a fight, either as a result of the impending physical loss of life or as a result of inflicting physical damage on another.

V. Effort

The experience of playing elements of physical effort can often cause vocal tension leading to areas of vocal misuse and breath constriction. It is your task to be able to create the physical and vocal *illusion* of hefting a heavy broadsword towards an opponent after a long fight while at the same time not actually damaging the vocal tissues within the larynx. Lifting oneself off the ground after a wound, carrying a dead body off the stage, pulling a sword out of a recipient – can all potentially be further supported by adding sounds of 'effort'.

The following suggestions will aid in the safe and effective vocal experience of playing 'effort'.

- Ensure the throat remains released and open rather than held and constricted.

- Initiate the open vowel sounds of effort with a silent /h/ prior to tone. Avoid hard Glottal Attacks.

- It is a helpful exercise to return to the 'Unbendable arm' exercise in Chapter 1 to aid your redefining of 'effort' as 'released extension'.

Teaching Tip: This silent /h/ is produced without any sound of the breath exiting the throat. If the students make this sound and there is the noise of air being expelled, this represents an unnecessary engagement of the vocal folds. It can potentially be a valuable choice to create this sound within a fight but better to first explore the facility of releasing the breath on a completely silent /h/ prior to the open vowel sound.

- There should be no effects of any pain or strain. Vocal muscles may tire but should be able to recuperate within 15–20 minutes.
- Explore short and subtle Fricative Consonant actions of /F/, /SH/, or /V/ in the playing of effort to keep the engagement of the voice above and away from the vocal folds.
- Throughout this work, it is helpful to recognize work on staged violence, regardless of how violent the choreography might need to *appear* to be, is about physically connecting with and protecting your partner. This simple reminder is often helpful in allowing the vocal responses and breath freedom to experience a larger degree of relaxed readiness.

VI. Death

The death of a character within dramatic conflict can be terrifying, relieving, surprising, uncomfortable, or even comedic. Depending on the style of production and the quality of the death, the actor and fight director need to be attuned to the breath and the qualities of the dying process that theatrically create the illusions desired.

The breath of death (30 minutes)

(I am grateful to Catherine Fitzmaurice for first introducing me to this exploration.)

1   One partner lies comfortably on his or her back, relaxed into the ground. The legs should be extended and the eyes closed.

2   Now slowly find a position that is comfortable but somewhat angular, in which the breath is still allowed to be relatively free and open. This position might resemble a prone position that a combatant might be in having recently expired as a result of wounds from a duel.

3   The partner not lying on the ground should position themselves off to the side of the partner or near the partner's head. All attention is placed on the partner lying on the ground.

4   The partners in the observer role should be prompted to ask themselves the question: 'How do I know this person is alive? What visual and energetic clues do I subtly receive that makes me know my partner is alive human being?'

5   The partner lying on the ground is only responsible for relaxing into the floor. Any attempt to 'demonstrate aliveness' to their observing partner should be avoided. Also, however, any attempt to appear 'dead' by breathing more shallowly than necessary should also be avoided at this point.

6   After a few minutes, without talking, have the partners switch and repeat.

7   Discuss what you observed and discovered.

8   Once again, switch who is lying on the ground. Partners who were observing now lie on the ground throughout the space in various 'dead' physical postures of death. Be careful to choose a position that is comfortable enough to remain in for an extended time, but does not appear physically as 'sleep'.

9   Each participant on the ground will close his or her eyes as an option, or allow the eyes to be 1/3 open softly as a secondary option. The eyes should not be open wide as this tends to quickly dry the eyes.

10 Ask the participants to allow the ribs to release to the breath on an easy but extended outwards rib release as the breath easily falls into the torso. With the ribs remaining gently extended, the 'dead' participants will breathe very shallowly.

11 The energetic holding of the ribs in their outwards position allows the lungs to use their full capacity of the little breath that is being employed by the body.

12 Allow the Autonomic Nervous System to organize the timing of your breath. *Wait* for the impulse to breathe. The breath can be very shallow in its inhalation and exhalation.

13 While the 'dead' participants shallowly breathe in their death position, instruct the other half of the class to slowly walk around the space and observe the 'dead bodies'.

14 Have each student carefully observe the qualities of death portrayed and the nature of what differences they note in a body that gives the impression of no longer breathing.

15 Repeat with the observers now taking on the roles of dead bodies.

Discussion

- What did you specifically observe in the breath pattern of the exercise?

- How does the illusion of the absence of breath in this exercise affect both partners?

The process of a character dying occurs in many plays. In Shakespeare's plays for example, characters frequently die on stage: Romeo, Juliet, Roderigo, Desdemona, Macbeth, Hamlet, Gertrude, Hotspur – just to name a few – all experience their deaths in full view of an audience. This process of dying can be a powerful and moving experience for an audience or inappropriately comedic. The quality and timing of the breath in relationship to the illusion of dying must be carefully and specifically choreographed. Care should taken to not allow the death become a vaudeville act of heavy breaths which suddenly and unexpectedly stop.

However, one of the characteristics of comedy is the introduction of the 'unexpected'. Death can be funny when the actual moment of dying is played as a sudden stopping of the breath and a collapse of the body. Clearly, in the scene from *Henry IV Part I*, the breathing pattern within the death needs to be played more subtly. Allowing the breathing to slowly decrease in rate and length is often useful in these final moments. The final death moment is often aided by a final breath that is slowly and gently exhaled with almost imperceptible subtlety as to whether that was indeed the final breath or not. It is useful to consider how Hotspur is trying to stay alive, and the loss of his ability to breathe is a primary obstacle.

In this scene from *Henry IV Part I*, Hal kills Hotspur at the end of a long fight. Hotspur has nearly 10 lines of text to progress from mortally wounded to fully expired. The quality and nature of the actor's breathing patterns can be a significant part of how this death proceeds. With a partner, read the following scene out loud, paying particular attention to where in this final speech of Hotspur the breaths may be artistically chosen without overwhelming the sense and structure of the language. Too frequent breaths can disjoint the text to such a degree that we no longer hear the meaning but only are seduced by the emotive content. Care must be taken to ensure that the actor's intention to communicate remains stronger than the need to play an overly realistic death scene. Explore how Hotspur's breathing can primarily occur at the end of his verse lines.

Henry IV Part I – Act V Scene IV

HOTSPUR: If I mistake not, thou art Harry Monmouth.
PRINCE: Thou speak'st as if I would deny my name.
HOTSPUR: My name is Harry Percy.
PRINCE: Why then I see
A very valiant rebel of the name.
I am the Prince of Wales, and think not, Percy,
To share with me in glory any more.
Two stars keep not their motion in one sphere,
Nor can one England brook a double reign
Of Harry Percy and the Prince of Wales.

HOTSPUR: Nor shall it, Harry, for the hour is come
To end the one of us, and would to God
Thy name in arms were now as great as mine!
PRINCE: I'll make it greater ere I part from thee,
And all the budding honours on thy crest
I'll crop to make a garland for my head.
HOTSPUR: I can no longer brook thy vanities.
[They Fight]
HOTSPUR: O Harry, thou has robb'd me of my youth!
I better brook the loss of brittle life
Than those proud titles thou hast won of me.
They wound my thoughts worse than thy sword my flesh.
But thoughts, the slaves of life, and life, time's fool,
And time, that takes survey of all the world,
Must have a stop. O, I could prophesy,
But that the earthy and cold hand of death
Lies on my tongue. No, Percy, thou art dust,
And food for –
[Dies]
PRINCE: For worms, brave Percy. Fare thee well, great heart.

Teaching Tip: Two excellent books to refer to are *On Killing: The Psychological Cost of Learning to Kill in War and Society* and *On Combat: The Psychology and Physiology of Deadly Conflict in War and in Peace*, both by Lt. Col. Dave Grossman. These books detail the physiology and psychology of killing in helpful ways for the fight director and actor involved in fight scenes.

Discussion

- How does the nature, quality and timing of the breath itself affect the meaning of Hotspur's last dying speech?
- Is there an opportunity for Hal's line ('For worms, brave Percy') to finish not only Hotspur's last thought but to also fulfil Hotspur's last failing breath?

Vocal extremes

Where and how the body breathes and vocalizes in relationship to a theatrical stab, a twist of the blade, and a retraction of the weapon from a wound – all offer the opportunity to act the fight with a depth of humanity and presence. Telling the story of the fight requires your skilful use of the breath and an awareness of the potential voluntary and involuntary sounds that support the physical work of the choreography.

A tendency when first introducing sound into a fight is to add a vocalization for every attack and defence. This not only is an inaccurate human representation of theatrical storytelling but it also tends to slow fights down to a 'plodding' regular tempo that can reduce the effectiveness of your full physical engagement. The body tends to move at the same rhythms as how the voice is engaging. If the voice is making a strong grunt on every move, then the body can only stay within that predictable rhythm. Instead, look for the voluntary and involuntary sounds that occur in the fight. Specifically choose and heighten specific vocal moments that support the unique story of the violence.

Voluntary and involuntary sounds

Voluntary sounds within a fight are those responses that are the direct result of playing a conscious intention. These aggressive sounds are often intended to startle, unbalance, freeze, or surprise an opponent. The following list of tactics describe those times in which voluntary sounds within a fight might be used:

- To scare an opponent
- To intimidate
- To knock off balance
- To disarm
- To push away
- To lure
- To deceive
- To disengage

- ○ To feint
- ○ To seduce into a trap.

On the other hand, involuntary sounds are mostly unconsciously originated and are largely without thought or conscious control. Examples of Involuntary Sounds include:

- ○ The in-breath of air when we witness a near accident and immediately audibly inhale.
- ○ When we experience an injury, or fear bodily harm.
- ○ When we narrowly avoid injury and the result is either an audible inhalation of the breath or a vocalized exhalation.
- ○ Extreme effort when we are physically extending ourselves in times of athletic rigour. The sounds and grunts of exhaustion and physical challenge will often create involuntary sounds of the breath and voice.

Vocal volume

When you are playing scenes of violence, due to the nature of the high stakes involved, you might be tempted to engage the voice consistently at the highest of volumes possible throughout a fight. The temptation to allow every moment to have the same vocal value is akin to an actor stressing every word in a sentence with the same emphasis. To emphasize every word in a sentence is to emphasize nothing. The same is true about vocal usage within staged combat. The intentions and physical tactics in a fight must reflect vocal responses that are specific, and reveal character thought and feeling.

Renowned Broadway Fight Director, B.H. Barry, advises that actors and directors examine what would be missing from a dramatic text if the fight were removed. Clearly, basic storytelling elements wouldn't happen without the fight between Mercutio and Tybalt (i.e., the death of Mercutio), however, the question remains of what *specific* aspects of character must be revealed through the vocal and physical storytelling elements of the fight. A variety of vocal volumes are one of many vocal choices that are possible to clearly embody the story of the fight and the journey of the character.

A practical method of exploring vocal volume possibilities is through an exercise in a non-contact slapping technique.

Basic non-contact slap with voice (30 minutes)[4]
(https://vimeo.com/132085711)

Practice the vocal volumes of the slap in isolation prior to engaging with partnered work. If vocal tension is present at any level, ensure that you can connect with your voice through a freely aligned spine and relaxed throat prior to engagement with a partner.

Accidental contact with a hand to the face can result in serious injury, including dislocation to the jaw, damage to the eardrum, broken nose, scratched cornea, or damage to the lymph nodes within the neck. Engage with the work with precision and with a full focus on safety. Fingernails must be trimmed and short. All jewellery must be removed. *At least* 6″–10″ must be maintained by partners at all times within this exercise.

> *Teaching Tip:* Often, when teaching larger groups in workshops or with younger students of high school age, I will increase the level of distance to ensure all students remain 100 per cent safe.

This non-contact slap focuses on three distinct steps:

1 Eye Contact
2 Preparation
3 Follow-Thru

> *Teaching Tip:* Ensure all students speak aloud these three steps with their partner while they are slowly learning the action.

You should remain standing and neutrally balanced for this exercise. Falling, stumbling, and physically reacting away from a slap requires specific training. Keep in mind that there are a great many variations of how to perform a safe non-contact slap on stage.

1   Be sure to engage with a thorough vocal and physical warm-up that energizes, relaxes and readies the muscles of the neck and shoulders for the technique to follow. Several warm-up exercises from Chapters 1 and 2 should be undertaken prior to engaging with this exploration.

2   Partner A will place the left leg forwards, their right leg behind, and gently soften the knees.

3   With a partner, establish a safe distance of at least 6″–10″ of the slapping hand from your partner's face. With an outstretched right arm and hand (with fingers directed upwards rather than at your partner), ensure at all times that this distance rule is maintained.

4   Partner A (the partner who will perform the action of the slap with their right hand) will be off-line (to Partner A's right) of Partner B. Left shoulder of Partner A should be facing the left shoulder of Partner B.

5   The 'Attacker' is facing downstage, and the 'Recipient' is facing upstage.

6   Both partners will establish eye contact, as they allow the breath to release naturally on both the in-breath and the out-breath.

7   Partner A will bring their right hand up towards their own right shoulder. This cued position needs to be fully visible to Partner B. This serves as a visual preparatory cue to the partner who is receiving the action. At this point, Partner B should look at the cued slapping hand, as he or she plays the threat of this imminent attack.

8   Partner A will slowly bring their right slapping hand across the area of their partner's face ensuring at least 6″–10″ distance from the face is maintained throughout the action. During the action of the slap, the fingers remain oriented towards the ceiling rather than directed at your partner's face. This hand will cross the partner's face – at safe distance – in a curving arc. The slap proceeds in a perfectly horizontal line rather than being angled upwards or downwards. Both partners must avoid leaning in to each other nor allow the feet to come off the ground. The

tendency will be, for the partner slapping, to over-rotate and bring the back foot off the ground. Ensure that both feet remain grounded to maintain balance and a safe distance between you and your partner.

9 The 'motor' of the slap occurs at Partner A's centre – the hips – rather than the arm.

10 After several times of slowly passing through the safe target area to ensure distance is exact and always maintained, start to add the physical reaction of Partner B, accompanied only by an exhalation of the breath. The reaction of the head and neck needs to stay relaxed and free. Allow the head to turn in the direction of the slap's trajectory to only a 45-degree angle from one's partner. Avoid the tendency to over-rotate the head to a 90-degree angle, at which point whiplash to the muscles of the neck is a possibility. The partner being slapped will crisply perform a 'Clap Knap' near their centre and in front of the body to create the sound of the hand making contact with the face. This 'knap' (the sound of the 'slap') is made by crisply clapping the fingers of one hand onto and past the palm of the other hand. This action of the knap should remain completely hidden from an audience's perspective.

11 Continue to explore the action of the slap with the accompanied vocal reaction after the knap has taken place by starting to add sound to the breath. Initiate the vowel sound of accepting the slap or delivering the slap with a silent, unvoiced /h/ prior to the open vowel sound.

12 After the slap and reaction have occurred, Partner B can explore options of lightly touching the jaw or cheek in a specific location to play the localization of pain. Alternatively, bringing one hand to the face is not necessary after the slap has occurred. What is important is to play the evolution of the relationship *between* you and your partner after the slap has occurred rather than being seduced into playing pain reactions at the exclusion of your acting partner. After the slap has occurred, reconnect with your partner.

13 Allow the possibility that the breath alone, or in connection to the voice, can be uniquely affected within this exercise.

14 After several rounds of experiencing this silent /h/ prior to the vowel sound of a slap, start to communicate with your partner the 'volume' of the slap and the vocal responses needed. Explore the volume variations described below between 1 and 10.

15 Within this work, explore the possibilities of the 'Attacker' having the majority of the vocal response. Reverse the scenario and allow the 'Recipient' to be responsible for the vocal response.

- **Volumes 1–5:** Both feet remain firmly planted on the ground throughout the action. The vocal reaction has a tendency to increase in volume throughout the increase of physical commitment.

- **Volumes 6–10:** As the 'acted volume' and 'knap volume' of the slap increases, the distance between the partners must increase as well. As before, both feet should remain grounded throughout the entirety of the action. The vocal reactions have a tendency to increase in both volume and pitch as the intensity of the slap increases. An image of a large empty pipe through which breath and voice can pass without impediment is helpful to imagine throughout the exercise.

Discussion

- In what ways could these physical and vocal variations affect the story of the fight?
- In what ways does the breath and voice of this stage combat illusion combine to increase the effectiveness of the technique?

Framing the knap and pain reactions (20 minutes) – Written by Brian Evans

(Special thanks to Payson Burt, who first introduced me to the phrases 'Framing the Knap' and 'Masking the Knap.')

The rhythm of the fight is every bit as important as the types of sounds that are being produced. Too many overlapping sounds, important lines being lost, as well as predictable rhythms can diminish an otherwise compelling stage fight. Being able to perform vocal reactions with a variety of rhythms is an important skill to be developed.

The 'knap', or sound of impact, is often mistakenly 'masked' by the vocal reaction of the victim in stage combat. The actor receiving the blow will vocalize at the same time as the knap. This can muddy the technique. When someone experiences real pain, the following chain of events occurs:

1 Pain receptors in our skin send an impulse to the spinal cord, brainstem, and brain where the sensation of pain is registered.

2 The information is interpreted.

3 The pain is perceived.

This takes time – not a lot, relative to the time of the whole fight (maybe just a fraction of a second) – but it does not happen simultaneously with the knap. More realistically we can react vocally *after* the knap to express the pain. This 'Pain Reaction' is one side of Framing the Knap.

1 As the 'Victim' of a 'slap', perform the 'Clap Knap'.

2 Practice breathing in while performing the knap.

3 Alternately, practice exhaling while performing the knap.

4 After inhaling with the knap, vocalize the reaction of pain.

5 After exhaling with the knap, inhale, and then vocalize the reaction of pain.

6 Experiment with different lengths of delay before vocalizing.

7 Explore different volumes in the reaction to the pain.

Now, with a partner perform the Slap with Voice exercise to incorporate the Framing of the Knap with the voiced reaction of pain.

1 Fill each moment after the illusion of impact with intention. Let one hand immediately move to touch the face with the goal of soothing the face. Voice the pain in spite of your attempt to ease the pain.

2 Voice the pain as you make eye contact with the 'Attacker'. Shame them for being so brutal.

The other side of Framing the Knap is the preparation for the actor who is slapping. The 'Attacker' or the 'Recipient' can make this sound. It occurs before the knap and can include text, non-verbal sounds, or both.

1 Refer again to the directions of the Slap with Voice exercise earlier in this chapter.

2 As the 'Attacker,' experiment with voicing during the preparatory cue.

3 Practice inhaling prior to lifting the hand for the preparatory cue. Then, as the right hand is lifted as a cue to the right shoulder, experiment with voiced sounds until the shared action of the slap occurs. Continue to exhale but unvoiced during the Slap.

4 The 'Attacker' can play with vowel and consonant sounds as well as one word phrases such as 'No!' or 'Wait!'

Now practice both participants Framing the Knap. Be sure that the sequence of safe technique is followed from the Slap with Voice exercise, described earlier in this chapter.

5 The 'Attacker' will make the initial vocal sound on the preparatory cue. As both participants perform the action of the slap together, the 'Recipient' will make the knap. After the knap, the 'Recipient' will voice a sound of a reaction.

6 The 'Recipient' can practice making both sounds of the Frame. As the 'Attacker' performs the preparatory cue, the 'Recipient' will experiment with voiced inhalations, non-verbal sounds, and partial words. Continue with the shared action of the slap, knap, and 'Victim' making the pain reaction sound after the knap.

7 Now incorporate text. Practice a short scene in which the 'Recipient' says 'No!' on the 'Attacker's' preparatory cue; the 'Victim' performs the knap and the pain reaction; and the 'Attacker' states: 'I told you!' after the pain reaction.

8   Another variation:

> 'Attacker': 'don't you ever...'
>
> Perform the Slap
>
> 'Recipient': Pain reaction sound
>
> 'Attacker':'... come here again!'

9   There are countless variations of Framing the Knap. Practice each variation with the same care and attention to detail as in the previous exercises. Framing can also apply to 'Forced Reactions' as described in the exercise below.

Another possibility is that the vocal reaction occurs at the same time as the 'impact' of the stage combat technique. This often makes the most sense when the target is on the torso of the 'Recipient'. The idea is that the 'blow' of the 'Attacker' forces the breath from the 'Recipient' on the moment of impact. When we voice that breath, it is a 'Forced Reaction' that occurs at the same time as the stage combat technique. This can 'Mask the Knap' or cover the absence of a knap. The torso can be defined as any part of the chest or abdominal cavities. The stomach, back, chest, and sides could force breath from the body upon impact. Techniques that safely give the illusion of forcefully 'landing' on these areas are most appropriate for the Forced Reaction.

Many of the opportunities to use the Forced Reaction will be with Contact Techniques of stage combat. A 'Contact Blow' in stage combat is a technique that safely makes contact with the receiver, delivered to a large muscle group or muscle mass. It must be learned and practiced under the supervision of a qualified stage combat instructor. The Laban Knife Stab, from later in this book, is a technique that would work well with the Forced Reaction.

Battle sounds 101 (30 minutes)

It is important to allow the body and breath to be released with physical alignment that allows a deep engagement with the breath. It is this appearance of acted aggression while remaining energetically relaxed that is very important to find the balance of within theatrical violence. When the actor is able to find ease and flow within the heightened energy of physically violent storytelling, he or she is capable of extending the work beyond technical skill into fully revealing the universality of humanity within violence.

Follow all of the warm-up procedures in this book, ensuring the jaw, shoulder, neck, and tongue are released and free. Take the time to warm-up the forward and focused placement of the voice. Remember that the breath support originates from deep within one's torso rather than from high in the chest. Allow the ribs to be responsive to the breath by their ability to release outwards as they swing up and out on the in-breath. However, on the battle cry exploration below, imagine the ribs continuing to release outwards throughout the committed sound. As a reminder, the tendency within a battle cry is to squeeze your ribs inwards through the breath and thereby sending an excessive amount of forced breath through your throat to such an extent that the muscles within the larynx can constrict, thereby creating vocal tension. The engagement of the ribs continuing to release outwards on the out-breath of the battle cry (with a reminder to allow the throat to remain free and open) can aid the muscles within the throat in maintaining a healthy openness throughout the expression of this type of heightened sound.

Teaching Tip: It is helpful to have all students with water near them throughout this exercise. Maintaining frequent hydration of the vocal folds is helpful. Students should be encouraged to frequently rest and take sips of water rather than 'muscling' through the exercise. In addition, limit the initial work on this extreme vocal engagement to relatively short periods of time to avoid potentially injuring the voice.

---

1 In partners, each student will choose one of the battle cries listed below.

2 Read through your battle cry silently to yourself.

3 Now start to gently speak your battle cry to your partner, paying particular attention to supporting the voice through those deep muscles of breath support.

4   Slowly add more vocal volume in increments of 10 per cent by
    increasing the level of vocal support. If tensions start to creep
    into the throat, decrease the amount of volume to the last level
    of voice that felt supported and without strain.

5   Remember to keep the throat and the jaw open and released.
    'Loudness' is not the goal. The exploration is focused on
    committing to the vocal sounds of violence placed forwards
    while engaging with a released and full level of vocal support.

Henry IV Part I: (Act II, scene 3, line 96)

* We must have bloody noses and crack'd crowns,

  And pass them current too. God's me, my horse!

Henry V(Act III, scene 1, line 1)

* Once more unto the breach, dear friends, once more;

  Or close the wall up with our English dead.

Henry VI Part III (Act II, scene 2, line 173)

* Sound trumpets! let our bloody colours wave!

  And either victory, or else a grave.

Macbeth (Act V, scene 8, line 33)

* Lay on, Macduff,

  And damn'd be him that first cries, 'Hold, enough!'

Richard III (Act V scene 4, line)

* A horse! a horse! my kingdom for a horse!

Henry VI Part I (Act I scene 2, line 325)

* Why, no, I say, distrustful recreants!

  Fight till the last gasp; I will be your guard.

It is very possible to create the ugly and disturbing 'noise' of vocal extremity within fight scenes. The actor can safely recreate the harsh sounds that can be released from the human body when engaged with violence without harming the vocal folds. The focus on this specific engagement is on finding areas that can be slightly constricted to create these types of unique sounds that clearly characterize distress.

These areas will generally be found near the uvular or velar areas of the vocal tract. Areas of the vocal tract at or near the vocal folds are to be avoided. The tongue, lips, and teeth – can be effectively employed to create disturbing sounds and breathing patterns that can create the illusion of vocal strain within violence.

(Note: The following exercises on heightened vocal use are intended to be used as reminders and as a reference, under the guidance of an experienced teacher of voice work.)

Vocal extremes – Written by Brian Evans

At the very limits of vocal potential are extreme expressions that can test the abilities of the voice. 'Vocal Extremes' such as shouting, screaming, keening, wailing, screeching, crying, laughing – and a host of others – offer unique challenges for the actor. They are integral to the full range of the voice, and at the same time they can be the least understood and sometimes most harmful aspect of performance. It is often the case that actors injure their voice in stage combat rather than an ankle, arm, or wrist as might be expected. It is therefore vitally important that actors train their voices to perform extremes with the same patience, rigor, and safety that is often afforded to stage combat training.

There are different definitions of shouting and screaming. For the purposes of this book, shouting will refer to the full use of power as expressed through volume. Shouting is loud. Just like a wind instrument, more breath can produce more sound. But just as a great musician uses the breath with maximum efficiency, so must actors manage the breath to support shouting without excess tension or straining.

Support exercise (20 minutes) – Written by Brian Evans

Practice the following exercises earlier in this chapter again as a reminder to always work from deep breath support.

- *Finding your Breath for Fight Work*
- *Vocal support for fight work*
- *Hey you, get away from my car!*

The foundation for good screaming technique is a solid understanding and practice of breath release and support. Without the skills and awareness developed from exercises such as those listed above, the specific exercises described below may not be beneficial.

'Screaming' can be defined as distinct from 'Shouting'. What we often do in highly emotional states of fear, anger, or pain is scream. Screaming is a fight or flight response to dangerous situations. It is extremely expressive in stage combat scenes (many scenes, for that matter) but also an incredible challenge for the actor. Actors may experience greater muscle tension in fight or flight situations, and often this tension interferes with the free play of the vocal folds.

The scream can be distinguished from shouting by the 'noise element'. The noise element is the chaos in the voice, the breaking up of pure tone. It is a gravel-like quality that is created by tension in the vocal tract and, if performed incorrectly, can be harmful to the voice. Often a scream is defined as high-pitched, but for this exploration we'll focus on the noise element as a distinguishing factor and a particular vocal skill. You can hear this noise in the recordings of Louis Armstrong (called a vocal growl), Janis Joplin, or Kurt Cobain.

It has been shown in numerous experiments that this noise element can be created by areas of the vocal tract that allow the vocal folds to remain free of injury. This is accomplished by focusing the tension of the noise element as far forward in the vocal tract as possible when performing a scream. The most important factor to consider when screaming is that it is safe. The noise should not be produced in the larynx because this high level of tension can damage the vocal folds.

First, let us experiment with a defining characteristic of screaming: the 'noise' element. To create the noise, make sure that you are hydrated and have warmed up the voice with the guidance of a qualified voice instructor.

Making noise (10 minutes) – Written by Brian Evans

1   Applying the exercise 'Vocal support for fight work' from Chapter 2, say 'Hi' at a lower volume.

2   Do an imitation of Louis Armstrong, or Marge Simpson, or Yoda saying 'Hi' at the same lower volume. It is this 'gravelly' quality that is one version of a noise element. Notice where in

the vocal tract you feel the noise is being produced. Take a sip of water.

3 If making the 'character voice' hurts and/or makes you want to cough, stop immediately. Modify the placement of the noise element further forward in the vocal tract (away from the vocal folds) so that there is little to no discomfort.

4 Play with different phrases such as 'Hey you' or 'Wait for me', while experimenting with a variety of noise qualities. Keep the volume of the voice at a conversational level. Remember to not push the voice while experimenting with the noise element. Take a sip of water.

5 Play with different pitches up and down your expressive range. Start gradually and continue only if there is still freedom from discomfort in the vocal tract and a sense of ease throughout the upper chest, shoulders, and neck.

6 Play with a specific text that you may have memorized or one from a previous exercise in this book. Take a sip of water.

7 Practice the exercises earlier in this chapter of the Healthy Cow and the Modified Cobra, while performing the text and experiment with and without the noise element. Be aware of how your body engages the muscles in both the noise and pure tones. Allow the same freedom from extraneous tension in the pure tones to provide a basis for healthy screaming while producing the noise element.

8 Take a break. Just like working any other muscles in the body, overuse can be as damaging as improper use. Take a sip of water. Hum gently up and down the vocal range. Rest your voice.

Supporting the noise (10 minutes) – Written by Brian Evans

1 Explore the healthy cow and modified cobra as described in Chapter 3. Notice how your ribs swing outwards and upwards on the in breath. Place your hands on your lower ribs with your thumbs forward and your fingers towards your spine. Feel the coordination of your diaphragm and your ribs as you allow the breath to find all of the space in your torso.

2   Notice how your belly, sides, and lower back all expand as your diaphragm descends in concert with the swinging of your ribs.

3   Engage the Transversus Abdominis on the out-breath. Practice this out-breath on a voiced 'Hey!'

4   Focus this sound from your pelvis, up your spine, over the back and top of your head and out of your forehead.

5   At ¼ of your vocal power, repeat this process of supporting a 'Hey!'. Add the noise element and remember to stop if there is any pain at all. Drink more water.

6   Paying special attention to the release of your upper chest, shoulders, and neck, increase the power to half of your potential. Increase the phrase length to 'Hey you!' or 'Hey wait!'

7   Practice longer phrases such as 'Hey wait, that's my bike!' or 'Hey you, get away from my car!' Keep the power at half of your potential. Initiate the noise element for *only part of the phrase* such as '…. my bike!' or '… my car!'

8   By alternating the practice of both shouting and screaming, you add more variety of vocal expression within the voice. The impact of a good scream is diminished if screaming occurs throughout an entire scene. Less is more.

9   Take a break and discuss what you have discovered.

Teaching Tip: Ideally, time should be devoted to the study of vocal extremes over the course of several short classes.

Once a familiarity with the process of creating a scream, or 'supported noise' is learned, you can experiment with three-fourths of your potential power. Always keep a little in reserve. It's the same idea with stage combat. If you rehearse at full power or speed, you'll go faster that you are safely able to when the adrenalin of performance kicks in. If you practice with an element of control, your muscle memory will recall this awareness when you perform. You will be able to safely recreate your rehearsed scream without increasing the risk of injury.

Holding the breath (10 minutes) – Written by Brian Evans

It is common to hold one's breath when lifting, pushing or pulling a heavy object. This is due to the internal pressure of both forcing the breath outwards and holding the breath, creating a sense of an 'internal weight belt'. This pressure can help to stabilize the spine so that in dangerous situations where you need all of your strength, your body remains structurally sound. Though it may help us in real-life fight or flight situations, it shouldn't be repeated often. The internal pressure could burst blood vessels, create damaging pressure in the larynx or strain muscles in the chest or neck.

Holding the breath and grunting are effective sounds in staged violence. Just as the visual illusion of combat is created through safe technique, the aural illusion of struggling combatants must be learned and practiced.

1   Stand facing a solid wall with enough distance to lean forward and push against the wall with your hands. Push as hard as you can without any risk of hurting yourself.

2   Notice whether you are tempted to hold your breath while pushing. If you do, you're not unlike many who add this extra internal pressure to help stabilize your core. Breathe through the temptation to hold your breath.

3   Now, release as many of the muscles in your neck and abdomen as you can. Still push against the wall as hard as you are able while paying attention to your limits.

4   Allow a balance of as much force as you can exert on the wall and as much ease as you can allow in your breathing.

5   Now take a large breath and hold it while you push. Return to breathing. Notice the expansion of the rib cage with the large intake of air.

6   Alternate between breathing and holding your breath while pushing against the wall. Expand your rib cage as you would before holding your breath, but this time, allow short small breaths in and out while keeping the ribs expanded. Simulate 'Holding the Breath,' but actually breathe.

7   When experimenting with actually holding the breath, notice
    where extraneous muscle tension may appear. It might be facial
    expressions, extra shoulder tension or tension in your chest.
    When simulating 'Holding the Breath,' try to recreate some of
    the extra tension that you found from actual holding. Allow the
    breath to release through as much ease as you can (of course,
    you're pushing on a wall with all of your might, so there will
    still be tension). It's the balance of tension and release that will
    create a healthier illusion of 'Holding the Breath.'

Grunting (10 minutes) – Written by Brian Evans

If you say the phrase 'uh oh' you will notice that the beginning of each
'word' has a sharper onset than if you were to put an 'h' before each,
as in 'huh hoh'. This is because you are beginning with a 'Glottal
Attack'. With low pressure and muscle release, this Glottal Attack will
not likely be harmful. But when we strain muscles such as those in the
neck, chest, and shoulders or if we push past an efficient use of breath
support, we run the risk of damaging the voice.

A grunt can be created using a Glottal Attack and then letting a
breathy non-verbal sound (such as 'uh') escape. Grunting expresses
effort, so it is often part of the sounds of stage combat. As with 'Holding
the Breath', it is worthwhile to take time practicing 'Grunting' in order
to develop the skills needed to do it without excessive risk to the voice.

1   Go back and forth between 'uh oh' and 'huh hoh' until you
    understand how you are making the Glottal Attack with 'uh oh.'

2   Hold your breath easily, without creating too much pressure,
    and release with a gentle Glottal Attack. You can experiment
    with different vowels, such as 'uh,' 'eh' or 'aw.'

3   Try releasing the Glottal Attack only on breath, without voicing
    it. Experiment with this breath by shaping the articulators into
    different 'vowels.'

4   Mix this 'breathy release' with voice. Find a balance between
    voice and pure breath on the release. Find a variety of different
    'Grunts' by playing with the 'vowel' shapes and mixture of
    breath and sound.

5   Pay special attention to the muscles in the neck and upper chest. It may be habitual for you to 'squeeze' these sounds out. Remind yourself to support your breath from lower in the body.

6   Simulate 'Holding the Breath' and then, just before grunting, bring the vocal folds together to actually hold your breath. Grunt and then return to 'Holding the Breath.'

7   Push against a solid wall as described above and add grunting to 'Holding the Breath.' Take this opportunity to develop more variety in these non-verbal sounds. Some of the sounds won't work, some will.

'Grunting' and 'Holding the Breath' are two overused and under-practiced skills in stage combat. Take time to develop these skills in an environment that allows for safe and helpful experimentation.

Summary

Below is a summary of reminders regarding the elements of vocal extreme usage as it applies to theatrical violence. Practice the skills of vocal extreme as a separate skill from the emotional work within a fight.

1   Ensure the throat and body are well hydrated prior to any demanding tasks placed on the voice. Cool, room temperature water is best.

2   Fully warm-up to release the breath and the voice prior to the work on vocal extremes. Ensure you warm-down the voice as close to the conclusion of the work as possible.

3   Allow the 'muscle' work to be engaged with only the deep muscles of vocal support in the abdomen. Release tension from the muscles of the jaw, the larynx, and the root of the tongue.

4   Initiate heightened vocal moments with an unvoiced /h/ prior to the open and released vowel sound.

5   Allow the focus of the vowel sound to bounce off of the hard palate at the roof of the mouth.

6   In isolation to the physical fight choreography, explore the effective vocal placement of pitch, volume and resonance. Play

with the pitch and where you feel the most focus in your facial mask.

7   It can be helpful to allow the onset of the heightened vocal sound to have a hint of a yawn. One can also think of a gentle smile towards the rear of the mouth, near the soft palate.

8   Support the breath from deep within the centre of the body. Imagine the breath as originating at your pelvic floor. Imagine the larynx to be a large and empty hollow tube through which the breath and voice can pass without impediment.

9   Feel your head floating on top of your neck. Visualize the strength of your spine running from your pelvis all the way up to nearly between your ears. Feel your feet making full contact on the floor. Imagine your back lengthening and widening, your chest softening, and your knees as soft.

10 Never hit your top of volume. Always allow an inner sense of ease and control within the work, regardless of how full or out of control the voice may need to sound.

Follow-up

Explore the following Follow-Up questions.

- In professional baseball games, notice that before the pitcher throws the ball – there is inevitably a settling of the breath and body. Similarly in all high-functioning athletes, notice that their physical engagement transcends 'technique' alone. Professional athletes are connecting technique and the ability to have a level of spontaneous reactions through a fluid and supportive breathing system. In what ways can the actor transcend 'technique' in a similar manner?

- In your everyday conversations, become aware of when you are grounded and breathing freely. What happens when we engage and the person we are speaking to is disconnected from the breath?

- In what ways might an actor who is not allowing the breath to be present unconsciously be affecting the audience's engagement?

Notes

1   Of course, the torso is not 'empty' and the mouth is full of fascinating parts of our anatomy that enable spoken communication to occur. Nevertheless, it can be helpful to imagine the mouth, throat, and torso as empty vessels containing the possibility of freely released breath and vibration. This type of imagery often allows actors to more fully experience vocal freedom and flexibility.

2   I have been inspired by the work of Lorna Marshall. Her book, *The Body Speaks,* contains many helpful exercises that can be usefully applied with the work of the Stage Combat Arts. See the Appendix for more information.

3   A swipe across the head that originates from your right would proceed with the palm held in 'supination' or palm upwards. In the exercises described in this book, the 'true edge' always leads on all cutting and swiping attacks.

4   Refer to the DVD video series titled *Unarmed Stage Combat I: Learning the Basics, Unarmed Stage Combat 2: Perfecting the Fundamentals,* and *Unarmed Stage Combat 3: Mastering the Techniques* by SAFD Fight Masters David S. Leong and J. Allen Suddeth and published by First Light Video. These videos offer helpful tutorials in the safe and effective performance of a variety of unarmed stage combat techniques, as taught by master teachers of the art. See the Appendix for more information.

Further reading

Amberger, J. Christopher, *The Secret History of the Sword*, Unique Publications, Burbank, CA, 1999. Part 1 – Interlude (Ultimate Male Bonding: A Schlager Mensur at Gottingen, A.D. 1987), pp. 47–53.

Carey, David; Carey Rebecca, *Vocal Arts Workbook and DVD*, Methuen Drama, London, 2008. Chapter 3: Breath and Voice – Supply and Support, pp. 76–109. Chapter Four: Resonance and Range, pp. 110–161.

Cazden, Joanna, *How to Take Care of Your Voice*, Booklocker.com, 2007. Chapter 1: Foundations of Voice Care, pp. 5–42.

De Becker, Gavin, *The Gift of Fear*, Random House, New York, 1997. Chapter 1: In the Presence of Danger, pp. 1–23.

Feldenkrais, Moshe, *Awareness Through Movement*, HarperCollins, New York, 1977. Lesson 3: Some Fundamental Properties of Movement, pp. 91–99.

Gelb J., Michael, *Body Learning*, Henry Holt and Company, New York, 1994. Part 3: Utilizing Potential, pp. 91–110.

Girard, Dale Anthony, *Actors On Guard*, Routledge, New York, 1997. Chapter: Acting the Fight, pp. 433–452.

Houseman, Barbara, *Finding Your Voice*, Routledge, New York, 2002. Chapter
     5: Releasing the Sound, pp. 118–161.
Houseman, Barbara, *Tackling Text*, Nick Hern Books, London, 2008. Part 2:
     Text, pp. 35–150.
Knight, Dudley, *Speaking with Skill*, Bloomsbury, London, 2012. Chapter 4:
     The Muscles That Shape Sound: The Tool Kit, pp. 35–63.
Kotzubei, Saul, *You're Getting Warmer*. http://www.voicecoachla.com/writing/.

4
ACTING THE FIGHT

Framework

The challenge is to explore the specific ways in which the acting of heightened reality can be both full and at the control of your artistry. Safety, specificity, clarity of choice, and the artistic arrangement of heightened moments are a few of the several primary goals of work within fight scenes. The authentic engagement of any given theatrical moment has a direct correlation to the scale necessary, and indeed the balance tipped one way or another produces a theatrical truth that is skewed in its communication. Othello's murder of Desdemona and consequent deep grief cannot be realized if the actor presupposes that his or her 'truth' must live in the scale of the 'everyday human experience'. The theatrical truth will be off balance. Authenticity is largely a result of an informed understanding of the needs required by the text.

In the context of fight scenes, though the actor may understand that a heightened visceral commitment needs to be released within the context of physical conflict, it is of little use if this understanding leads the actor to playing generalized or over-wrought emotion. The death of Hotspur at the hands of Harry Percy in *Henry IV Part I*, for instance, cannot be so true to life with the ultra-realistic groans and gasps of a soldier suffering from a sucking chest wound, that the language becomes a wash of unintelligible sentimentality.

Exploration

1   Our intentions and behaviours, changes depending on where we are, whom we are with, what time it is, and what we want

from the given situation. Interactions with our family are different than interactions with our colleagues. These changes of behaviour are the result of different 'intentions' we hold within different groups or between individuals. Become aware of how these intentions and tactics affect you in your daily life. Explore how this basic human behaviour can be directly applied to your work as an actor.

Exercises

Teaching Tip: The work of this chapter engages the actor with tools to theatrically explore the high stakes of physical conflict. The exercises in the chapter are organized under six headings: *Fighting with Intention; Variety in a Fight Scene; Exploring Physical Volumes; Exploring Physical Rhythms; Connecting to Thought;* and *Engaged Play.* This chapter will provide exercises that promote greater freedom, specificity, and flexibility of intention-based acting as it relates to stage combat. In addition, exercises that connect the imagination to the body will be explored in detail.

Fighting with intention

(In this work I have been inspired by Professors Dr Robert Cohen, David Lee-Painter, and Scott Kaiser from the Oregon Shakespeare Festival).

In life, the mother weeping and fighting for the life of her child, the soldier feeling the fear and sweat of going into battle, the lover desperately mourning the loss of their relationship – all feel emotional responses but the feelings occur as a result of a *thought*, of a *predicament*, or of a *need* unfulfilled. The weeping mother or the spurned lover has no need to express his or her emotional life. Their focus is on the 'other', the object of their needs or desires. Feelings are a by-product of those thoughts. This basic pattern of thought-oriented behaviour is at the heart of what makes us human. It is the way we behave every day of our lives. The clothes we wear, the language choices we make, the manner in which we speak and move, the totality of our behaviour we engage with – are changeable based on whom we are with at any given moment and how we are wishing to influence another or how we wish to be perceived.

Focus on affecting your acting partner and the intentionality of the moment. This fundamental principle of acting can be defined by exploring the following questions:

1   What do I *want*, or *need*? What am I fighting for? What is my character's goal in this scene or monologue?

2   What are the *obstacles* to what I am fighting for? Why is it difficult to fight for what I need?

3   What *tactics* will I use to overcome any given obstacle? For instance: will I manipulate, neutralize, or disarm my obstacle to fight for what I need? Tactics are visceral verbs that allow fully invested choices to be explored.

4   What will it specifically *look like* when I have succeeded? What will I see, hear, taste, touch, and smell to let me know that I have been successful in accomplishing my goal?

5   Allow the answers to these questions to be visceral and compelling. Answer these questions vividly and imaginatively – rather than academically.

One of the benefits of the study of the Stage Combat Arts is that it provides an interactive, intention-oriented approach to the study of acting.

Connecting thought to action can be a very helpful exploration for your work in stage combat. As an actor, it is not enough to intellectually consider the questions posed above, they must be fully embodied and lived. This chapter will provide exercises that explore integrating the body, the voice and the text. In real life, 'thought' precedes 'text'. If we are asked to describe what our home looked like when we were five years old, the thought of the house initiates the breath, which initiates the voice to engage with the text. Thinking happens, consciously or unconsciously, prior to all other emotional response or physical action.

When actors approach text work, the task of memorizing lines can mistakenly reinforce the misconception that the text *precedes* the thought in ways that are inauthentic. It is a thinking process that leads to all action and text. There is often nothing more fascinating in the theatre than watching a character try to work out a predicament through thought, text, and physical work. There is nothing less interesting in the theatre than watching an actor pretending to give the appearance of 'thought' or 'feeling'.

In staged fights, a character's thinking process – preceding the physical conflict – is often a lightning quick reflexive reaction or a learned automatic response. Thought and response within conflict can occur at speeds beyond our ability to logically process. Nevertheless, in a choreographed fight sequence, it is helpful to differentiate between 'Semi-Conscious Thought' and 'Automatic Response' as two distinct possibilities within a response to violence. With thought that occurs consciously, the character *decides, intends, or realizes* an opportunity to specifically engage in a fight or in a moment of physical conflict. Moments of conscious or semi-conscious thinking may occur at the following points of a choreographed fight:

1   Prior to a fight beginning – *'My opponent is a better fighter than I.'*

2   Between the phrases of a fight – *'I realize that I have the upper hand.'*

3   At the conclusion of the fight – *'I am dying and can hardly believe it.'*

On the other hand, Automatic Responses can occur during the fight in moments when the body is responding according to how it was trained or as a result of a natural human response – evasions, parry-riposte actions, looking for and taking advantage of openings. These types of physical actions are subject to processes that have become ingrained to such a level – or are basic human responses to threat – that they are essentially automatic in nature. However, this is not to imply that in stage combat the illusions of Automatic Responses are neutral and emotionally disengaged choices. In this chapter, exercises will be explored that sensitize the actor to playable options within both Semi-Conscious Thought and Automatic Response.

Professor, director and author of acting texts – Robert Cohen[1] – has developed a useful acronym that sums up a basic principle of acting: 'GOTE':

1 Playing a visceral GOAL.

2 Overcoming substantial OBSTACLES.

3 Employing a variety of TACTICS.

4 Imagining the EXPECTATION of success.

In your work on scenes of violence, all action must be played for success. Your character is striving to win the heart of her love, to defeat the despotic ruler, to persuade the foe to join his side. You must believe in your potential for success. Even in those moments in which you are fearing the worst, in which utter ruin seems likely, you are well served by imagining the *hope* that victory will nevertheless be achieved.

Group goals (20 minutes)

(I am grateful to Chris Villa, for first introducing me to this exercise that I have subsequently adapted in my own work.)

Teaching Tip: This exercise aids your students in developing a physical connection of pursuing interactive choices based on intention. It can be an ideal exercise to begin a stage combat class in preparation for more specific intention-based stage combat explorations.

A large open space is ideal for this exercise. Ensure that all furniture in the room has been cleared away.

---

1 As a group, start walking in the space.

2 Stay in your own 'bubble' of energy without making contact with anyone else in the group, verbally or physically.

3 Walk, jog, and skip.

4 Skip for distance.

5 Skip for height.

6 Skip for style.

7 Skip for height and style.

8 Walk.

9 Freeze and close your eyes. As a class, you have ten seconds to create a group circle as an ensemble, with your eyes closed. There can be no talking and all must move in slow motion.

10 After ten seconds, open your eyes, and celebrate the success of the shape created.

11 Continue walking. Freeze. Change directions. Walk. Jog. Run.

12 Freeze! Close your eyes.

13 As a group, you have ten seconds to create a triangle. Try not to use your voice to communicate as you do so.

14 After ten seconds, open your eyes and see what shape has been created.

15 Continue walking. Walk with someone.

16 Walk on your own.

17 Walk towards someone.

18 Walk away from someone.

19 Explore the distance between yourself and one other student. Explore close, medium, and far distances. How do these different sets of distance affect your imagination? How do these distance differentiations affect the relationship between you and a partner?

20 Jog randomly in the room. Ensure you don't make any physical contact with any other objects or persons in the room.

21 Freeze! Close your eyes.

22 As a group, you have fifteen seconds to create – without talking – a triangle within a circle. Go.

23 After fifteen seconds, open your eyes. Once again, celebrate the shape that has been made.

Discussion

- Discuss in what ways this exercise relates to the tasks of the actor.
- What was the goal for the group?
- What was the goal for the individual?
- What made these goals difficult? What were the various obstacles present?
- What tactics did the group use to accomplish the goal?
- What tactics did certain individuals employ?
- What were the expectations of the group?

The single sword salute (20 minutes)
(https://vimeo.com/132085799)

(I am grateful to SAFD Certified Teachers Ted Sharon and Heidi Wolf, SAFD Fight Director Emeritus Richard Lane, and Professor Robert Cohen, from whom this exercise has been inspired.)

As a group, a neutral Salute with an epee-bladed single sword[2] will be learned and applied as a basic foundation for the physical exploration of intention-oriented choices.

1 For a right-handed student: stand with the right foot facing forward and the heel of this foot touching the heel of the left foot, which should be pointed towards a 90-degree angle to the left.

2 With the left hand easily by the left hip, bring the sword's hilt gently towards one's own lips.

3 After a moment, lift the hilt and point of the sword to the heavens.

4 After a moment, lower the hilt to the heart with the point remaining vertical.

5 Lower your sword so that it is now horizontal and pointing to your left, at about heart level. Extend outwards and diagonally downwards and low to your right. The point of the sword never crosses the face, head, neck, breasts, or groin of your imaginary partner.

6   Lastly, crisply step forward with your right foot into an en garde stance with the point of the weapon directed offline of your imaginary partner's left shoulder. The point should be *no higher* than the shoulder (or armpit level) and make sure it remains below the head. At no time does the tip of your sword ever cross in front of your partner's head or face.

As a class, explore this Salute several times until the basic pattern is thoroughly learned. It is helpful for the instructor to call out the following sequence for the students to follow:

1   Salute!

2   To your lips.

3   To the heavens.

4   To your heart.

5   To your imaginary partner.

6   En Garde!

> ***Teaching Tip:*** Only teach this exercise with pool noodles, unless a qualified teacher of stage combat is present.

Exploring goals (20 minutes)

1   Once this Salute pattern is thoroughly learned, explore the following goals for each Salute performed.

2   Explore differences in timing, rhythm, and the possibility of physical stillness within the actions of the Salute.

Goals

- *Apologize to me.*
- *Kiss me.*
- *Worship me.*

○ *Leave me.*

○ *Bow down to me.*

As simple an action as a basic Salute is, it nevertheless becomes full of specific playable moments when a goal is imagined fully and with commitment. The same is true for any piece of choreographed violence. Overly complex fight choreography can lead to a fight the actors can only barely manage to perform with safety and confidence. A less-complex fight, more fully and specifically acted, permits actors to engage in more deeply connected choices and frees the voice for supported engagement within the fight's vocal reactions. The balance is on revealing the action of the story through exciting and plot-driven physicality that allows the actors an opportunity to engage with specific and visceral choices that affect their acting partner.

Discussion

- How do playing these goals affect your physicality?

- In what ways is the inner life of your imagination made manifest through the body?

- How might playing different goals affect your physicality in a fight scene?

Exploring obstacles (20 minutes)

The element of obstacles raises the stakes of the goals that are being pursued. It is the struggle to achieve the goal *despite the fact that it is difficult* that is ultimately compelling. The more full and imposing your obstacle, the more engaged your goal will need to be and the more visceral your tactics will become. What often reveals the humanity of the character is the honest portrayal of physiological and psychological obstacles in the depiction of violence, not athletic displays of prowess and superhuman abilities to withstand multiple injuries without consequence.

1 Using the single sword salute and having chosen one Goal, choose one Obstacle from the list below.

2 How does the obstacle make the playing of your goal difficult? How does this affect your performance of the Salute with an imaginary partner?

3 Explore timing, speed, physical pauses, and the possibilities for physical stillness within the Salute.

Obstacles

    ○ *I don't want to hurt you.*

    ○ *I don't want to appear foolish.*

    ○ *I am afraid of what I know.*

    ○ *I am too injured/too old/too young.*

    ○ *Someone I love doesn't want you to die.*

Exploring tactics (20 minutes)

Tactics are what enables action to be played with the greatest commitment. The tactics you engage with are the kindle that can ignite your interaction with your partner. It allows you to truly pursue the Goal vigorously, with no room for self-absorption or paralyzing self-analysis. Within all art, it is the artistic engagement of creative variation that allows the artist to bring the work to its full resonance and meaning. It is the *variety* of tactics (not just one or two) that allows you to invest fully in the outward-directed focus of achieving your goals as the character. When one tactic fails, another must be employed to find your way to success.

1 Choose a goal, an obstacle, two threatening tactics (i.e., tactics that repel, attack, confront), and two inductive tactics (i.e., tactics that draw a partner closer, encourage, and attract).

2 Perform the single sword salute to your partner, allowing the tactics chosen to physically inform the actions of the Salute.

Threatening tactics

    ○ *To Scold*

    ○ *To Terrify*

    ○ *To Assault*

- *To Intimidate*
- *To Impede*
- *To Torment*
- *To Baffle*
- *To Belittle*
- *To Trick*
- *To Perplex*
- *To Poison*
- *To Harass*
- *To Scold*
- *To Eliminate*
- *To Lacerate*
- *To Defile*
- *To Batter*
- *To Petrify*
- *To Destabilize*
- *To Provoke*
- *To Ram*
- *To Unnerve*
- *To Deflate*
- *To Drown*
- *To Cripple*
- *To Horrify*
- *To Press*
- *To Gouge*
- *To Mock*
- *To Freeze*
- *To Reduce*
- *To Flatten*
- *To Confront*

- o *To Dismiss*
- o *To Obliterate*
- o *To Control*
- o *To Agitate*
- o *To Malign*
- o *To Shame*
- o *To Dissuade*

Inductive tactics

- o *To Amuse*
- o *To Incite*
- o To Allure
- o *To Encourage*
- o *To Awaken*
- o *To Astound*
- o *To Elevate*
- o *To Entice*
- o *To Fascinate*
- o *To Honour*
- o *To Cheer*
- o *To Strengthen*
- o *To Seduce*
- o *To Enlighten*
- o *To Caress*
- o *To Stroke*
- o *To Rouse*
- o *To Stimulate*
- o *To Assure*
- o *To Pacify*
- o *To Tease*

- *To Awaken*
- *To Delight*
- *To Enliven*
- *To Caution*
- *To Revere*
- *To Engage*
- *To Captivate*
- *To Stimulate*
- *To Hypnotize*
- *To Congratulate*
- *To Entertain*
- *To Probe*
- *To Impress*
- *To Pity*
- *To Lure*
- *To Tempt*
- *To Bribe*
- *To Foster*
- *To Shelter*

Discussion

- In what ways did the basic actions of the Salute change as Goals, Obstacles, and Tactics were added?
- How did the subtle physical timing variations within the Salute affect your imagination and emotions?

Teaching Tip: For teaching and learning aids based on this approach to exploring the acting process, visit http://mindtoolsinnovations.com to purchase helpful materials that aid students' integration of Goal-oriented work.

Preparing for a fight scene

(I have been inspired by the writings of Anne Dennis, Jean Sabatine, and Anne Bogart. See the Bibliography section for helpful additional resources.)

Use the following guidelines for your work on specific scenes that contain violence. Use lists, statements, words, and images – but ensure that they are visceral, engaging, and surprising rather than academic. The goal is to find those prompts that most fully compel your imagination with specificity and intent that propels you into the given circumstances of the scene with variety, flexibility, and heightened authenticity. The goal is to open the possibilities of your own creative discoveries rather than to box you in within academic 'correctness'.

1 CHARACTER BIOGRAPHY
   a List the history of the character.
   b Examine pertinent relationships.
   c Pursue potential intentions.

2 BASIC INFORMATION
   a Name
   b Sex
   c Age
   d Marital Status
   e Educational Level
   f Economic Status
   g Social Status
   h Describe your physical silhouette:
      i. Where is your physical centre? (Possibilities include: forehead, nose, chin, neck, chest, back, belly, groin, knees, and feet ...). Be aware that this is not necessarily where a character actually physically 'leads' from, but also where the character's energy or focus feels to be physically located.
   i Characteristic manner of walking, sitting, standing.

j   What is the typical physical tempo (i.e., fast, slow, moderate) of the character?

k   How long does the character tend to stay within a given choice of tempo?

l   What are the behavioural gestures of the character, and how might this physicality inform a fight? Explore what possibilities exist within a fight to embody these gestural actions:

   i.   Examine gestures of body (i.e., wounds, disabilities, pain, gestures related to temperature, etc. ...).

   ii.   Examine gestures of Period (i.e., Elizabethan vs. Restoration vs. gestures of the 1950s that might occur before, during or after a fight).

   iii.   Examine communicative gestures that might occur before, during, or after a fight:

     1   Screw you!

     2   Come here!

     3   Enough!

     4   Hi ya!

     5   Stop!

     6   Obey me!

   iv.   Explore how these gestures can be subtly communicated with only specific parts of the body, including:

     1   Hands

     2   Eyes

     3   Back of the neck

     4   Chin

     5   Nose

     6   Shoulder

     7   Hip

     8   Knee

     9   Foot

3 RELATIONSHIP TO YOUR PARTNER

    a What is at stake in the relationship? How, why, and specifically when might your character be emotionally vulnerable within the fight?

    b How is the relationship status manifested in your body?

4 MOMENT BEFORE

    a What fuels the moment before the scene begins?

    b What is the spark that engages the *need* to fight? This needs to be clear. The choice to resort to violence may be a result of conscious planning or an unconscious explosion of physicality. Make the choice knowingly and fully.

5 GOALS

    a Strive for the highest stakes possible. What will happen if you lose the fight? What will become of your honour? What will it mean for you, for your family, and for the generations to come?

    b What will it *exactly* look like for you to achieve your goal? How does your acting partner specifically respond in the scene prior to the fight? The fact that they don't respond as you wish is part of what compels the fight to occur and to continue once it has started. The visceral understanding of *what* you want and *how* it would look and feel like to achieve your goal needs to be specific. When it does not occur, the violence erupts out of your unfulfilled needs.

6 MOMENT TO MOMENT

    a Find the variety of tactics you can play within a fight scene. How can you guilt, seduce, confront, and terrorize? Find the specific moments in which the tactics change. What word or phrase within the text does the scene start to evolve from verbal conflict into physical?

    b Allow this specificity in the text to transform naturally into the tactical variations within the fight. Where are the specific physical points in the fight when tactical changes occur?

   c   Use the tactics presented earlier in this chapter to find the
        most playable actions within the fight. Look for variety rather
        than settling on one or two choices.

   d   Use physical tactics of proximity, variations in eye contact,
        and variations in physical contact prior to the fight and after
        the physical conflict has occurred.

   e   As an actor in a scene, it is an act of creative generosity to
        present as many psycho-physical and emotional obstacles
        for your partner as possible. It allows the possibility that your
        partner will need to change tactics frequently and viscerally.

7   AS IF …

   a   We all have the *capability* to be Richard III. We must be
        able to see ourselves as the character, rather than seeing
        the character as something outside of us that we need to
        'become'.

   b   Your acting is only as full as is your ability to personalize the
        work. Imagine yourself in the situation of the character, or
        'As If' *you* were faced with the same predicaments, living at
        the same time, and versed with the same fight skills, or lack
        of fight skills, as the character.

   c   There is no Hamlet, Desdemona, or Joan of Arc. Though
        many dramatic characters did exist historically, in your work
        as an actor, they exist now as words on a page that need
        to be fuelled by your imagination. Your opportunity as an
        actor in a fight scene is to reveal your own humanity through
        the work rather than hiding what makes you unique to fit a
        narrow vision of what you may feel the 'character' should be.

8   REHEARSING THE SCENE

   a   In your scene, take big swings with your intentions. If you
        could play a more committed intention, take the opportunity
        to do so. Experiment with intentional and tactical choices.
        Rehearsals are about productively failing so that the most
        fully authentic choices can be found.

   b   Fight scenes are not about playing continuous, generalized
        aggression, vocally and physically, throughout an entire

scene. Look for the vocal, physical, and tactical variations within the scene that inevitably leads to the violence.

c   Avoid speed. It is tempting to want to go fast. Stay in half-speed tempos to find the subtleties of how the fight is an extension of thought, intention, and language. Find how the fight is a physical conversation rather than a display of athleticism outside of the context of story.

Given circumstances: Who, what, when, where, and why[3]

It is important to ask yourself the question of what story needs to be told by the specific violence required in any given moment within the scene. In the context of a fight scene, the more specific your answers are to the following questions, the more imaginative your work will be, and the more you will be able to contribute to engaging the story with clarity and specificity through the fight.

These basic questions will help you begin to arrive at the answers that each production or scene needs to answer:

1   WHY does the emotional conflict erupt into physical conflict?

2   HOW does the violence further the action of the play?

3   WHAT would be missing in terms of character and story development if the fight were removed?

It can be tempting to occasionally imagine dramatic justifications that extend beyond what is provided by the text. You may be excited to make choices within the acting of a fight scene that are compelling but that ignore the text or even contradict textual clues. Remember that everything you need to know, or can infer, can be found within your textually informed imagination.

A helpful way to start examining the text is to consider the answers to the following three questions:

1   What do I know about my character based on what others say about me?

2   What do I know about my character based on what I say about myself?

3   What actions or behaviours do I actually engage in that may
      contradict or support the answers from #1 and #2?

Who

Who are you, *who* in the play or scene can hurt you, *who* in the play or
scene can help you, *whom* are you fighting for or against, and *who* will
be affected both directly and indirectly by this violence?

What

The *What* of any scene includes such questions as: *What* just happened,
what kind of fight is it, *what* are the given circumstances of the fight,
what are the animate and inanimate objects in the space, and *what* are
the emotional and physical considerations of the fight?

1   What just happened?

    a   My best friend was killed.

    b   I suffered a major wound.

    c   My wife and children were slaughtered.

    d   I just saw my army destroyed.

    e   I suspect my wife/husband is cheating on me.

2   What kind of fight is it?

    a   A private duel.

    b   A battle.

    c   A trial by combat.

    d   An ambush.

    e   A friendly bout.

3   What are the given circumstances of the fight?

    a   It is at night.

    b   My weapons are old and dull.

    c   I have already suffered several wounds and fatigue is setting
      in.

    d   My opponent is more skilled than I.

    e   The ground is muddy.

4   What are the animate and inanimate objects in the space?

    a   What is in my way physically that must be either avoided for safety purposes or taken advantage, safely, within the choreography?

    b   What are the weapons being used and what is the character's specific relationship to the weapons? Are they old or new? Rusty or recently sharpened? Is the character very familiar with the particular weight and size of the weapons or are they foreign to the character?

    c   What are the physical levels in space?

5   What are the emotional and physical considerations of the fight?

    a   I am drunk but fighting for my life.

    b   I am extremely frightened but am trying to hide it.

    c   I am exhausted and feel my energy is waning.

    d   I have not fought before.

    e   I love my opponent even though he or she must die.

    f   I enjoy fighting.

    g   I hate fighting.

    h   I am very good at fighting but don't want to hurt my opponent.

    i   I am very bad at fighting and don't want to hurt my opponent.

    j   I must strive to hide the effort it takes for me to fight.

When

The *When* of a fight can inform a fight with important specificity. The year, month, day, and time all have both conscious and unconscious effects on our behaviour and our methods of violence.

1   Is it light or dark?

2   Is it cold, warm, or unbearably hot?

3   How does the time of day affect your energy?

4   Is it a time of day that noises will be overheard or would sound
be a common occurrence?

While the capacity for violence is a universal trait of all humans, the
specific ways and means by which violence occurs both differs and, in
many psychological ways, remains the same throughout history. How
cultural, social, political, and economic factors influence your choices are
informed by researching the period of the play and the history of violence.
However, in the end the actor and fight director must answer the question,
'Does it work for this story and this theatrical interpretation of the story?'

Where

Where the fight takes place can provide the actor and fight director with
many clues about how to physically engage in the work and how the
concept of 'place' informs violence.

1   How does the violence in a play reflect or stand in counterpoise
to the environment in which the fight takes place? Is the
environment a location in which violence is common or
uncommon? How do these elements affect the characters
fundamental ability or willingness to fight?

2   Is the ground smooth and easily fought on or rough and
natural?

3   Is it a private area or public?

4   How easy is it to see, or is there smoke, haze, dust, or
darkness that impedes vision?

Why

The question of *Why* is a deeply important element to delve into as it
more fully probes the important questions of *why* this fight now, *why*
these weapons, *why* does the fight happen in this place, at this time,
and end in this way. *Why* doesn't one character simply give up? *Why*
are the causes to fight too overwhelmingly strong to prevent surrender?
Potential thoughts to consider in answering the questions of why the
violence occurs are:

a   To revenge my honour.

b   To make amends.

c To find a supporter.

d To hide from the enemy.

e To protect my children.

f To assert my rights.

g To follow through on my promise.

h To prove my strength.

i To survive.

Variety in a fight scene

In all art, variation is one element that makes the art compelling or appealing to the viewer or listener. For instance, the Renaissance master Leonardo da Vinci employed a great variety of line weights and tones in figure drawings. He used heavy, strongly stroked lines as well as very faint markings and sometimes 'lost and found' lines that seem to disappear altogether.

Variety is inherently human in its nature, and our minds will seek to generate multiple solutions to the same problem. The child begging for candy from a parent uses multiple tactical variations to try to achieve his or her goal. The same basic human principles are true for any art that is compelling. In the following exercises, we will explore ways in which the actor can bring variety to his or her fight scene work – specifically, authentically, and artistically.

Smooth and sharp single sword (30 minutes)

(I am grateful to SAFD Certified Teachers Tiza Garland and Brian Evans, as well as Sensei Michael Friedl, from whom this exercise has been inspired and adapted.)

Movement that is characterized by a high degree of flow and fluidity as opposed to movement that is defined by sharp extensions and angular engagements, and the combinations thereof, greatly affects an actor's internal energy. Identifying where the movement might have a quality that is 'sharp' and where they might be 'smooth' physicality can hold resonance for an actor exploring the internal dynamics of a staged fight.

Using the prompts provided, allow the energy of this drill to suggest possible scenarios and intentions. Allow the physical engagement to inform your imagination.

The tendency will be to add unnecessary tension and muscled effort to 'sharp' actions. The inquiry is about exploring the possibility that strength and full engagement does not necessitate a loss of safety and control. Sharp actions are connected to a release of energy and intent rather than muscle and force. If you are having a difficult time differentiating these actions, the Unbendable arm exercise from Chapter 1 can re-establish the process of connecting to a sense of full energy without excess muscular tensions.

(Note: Partnered stage combat cannot be thoroughly or effectively learned from reading a book, as there are many safety considerations of distance, targeting, cues, and blade pathways that can only be fully understood in the context of experiencing the work physically. Therefore, it is important to engage with the remaining stage combat exercises in this chapter only as a reference to your in-class work with a qualified teacher of this discipline.)

Finding safe distance (10 minutes)
(https://vimeo.com/132085800)

Prior to learning the basic choreography below, both partners will check distance to ensure that the point of the weapon, at full extension, is never closer than 6″–10″ from your partner. In this exercise, at no time may the actor close the level of this distance.

1   Both partners will stand in an en garde stance, with their right feet forward (for right-handed actors) and with their knees bent.

2   The sword of Partner A is held with energized ease in the right hand with the point of the weapon directed offline of their partner. Partner B will stand neutrally in an en garde stance with the weapon held point down and at the side.

3   Partner B will weight shift back and will place his or her thumb, with the pinkie finger extended, at the level of their sternum.

4   Partner A will slowly extend their sword *outside the body-line* of Partner B.

5   Partner A will slowly bring the sword from its offline position to point towards Partner B's sternum and will then slowly weight shift forwards. The point of the sword *strictly* stays at sternum level and never comes into close proximity to Partner B's face or neck.

6   Both partners will ensure the point of the extended sword of Partner A is at, or just out of distance, from the pinkie finger of Partner B. The distance from the sword point of Partner A and the pinkie finger of Partner B is approximately 6″–10″ distance from Partner B's body.

7   After this distance has been found, Partner A will safely lower their own sword and weight shift back. Partner B will weight shift to a neutral stance. Both partners will ensure that the tip of the sword never crosses the plane of the face or neck at any time during this action of checking distance.

Single sword choreography (45 minutes)
(https://vimeo.com/132085801)

For the partner attacking, the targets described below of 'hip' and 'arm' are directed *past* their partner. All weapon-to-weapon contact on the attacks and parries should occur lightly, with precision, and control. As a reminder, it is important that the 'targets' described below are never actually threatened. When working with a teacher of stage combat, various safety procedures governing safe distance and the casting of one's energy *past* the partner, always ensure that what looks like 'attacks' to specific body targets are illusory in nature. [4]

Teaching Tip: The martial logic of an attack (either at the beginning of a fight or throughout the course of a choreographed sequence) necessitates that the target is open and available to be attacked. A variety of choreographic techniques are employed by fight directors and teachers to build this martial logic into their work. While working with a teacher of stage combat, be aware that choreography is grounded within martial logic and sound bio-mechanical movement.

---

1   Both partners will establish an eye contact cue to ensure each
     partner is ready. Each partner will have their right foot forward
     (for right-handed actors). Partner B will perform an 'in front
     of the body' cut to Partner A's right hip. At the cue of Partner
     B, Partner A will begin to initiate the parry of the right hip (the
     target being at the height of the upper thigh). Partner B, seeing
     Partner A beginning to engage with a single pass backwards
     with the right foot and initiating a parry of 2, will follow through
     with a single pass forwards with the left foot and the controlled
     fishing line cut to Partner A's right hip, extending the energy of
     the cut *past* Partner A's right hip.

2   After light contact of the blades has been made, Partner B will
     bring the sword in front of their own body and cue a fishing
     line cut to Partner A's left arm (the target being the middle of
     the upper arm, at the mid-point between the elbow and the
     shoulder). Partner A, from the parry of 2, will engage another
     single pass backwards with the left foot, coupled with the
     action of protecting the left arm by bringing the weapon up from
     a parry of 2 to the parry of 4. (The weapon, from the parry of 2,
     continues to extend out to the right and the point raises *outside*
     Partner B's body-line to then allow the blade to vertically and
     safely cross the centre-line. The point of Partner A's weapon
     never crosses any part of Partner B's body during this transition
     from Parry 2 to Parry 4. The action ends in Parry 4 with the
     point directed upwards.) Partner B will ensure to send the
     energy of the fishing line cut *past* Partner A's left arm with a
     single pass forward with the right foot.

3   After light contact has been made, Partner A will now perform
     a bind from the parry of 4 to the parry of 2, with an expulsion.[5]
     This action transports the attacking blade, from a high line
     (Parry 4) to a low line (Parry 2) and crosses the centre-line of the
     body. Both blades stay connected throughout the action.

4   Following the action of the bind with expulsion, Partner A will
     bring his or her weapon around the body and will cue a cut
     to Partner B's right hip. Partner B will engage in a single pass
     backwards with the right foot and initiate the action of protecting
     his or her right hip in the parry of 2. Partner A will extend a slow

horizontally placed cut, sending the energy past Partner B's right hip, with a single pass forward with the left foot.

5   After light contact has been made with the parry of 2 for Partner B, Partner A will bring the sword in front of his or her body and cue a fishing line cut to Partner B's left arm. Partner B will again engage the action of a single pass backwards with the left foot, protecting the left arm (the target again being located in the middle of the upper arm) by initiating a parry of 4. Partner A will follow through with the cut, sending the energy past Partner B's left arm, with a single pass forward with the right foot.

6   As before, in the transition from the parry of 2 to the parry of 4, the action of the blade continues to the right, the point raises *outside the body-line* of the partner attacking, and travels safely and vertically across the body with the point up to protect the left arm. The point of the weapon never crosses either the body or face of Partner A during the action of this, or any, parry.

7   From the parry of 4, Partner B will weight shift forward and perform a croise with expulsion, which transports Partner A's sword from a high line (parry 4) to a low line but does not cross the centre-line of the body, but rather it stays on the same side of the body. Partner A will weight shift back on this action. At all times throughout this action the area of the face and body are never threatened or crossed by the points of either weapon. Partner A's sword stays in connection and extension with Partner B's sword throughout the action of the croise, prior to the expulsion. Partner A maintains a relaxed but energized extension through the arm while receiving the croise rather than breaking at the wrist. Partner B's sword, on the action of performing the croise, firmly glides down the blade of Partner A, moving Partner A's blade down and away.

8   After the basic choreography has been learned, begin to slowly incorporate 'smooth' and 'sharp' physical energy. With your partner, explore speaking out loud the word 'smooth' when an action is smooth, and speak out loud the word 'sharp' when the action is meant to be so. Allow your voice to travel without impediment on your breath. Release excess tensions. Remember that 'sharp' actions within stage combat are not

performed with force or strength directed at your partner. Rather it is the coordination of increased intention, *casting* of one's energy past your partner and full-bodied commitment from your centre (with an inner sense of calm precision and control) rather than overly held tensions placed in your arm and breath.

9   After you have explored speaking aloud 'smooth' and 'sharp' during the choreography, explore what happens when the voice is silent. However, allow the breath to be freely engaged rather than held.

10 Explore other variations than 'Smooth' and 'Sharp', including: Float, Glide, Punch, Stab, and Slash. These can all provide you with subtle physical and vocal variations within this exercise. In addition, refer to the exercise found later in this chapter, 'Laban Exploration' for additional explorations that can be applied within this exercise.

A		B
1. Parry 2	←	Cut right hip **(smooth)**
2. Parry 4	←	Cut left arm **(smooth)**
3. Bind **(sharp)**	→	React
4. Cut right hip **(smooth)**	→	Parry 2
5. Cut left arm **(smooth)**	→	Parry 4
6. Allow	←	Croise **(sharp)**

Refer to shortened fight notation above as a reminder of the choreography. Arrows (→) (←) indicate the Attacker's actions. Ensure you proceed slowly through the choreography.

The martial art of Aikido employs a variety of smooth and sharp qualities to unbalance and control a partner's body. Watch this video of Sensei Michael Friedl discussing Aikido-based smooth and sharp variations. This video is intended for demonstration purposes only. As a reminder, the martial techniques shown on the video tutorials throughout this book can be very dangerous, and should only be practiced under the guidance of a qualified teacher of these disciplines.

(https://vimeo.com/132085804)

(The weapons techniques shown in this video are martial in nature and should not be duplicated on the stage or within stage combat choreography. The study of these martial techniques are potentially injurious and should not be undertaken without the supervision of a qualified instructor of Aikido.)

Eye contact variations (45 minutes)

(I am grateful to Dueling Arts International Founder and Master Teacher, Gregory Hoffman, from whom this exercise has been inspired and adapted.)

Frequently checking in with your partner through eye contact is one of the primary tools that helps maintain safety, connection, and effectiveness within stage combat choreography. Actors must frequently 'check-in' using visual cues to establish clearly communicated signals that help partners remain safe and connected. In addition to the safety procedures that eye contact cues provide, the manner in which the eyes are directed in connection with an acting partner directly affects the clarity of acting choices. As an actor, how you engage with these eye contact variations provides subtle clues to behaviour and affects your internal dynamics and energy.

There are many ways in which partners may employ eye contact within a fight. Two variations are listed below:

- Variation 1: The attacking partner looks at the target being attacked (i.e., with an attack to the right arm, the Attacker looks at the right arm). The partner who is performing the parry or defence (the 'Volunteer', 'Recipient', or 'Defender') has soft focus on the Attacker. The Attacker 'checks in' with their partner through direct eye contact between sequential attacks.

- Variation 2: The Attacker looks at the target and the Recipient looks at the attacking weapon. For instance, when the Recipient parries, he or she looks to see and follows the attacking blade. This method is often used in those instances of heightened effect or in creating the illusion of desperation within choreography.

Using the choreography from the 'Smooth and Sharp Single Sword' exercise, explore each of these two methods in turn. Place particular attention on the action of the breath and allowing the vocal tract to remain free and open. Allow the eye contact variations to affect the breath with variety, with an appropriate engagement of energy and release but without excess tension.

Discussion

- Each of these different methods of eye contact will uniquely affect you and will be subtly perceived differently by an audience. How is the breath affected in each variation?

- It is tempting to hold the breath within choreography. Explore this breath holding pattern in this exercise as a choice. What are the results of allowing the breath to release even within heightened moments?

Scenarios and fights (1 hour)

(I am grateful to SAFD Certified Teacher, Ted Sharon, for this exercise that has been adapted in my own work.)

Written scenarios in combination with in-class drills can help further the development of transforming even the most seemingly simple technique drills into exciting and imaginative moments of action and physical dialogue. The exploration throughout this book is training the body to be flexible, expressive, and responsive to the imagination. This exercise further develops an integration of the body and the imagination in your work.

Using the choreography from the previous exercise, with your partner choose one of the following scenarios. Proceeding slowly, explore the variations in physical dynamic that occurs when your imagination is engaged.

- Scenario 1: Partner A is the jail keeper and has discovered Partner B outside the prison gate. They fight …

- Scenario 2: Two opposing generals meet on the field of battle. They fight …

- **Scenario 3:** Two strangers meet in a darkened alley.
  They fight ...

- **Scenario 4:** A college student demands a better grade in a
  course. The professor insists that the student will fail.
  They fight ...

- **Scenario 5:** Partner A is a Sensei teaching in a dojo. Partner
  B is an opposing Sensei who has come to take the dojo over.
  They fight ....

Teaching Tip: Ensure students take their time within this
exercise to explore the complications and specific physical choices
that further develop relationship and story. The tendency will be to
revert to previously held habits of held breath, tight shoulders, excess
jaw tension, and locked knees. Encourage the students to continue
developing their capacity of engaging the imagination without
locking down on the breath. The task is about exploring a connected
engagement with their partner in which unnecessary tensions are
released and an appropriate expenditure of energy is developed.

Open-ended scene (1 hour)

Explore a scenario within the context of one of the two of open-ended
scenes below. Memorize both sides and alternate playing Actor A and
Actor B. Explore the same choreography from the previous exercise
in the context of one of these scenes. Now that more text is being
explored in conjunction with the physical work, continue to engage with
the previous exercises by allowing the work of breath, the voice, and an
appropriate release of controlled energy into the fight scene.

SCENE 1:

ACTOR A: Hello.
ACTOR B: Hi.

ACTOR A: *What are you doing here?*
ACTOR B: *You know what I'm doing.*
ACTOR A: *Why don't you tell me.*
ACTOR B: *I'd rather not.*
ACTOR A: *You shouldn't be doing this.*
ACTOR B: *You don't think so?*
ACTOR A: *No, I don't.*
ACTOR B: *That isn't my concern.*
ACTOR A: *I'm going to make it your concern.*

(They fight.)

SCENE 2:

ACTOR A: *Are you resisting?*
ACTOR B: *I might be.*
ACTOR A: *Are you ready?*
ACTOR B: *Yes. Are you?*
ACTOR A: *I suppose so.*
ACTOR B: *Then let's get started.*
ACTOR A: *I don't think we should.*
ACTOR B: *No? What's your plan then?*
ACTOR A: *Not sure I have one.*
ACTOR B: *Well, then, I guess we have no choice.*
ACTOR A: *I suppose we don't.*

(They fight.)

Teaching Tip: At the conclusion of a class working on these open-ended scenes, provide an opportunity for each pair to show the work they have been exploring within the scene. As a variation, within a 6–8 move phrase have each pair explore the possibility that the choreography is appropriately divided at 1 or 2 chosen moments *within* the context of the scene rather than occurring only at the conclusion of the scene.

Laban exploration (90 minutes)

Rudolf Laban [1879–1958], was a master teacher, movement innovator, and one of the leading founders of Modern Dance. He developed a systematic vocabulary of human movement. This work can serve as a powerful training tool for actors studying stage combat.

For our purposes, Laban defined three primary Effort Qualities that are particularly useful for our purposes:

1 *Weight*
   a Heavy
   b Light
2 *Time*
   a Sustained
   b Staccato
3 *Space*
   a Direct
   b Indirect

In the following exercise, you will explore a stage combat technique in relationship to these three basic variables. What is important is to allow the physicality to affect your internal energy, which in turn can affect your imagination. The body is not disconnected from the mind and vice versa. Placing your body into various physical postures, authentically and fully, cannot help but affect the authentic internal geography of your thoughts and emotions.

Teaching Tip: It is possible for students to engage with this exercise without allowing the physicality to affect their imaginations. This is a control that some students may exhibit in an effort to do the exercise 'correctly', or in an attempt at controlling emotions that they may perceive as being inappropriate. It can be helpful to remind students that the focus of the exercise is not on physical calisthenics but rather on allowing the physicality to inform their work creatively.

---

1   In a large open space, as a group start to walk in a random pattern within your own bubble of energy. Fill the space but avoid making any physical or vocal contact with any other students in the space.

2   Explore Direct Quality: Choose a location – a chair, a spot on the wall, a crack in the floor – and walk very directly in a straight line to that location.

3   Once you have arrived at your 'intention' of focus, immediately choose another visual target, and walk directly to that location.

4   Allow the physical directness of your movement to inform your internal life. Allow whatever thoughts and emotions arrive be a result of the nature of your physicality.

5   Repeat this several times.

6   Explore Indirect Quality: Choose an object to walk towards but arrive at the location indirectly. Use curves, zigzags, and ellipsoids. It is important that the object is arrived at; however, the pathway towards it is indirect and circuitous.

7   Once the item is reached, choose another object in the room and repeat the exploration of pursuing physical intention indirectly.

8   As before, allow the physical rhythm to affect your mind/body connection. Allow thoughts, scenarios, and emotions to arrive, develop, and transform.

9   Repeat three or four rounds of Indirect Quality.

10 Start to walk with a sense of Heaviness. This will have a tendency to decrease the pace. However, allow the possibility that a sense of heavy physicality is not necessarily slow.

11 Heaviness can involve increased connection to the earth through gravity. Explore uncommon elements of Heaviness: explore Heaviness while jumping up, extending ones 'Heaviness' upwards.

12 Interact with a partner with a subtle 'heavy' energy only through the eyes. Try to explore subtle variations of visual cues within this heavy energy. Allow the breath to respond to this energy.

13 Explore the physicality of Lightness, almost a floating sensation. Imagine gravity has suddenly greatly decreased and that your feet effortlessly skim on the surface.

14 Explore the possibility that Lightness doesn't necessarily mean that a demonstration of 'floating' is necessary, with your arms extended like a bird or hang-glider. Without making contact with anyone and staying far out of distance of any other students, explore how it is to powerfully strike out with a punch, with Lightness as the energy. Explore lying supine on the ground in a state of Lightness. Try 'jumping down' into the ground, lightly.

15 Begin again to randomly walk in space.

16 Start to explore variations in these Effort Qualities – when do you start and stop moving? Place pauses into your walk.

17 What are the lengths of the physical stillness that are habitual?

18 Start to walk with staccato energy. Explore quick, angular changes of direction.

19 As before, allow yourself to connect to the thoughts and emotional life that this energy inspires.

20 How is your breath affected? Where, physically, in your body is the breath centred? Chest, throat, belly, groin? Where do you feel the tensions – the places of breath-holdings – as well as where do you feel the areas of release?

21 Imagine an energy that is characterized by a freedom of sustained energy. Feel your feet make fluidly circular contact with the floor. Feel each micro-moment of weight distribution as you walk in the space. Flow through space sustaining your energy throughout all of your movement.

22 Return to neutral to discuss with the class what you discovered.

Discussion

- How were your thoughts and emotions affected by your physical explorations?

- In what ways did your relationship to others in the space change based on your explorations of various Effort Quality shifts?

- In what ways are fight scenes and choreography potentially influenced by Laban's system?

Now explore these eight different Effort Actions, which are the result of the combinations of the 'Space', 'Time', and 'Weight' Effort Qualities.

(I am grateful to Professor Maggie McClellan, for first introducing me to this chart that has inspired this exercise.)

Effort action:	Space:	Time:	Weight:
PRESS	Direct	Sustained	Heavy
FLICK	Indirect	Staccato	Light
WRING	Indirect	Sustained	Heavy
DAB	Direct	Staccato	Light
SLASH	Indirect	Staccato	Heavy
GLIDE	Direct	Sustained	Light
PUNCH	Direct	Staccato	Heavy
FLOAT	Indirect	Sustained	Light

Explore each of the variations by following the directions below. Explore these variations of Effort Actions before proceeding on to incorporate the techniques within the following exercise of the 'Laban Knife Stab'.

1 As before, within a large space, find your own bubble of energy in which you can explore without making contact with any other students.

2 Proceed through the list of explorations below. Allow the breath to be released and free within your work.

- **PRESS:**
   o Press away an imaginary attacker with your hand, your foot, and your chest.
   o Press on a wall or on the floor with your hands.
   o Press on a wall with your back.
   o Press imaginary dough between your hands.

- **FLICK:**
  - Flick your imaginary whip at someone across the room.
  - Flick an imaginary towel at someone across the room.
  - Flick a kick with your foot.
  - Flick a dog away from you with your foot.

- **WRING:**
  - Wring an imaginary partner's neck.
  - Wring the water out of a damp towel.
  - Wring and twist your entire body in despair.
  - Wring your hands together in worry.

- **DAB:**
  - Dab gently as an artist painting at an easel.
  - Dab with a wet cloth at an imaginary spot off of a piece of clothing.
  - Dab a gentle jabbing, teasing push at an imaginary partner.
  - Dab with your forefinger, dab with your knee, dab with your head.

- **SLASH:**
  - Slash with your arms as if they were steel blades.
  - Slash with your legs in slashing kicks.
  - Slash with your hips.
  - Slash with your elbows in slashing attacks at an imaginary partner.

- **GLIDE:**
  - Glide a slap smoothly towards the face of an imaginary partner.
  - Glide your centre through space as you walk.
  - Glide your arm, connected to your centre, through the arc of a roundhouse punch.
  - Glide your head and torso through space as if you were deftly avoiding multiple punching attacks.

- **PUNCH:**
  - Punch an imaginary floating punching bag.
  - Punch with your hips, elbows, forehead, knee, and foot.
  - Punch with variations of tempo, exploring fast/medium/slow variations.
  - Punch into imaginary warm sand.

- **FLOAT:**
  - Float your fists in your front of you like a boxer in a ring.
  - Float your head on top of your neck and allow that energy to gently move your body through space.
  - Float a round-house punch that sails over the head of an imaginary partner who has ducked.
  - Float your hips, your knees, your ankles, and the back of your head through space.

Teaching Tip: The use of specific music choices in a class helps the students to release into the physical explorations of this Laban-based work. As students explore varying Laban-energies, different pieces of music played can aid the depth of their engagement. In addition, within the development of choreography, a variety of musical choices played can be useful to help technique drills maintain a visceral imaginative energy. The development of choreography, the refinement of an actor's ability to release into the illusion of a weapon's vocabulary, and the honing of a specific fight's acted release can be aided by the inclusion of musical choices within a rehearsal or training environment.

Laban knife stab (60–90 minutes)

You will first learn a theatrical knife stab and then apply the Laban techniques that have been explored in the previous exercise to the movement of stage combat.

Teaching Tip: Always ensure you are working with safe theatrical weapons that are specifically designed by a professional experienced in their safe construction. A list of potential suppliers is listed in the Appendix. Depending on class size or maturity, for safety, explore this technique with a short (6″–8′) cut down section of a pool noodle. Retractable knives are not safe, and should not be used. The mechanism that retracts the blade can and does fail. Sharp knives are not safe. Do not *ever* use them. Do not attempt to dull a sharp blade yourself. In addition, the blade of the knife must be free of any burrs, projections, guards, and be completely blunt on the edges and tip. Injury can occur with even a blunt prop knife. Slow and safe precision must be consistently employed throughout the exercise.

Establishing safety, targeting, and distance

1   Partner A (the 'Attacker'), holding the safe prop knife of approximately 6″–8″ in their right hand, stands facing Partner B (the 'Recipient') with their left foot forward. Partner B is standing off-line from his or her partner. Partner A has their right foot slightly forward. Right shoulder of Partner A should be on-line with approximately the centre of Partner B's chest.

2   Partner A's left foot is just outside of Partner B's right foot.

3   In preparation for the technique, Partner B (the 'Recipient') will place the closed palm of the knife-holding right hand of Partner A (the 'Attacker') on Partner B's own belly. The placement of the hand is on the left side of the belly. The ribs or the hard bony areas of the hip are never contacted by either the hand or knife. This pre-placement of the hand and flat of the knife blade by the Recipient of the technique, ensures that the Attacker knows exactly where the exact target is located. It is important for Partner A to clearly see where this target is, to be able to spot this target, and to gently place the palm of their hand on this exact location.

Three-step process for the theatrical knife stab

1   There are three steps that must be followed in the course of this
action:

a   *Eye Contact* – Partner A and Partner B ensure that eye
contact is established prior to execution of the technique.
Allow yourself to breathe freely while you make eye contact
with your partner.

b   *Preparation and Spot the Target* – Partner A places their left
hand on Partner B's right shoulder. At the same time, the
hand holding the knife is cued just off of the right side of the
waist of Partner A. It is at this step that the point of the knife
must be clearly misdirected off-line from Partner B. Partner
A will ensure that the point of the knife will always remain
pointed slightly away and off-line from Partner B. At no time
is the tip of the knife pointed directly the Recipient's belly.

At the same time as Partner A cues the knife to their right side, he or she also will visually spot the target that was identified at the beginning of the exercise. The target must be clearly available and unobstructed, the left arm of Partner B must be removed by at least 24″ from the target area, and the point of the weapon is directed off-line from Partner B's body-line. Partner B should look at the knife in the playing of the danger, as it is cued by Partner A prior to the next step.

c *Follow Through* – Partner A slowly extends the palm of their hand and the flat of the knife blade (not the point) to the target area of the belly. It is very important that it is the *flat* of the blade that makes light contact with the side of the Recipient's belly, not the edge. Lay the knife blade gently on your partner's side, rather than whipping it against your partner. The hand, wrist, and forearm of the attacker remain in alignment on the action of the stab. It is important that the tip of the knife does not extend *past* your partner's body.

Only after the closed palm of the hand and blade has made controlled and specific contact, Partner B gently covers Partner A's hand with his or her left hand and places his or her right hand on the inside forearm of Partner A's right arm holding the knife.

(The correct audience angle for this stab is that the stabbing action occurs on the upstage side of the Recipient's belly, furthest away from the audience.)

2 It is imperative that the heads of both partners remain well separated from each other. For this reason, Partner A will isolate their abdominal muscles to contract only slightly over the hand and knife of Partner A. In addition, the bodies of both partners remain off-line from each other throughout the exercise. The partner being stabbed will ensure that the head and torso does not drop over in the playing of the wound. Both partners will

work together so that their heads remain off-line and always at least 18″ away from each other at a safe distance. In addition, both partners must maintain at least 18″ distance between heads and the shoulders of their partner.

3   Play the wound as if it is occurring in the centre of the belly rather than off to the side.

4   It is important to establish eye contact between partners after the contact has been made. An audience is primarily interested in the *relationship* between the characters within this moment of violence.

5   At this point, maintaining a safe distance from each other and ensuring that heads remain safely separated, Partner A will create the illusion of twisting the weapon further in to the body of Partner B. This is accomplished by a small rotation of the hips of the Attacker while *leaving the arm completely still and neutral*. There is no actual energy applied to the body of Partner B. The only action is Partner A's slight rotational engagement of the hips to the left but allowing the knife arm and hand to remain controlled and relatively still.

6   The left hand of Partner A remains on Partner B's right shoulder. This helps both partners remain stable and connected. Both partners must remain grounded, balanced, with knees bent, and both feet firmly on the floor at all times.

7   Partner B, whose contact on the hand and just above the wrist of Partner A has been very light, will allow Partner A to remove the knife down and away from Partner B's torso. Partner A will make sure the knife ends up pointing down and away from their partner after it is withdrawn. Partner A should take 2–3 steps away from Partner B, after the knife has been removed.

8   As Partner A removes the weapon down and away, Partner B's reaction is an isolation of the belly forwards in the direction that the knife has been removed.

9   Once the knife has been safely removed, the hands of Partner B immediately return to the placement of where the illusion of penetration has occurred, the *centre* of the belly. Partner B ensures that he or she stays on their feet without crumpling or

falling to the ground, which would require additional training with a qualified teacher of stage combat.

Within the basic sequence of the basic knife stab, you will now explore the Laban energies within each moment of the technique. Practice slowly to fully allow a thorough investigation of the artistic choices that are possible. It is tempting to settle for the overall effect of the technique without engaging in the specific playable choices that are possible.

Isolate the sequence into three distinct actions:

1 The Attack
2 Twisting the Knife
3 The Removal of the Knife

Each of these three moments in time can be explored from a different perspective of a Laban Effort Action. Stay in slow-motion, or 'Tai Chi speed', as you practice with these Laban Effort Actions. Copy the table below, and explore with your partner what effects the following combinations can create:

ATTACK	TWISTING THE KNIFE	REMOVAL OF THE KNIFE
PUNCH	Press	Slash
SLASH	Wring	Flick
DAB	Flick	Punch
GLIDE	Slash	Press
WRING	Float	Punch
FLOAT	Punch	Float
FLICK	Wring	Float

Come up with your own combinations, and explore what other micro-moments are possible within a sequence as short as this knife stab. Keep in mind that it is not how long and complicated a fight is that makes it compelling. The true resonance of a fight is in the depth of its acting components. A shorter fight, specifically played, is infinitely more compelling as a piece of storytelling than a long fight with complicated moves that cannot be effectively integrated – physically, vocally, or emotionally.

Discussion

- How do the different physical rhythms and energies of the Laban work affect your breath? How is your breath, in connection with the body, influenced by various Laban energies?

- Using the Laban work, in what ways can the breath and the voice be specifically integrated within a fight scene?

Exploring physical volumes

One of the qualities we most admire about great actors are their abilities to be available to the emotional life of the character. It is this availability that allows us to see our own foibles, our own fears, and our own capacities for compassion. When a character is in trouble – when he or she may be experiencing pain, fear, loss, and the possibility of injury or death – seeing this struggle played out is immensely compelling. In action movies, we thrill when the hero is beating the 'bad guys'. However, it is when the hero is faced with the possibility of mortality that we are most truly gripped by the story. The same holds true for the actor faced with dramatic violence.

As we explored in the previous chapter, vocal volume is a primary tool for the actor engaged with stage combat choreography. A high level of volume, consistently engaged with at the expense of other choices, is to be avoided. Without volume variations in conjunction with pitch and pace variations, spoken language would be very difficult to decipher. When Hamlet speaks the line: 'Oh, what a rogue and peasant slave am I ...', we understand the actor's point of view based on which words are given more or less emphasis. The actor often gives greater weight primarily to nouns and verbs as the words that most often carry the character's intentions, argument, and meaning.

In a similar way, in choreographed fights it is often more effective to select or choose specific moments of heightened physical volume.

A method of propelling actors into the playing of the realities of fights that are life and death affairs is to engage the voice with a cry of 'Help!' on every defence and a cry of 'Die!' on every attack. Vocal support, resonance placement, and an open vocal tract are vital to maintain throughout the exercise. Be sure that when engaging with the word 'Die' or 'Help' they do not become generic words voiced at the same volume. While maintaining vocal support and a free passageway of the throat, play with pitch, pace, rhythm, volume, and quality in the voicing of your words in connection with your physicality.

Help and die broadsword (30 minutes)[6]
(https://vimeo.com/132085877)

(I am grateful to SAFD Certified Teacher, Tiza Garland, from whom this exercise was originally inspired and has been subsequently adapted in my own work.)

1 Both partners will establish a safe stage combat distance. Refer to the exercise of 'Smooth and Sharp Single Sword' in this chapter, as a reminder for the procedure for establishing this distance.

2 Both partners come into an en garde stance, with both knees bent and weight grounded. There should be width and depth between the feet. As before, use the weight shifting action of your legs and smoothly move from your centre, forwards and backwards, to aid the action of the weapon on the attacks and parries rather than operating solely from the arms or leaning from the torso. The spine remains lengthened with relaxed shoulders. Remind yourself that the breath can remain free and flexible even within the demands of a weapon that has weight.

3 Partner A will bring the weapon to their own right side, with the point directed upwards. The point of the weapon never crosses the face or body of Partner B. Ensuring to then place the weapon on an imaginary flat, horizontal table and sliding it forwards in a cutting like action, Partner A will perform a fishing line cut towards Partner B's left arm, extending the energy *past* Partner B's arm, at a target located at the mid-point between shoulder and elbow. Partner A will vocalize the word 'Die' on this attack. Partner B protects their left arm in a vertical parry

of 4, and will vocalize the word 'Help'. Both partners ensure to never cross the body or face of either partner with their weapon.

Teaching Tip: As a reminder, ensure that with all attacks and parries, the 'foible' (last third of the blade) is the part of the blade that attacks and the 'forte' (the first third of the blade) is the part of the blade that parries. Distance between partners must be at the correct measure of 6″–10″ of safe distance from the furthest extension of the attacking weapon.

---

4   Once light contact has been made, Partner A will bring his or her own sword around the body to cast a horizontal fishing line cut towards Partner B's right hip, directed at the height of the upper thigh level. Be sure to avoid your own head and body with any part of the blade or hilt as it travels around your body. The cut to the right hip travels in a plane horizontal to the ground rather than being directed on any upward or downward angle. Partner B will slowly bring the broadsword downwards in a semi-circular manner to protect their right hip in a parry of 2. The true edge of the parrying blade is facing towards the incoming attack. As before, Partner A will vocalize the word 'Die' on the attack and Partner B will vocalize the word 'Help' on the parry. Continue to repeat these words as the exercise progresses.

5   Again, after light contact with the parry has been made, Partner A will slowly bring his or her sword around their own body to perform a horizontal fishing line cut towards Partner B's left hip. Partner B will protect their left hip by performing a direct parry of 7, with the true edge again facing the incoming attack.

6   After light contact has been made, Partner A will bring their sword once more around his or her own body to perform a horizontal fishing line cut to Partner B's right arm, again targeted

at the mid-point between shoulder and elbow. Partner B will protect their right arm by bringing their sword out to the left from the parry of 7, upwards, and vertically crossing their own centre-line to protect their right arm. This is the parry of 3. As a reminder, all of these parries are performed with the 'true edge'. Ensure that the point of the weapon never crosses the head, torso, groin, or knee area of Partner A.

7   After light contact has been made, safely return to an en garde position, being careful to never bring the point of the weapon across the face or neck of your partner.

8   Switch sides and repeat.

A		B
1. Cut left arm *(Die!)*	→	Parry 4 *(Help!)*
2. Cut right hip *(Die!)*	→	Parry 2 *(Help!)*
3. Cut left hip **(Die!)**	→	Parry 7 *(Help!)*
4. Cut right arm **(Die!)**	→	Parry 3 *(Help!)*

Variation 1

As a variation, explore a reversal of the above directions: on the attack vocalize 'Help!' and on the defence vocalize 'Die!'. As before, allow yourself to connect to your centre with your breath and voice. This exercise allows actors to release into the shifts of control and to explore the power struggles that occur in a fight. Avoid the same level of vocal commitment in each attack. Explore how variations within vocal pitch and volume can affect the internal geography of your exploration of this drill.

A		B
1. Cut left arm *(Help!)*	→	Parry 4 *(Die!)*
2. Cut right hip *(Help!)*	→	Parry 2 *(Die!)*
3. Cut left hip *(Help!)*	→	Parry 7 *(Die!)*
4. Cut right arm *(Help!)*	→	Parry 3 *(Die!)*

Variation 2

As a further variation, explore a shift that can occur within the middle of this basic drill. Partner A should vocalize 'Die!' on the first two attacks; however on the last two attacks, the vocalization of 'Help!' can now be vocalized by Partner A. In this variation, try exploring how these shifts in energy and connection between you and your partner can be specifically placed and carefully arranged to tell subtly different stories, even though the same choreography is being employed.

A		B
1. Cut left arm *(Die!)*	→	Parry 4 *(Help!)*
2. Cut right hip *(Die!)*	→	Parry 2 *(Help!)*
	SHIFT	
3. Cut left hip *(Help!)*	→	Parry 7 *(Die!)*
4. Cut right arm *(Help!)*	→	Parry 3 *(Die!)*

Explore the exercise with the inclusion of other words. A brief list could include:

- I Love You!/I Hate You!
- Stay!/Leave!
- Now!/Never!
- Go!/No!

Conflict is the basis of all drama and the actor must engage with the process of psychologically presenting significant obstacles for their acting partner. Unlike real life, where overt conflict is usually avoided, actors must actively look for the conflict and fully engage with the opposing goals of their scene partner. It is an act of creative generosity to engage with as much conflict in scene work as possible – safely and appropriately as will be dictated by the nature of the scene. The study of stage combat allows you to viscerally explore when and how a character is pursuing actions of intention to gain the upper hand.

> *Teaching Tip:* It is easy to mistake 'volume' for hitting harder
> or moving through the fight more quickly. Making hard contact
> results in broken blades and potential injuries. Rather than hitting
> harder, the student should be always making light contact ensuring
> energy of the attacks is directed *past* their partner rather than *into*
> a partner. 'Volume' is about intention, *casting* the energy past your
> partner, full-bodied commitment from your centre while allowing
> the breath to be free – rather than tension.

Discussion

- What discoveries did you make in the fight sequence by varying your physical volume?
- How can an exploration of physical volume begin to develop a clearer specificity of character thought and intent?
- Using this exercise, how can stage combat training serve as a visceral tool for actors connecting to text and scene work?

Finding physical rhythms

In David Carey and Rebecca Clark-Carey's book on text work for the actor, *The Verbal Arts Workbook*, the authors succinctly describe the importance of 'rhythm':

> We enjoy the rhythms of dance, of music, of skipping rhymes and football chants because rhythm is infectious; it affects us physically, emotionally and mentally, changing the way we think and feel. Rhythm can be hypnotic, sexual, dramatic, soporific, soothing, rousing and even aggravating.[7]

In the same manner that volume affects spoken language and contributes to a clarity of thought, so too does an actor's ability to employ elements of pace and rhythm allow an audience to fully follow the thinking process of the character.

Similarly to textual rhythms that the actor must be able to be responsive to, it is important to identify the physically based rhythmic choices that fully engage the actor in a fight scene. Each piece of fight choreography may have a different internal rhythm, each move may have a different energetic 'weight' (based on the pitch, pace, rhythm, or volume of the specific physicality). The rhythm of a fight can aid in the revealing of character thought and action within the choreography.

The musicality of the fight – these internal rhythms – subconsciously affects an audience's understanding of the emotional geography of the conflict. It is important to remember that though real violence may most often be characterized by a flurry of attacks without particular attention paid to the rhythmic qualities, everything on stage must maintain a heightened or 'placed' element, that allows an audience fully in to the event on a deeply intuitive level.

Rhythm also affects the internal reality of the actor as well. How the rhythms are placed within fight choreography will affect the character's psychology when performing the fight. How we speak, what words we choose to place emphasis on – are all 'behaviours'. The same is true for fights – the specific behaviours of the characters can be perceived and experienced by an audience rather than a wash of generalized physicalized aggression.

There are no right and wrong choices. There are only choices that are 'right for …' and 'wrong for …' particular situations, stories, productions, actors, rehearsal times, and directorial preferences. Though a fight director may work on dozens of productions of *Romeo and Juliet*, each production's choreography may have different emphases, qualities, rhythms, musicalities, and behaviours. In your work, allow the physical rhythms of a fight to affect your internal rhythms.

Rhythms of wrist/elbow/shoulder cuts (30–45 minutes)

Where an attack physically originates from can largely determine the rhythms that a fight develops. Cutting attacks from the three different anatomic points of origin – the wrist, elbow, and shoulder – inherently have progressively slower rhythmic qualities. Physical rhythms often affect the nature of the physical volume that is perceived within any given technique. As always, there is a great deal of variation available. In general terms, slower and more consistent rhythms may have the tendency to give the appearance of heavily muscled attacks, which may also be the result of characters nearing the end of their stamina limits. Quicker and more varied rhythms may have the ability to signify a fight in which the combatants are testing, probing, and responding to their opponent with full energy, stamina, and skill.

With a single rapier, Partner A explores attacks to the right hip and left hip of Partner B. Partner B protects the right hip (Parry 2) and protects the left hip (Parry 7 or 1).

1 (https://vimeo.com/132085878) Explore these two attacks from the standpoint of engaging the attack from three different locations: the Wrist, the Elbow, and the Shoulder. Allow the increased time it takes between each attack of the wrist, elbow, and shoulder to not only affect the rhythm and tempo but also to affect the potential emotional reality of this simple sequence.

Single sword rhythm (30–60 minutes)
(https://vimeo.com/132085880)

> *Teaching Tip:* The following exercise introduces several new technical elements and is meant to be undertaken only by students with significant previous stage combat training or those students currently studying stage combat. This exercise is to be undertaken only under the supervision of a qualified instructor of stage combat.

A caesura is a small pause or 'poise' within a line of dialogue. It can also signify a very small moment of pausing within a fight. These small caesuras can be effectively employed to specifically tell the story clearly and with precision. This is similar to the practice of the musician, who is trained to respond to the length of notes (e.g., whole-notes, half-notes, quarter-notes of increasing rhythmic speed) as well as the specific markings that notate lengths of silence. It can be useful for fight scenes to investigate these musical rhythms as well as where there could be a physical pause of either slight or long duration. These small moments of pause within a fight signify a physical realization, a last ditch effort, or a change of tactic.

Actors abilities to communicate text not only through speech but through their silence is equally important as their abilities to allow the contributions of pausing to affect the internal realities of a fight. Within text, if language is devoid of these pauses, an audience cannot follow the thinking. Similarly, if a fight is devoid of phrasing and subsequent pauses, the audience is lost within a flurry of perceived attacks that do not necessarily reveal the fullness of the character's intentions, fears, discoveries, and realizations. It is important to note that this can also become overdone and too many pauses can overstuff the fight with physical timings and well-intentioned minutia that also do not serve effective storytelling. As is true within language, pauses must be *earned* for them to have their full effect. In addition, not every fight holds significant rhythmic qualities. An absence of rhythmic variation can be a significant clue into the character's psychology. The choices, as always, are yours to make by design rather than by the default of an unconscious habit.

Using a Single Sword explore the following piece of choreography, with a focus placed on the rhythmic variations that are possible:

1   Both partners will have their right feet forward (for right-handed actors). After establishing safe distance of 6″–10″ and an eye contact cue, Partner A will perform an in front of the body fishing line cut to Partner B's right hip. Partner B will protect their right hip, in a counter parry of 2. The target is at the upper thigh level.

2   Immediately following the successful parry, Partner A will perform a small cut from the wrist to Partner B's right arm. The target is the middle of the upper arm, between the shoulder and elbow and approximately at the point of the bottom of the deltoid muscle. Partner B will perform a semi-circular blade pathway, being sure to never cross the face, neck, or body of Partner A, to bring their weapon upwards to protect their right arm in the parry of 3.

3   After light contact has been made in the parry, Partner A will now bring his or her weapon in front of their own body. After the

blade has cleared around their own body, Partner A will imagine sliding the weapon on a flat table and perform a fishing line cut to Partner B's left arm. Again the level of the imaginary target is the middle of the upper arm, at the mid-point between the elbow and the shoulder. Partner B will protect their left arm, in the parry of 4.

4   Following the successful parry, Partner B will perform a bind, from the parry of 4 to the parry of 2, with an expulsion. This action transports the opposing blade, in this case from a high to low line, across the centre-line of the body. The action of Partner B's bind originates at the elbow rather than the wrist. Partner A, who is receiving the bind, stays connected with the entire arm with Partner B's blade throughout the course of the bind. Partner A maintains the supinated position of his or her hand and arm during the bind. The foible of Partner A's weapon stays in connection with the forte of Partner B's blade as he or she performs the bind, prior to the action of the expulsion.

5   Following the bind with expulsion, Partner B extends the point of his or her weapon off-line of the right hip of Partner A, with the palm facing down. After this full extension occurs, Partner A weight shifts back. Partner B weight shifts forwards. Partner A then protects their right hip in a parry of 2. (For the purposes of this drill, the extension of the point of the weapon on the attack is directed just outside of the hip rather than on-line and directly at the hip. Only with the guidance of a qualified instructor, on-line targets are often employed in specific choreographic situations, in which distance is correct, blade pathways are safe, and partners are at a proper measure of at least 6″–10″ out of distance.)

6   Partner A now extends his or her weapon (palm down) towards an imaginary target off-line of the right hip of Partner B. Partner B weight shifts backwards. Partner A weight shifts forwards. Partner B then protects his or her right hip in a parry of 2.

7   Partner B extends the point towards Partner A's right arm, with the hand in pronation (i.e., palm down). The target is off-line of the right arm and at the height of the mid-point between the

elbow and shoulder. Partner A weight shifts to the rear. Partner B weight shifts forwards. As before, Partner A then protects their right arm in a semi-circular parry of 3. Be very careful and precise that the weapon does not cross the head or face of the partner in any action within stage combat.

8 Once Partner A has protected their right arm in the parry of 3, Partner A will execute a bind with an expulsion. This action transports the blade of Partner B, in this case, from a high line (parry 3) to a low line (parry 7) and crossing the centre-line of the body. A weight shift forward accompanies this action, with a corresponding weight shift back from Partner B. This weight shift occurs *after* the weapons have crossed the centre-line of both partners.

9 Both partners slowly reset into the en garde position, being careful to avoid crossing the face or neck with the point of either weapon.

10 Switch roles and repeat.

Teaching Tip: The next step to this process would be Partner B waiting only to see Partner A's *initiation* of their weight shift back, before Partner B would begin their weight shift forwards. The partnered weight shifting process with further training begins to give the illusion of partner's shifting weight forwards and back in what seemingly appears to be at the same time. However, in the early stages of training, careful safety practices are drilled, which fully solidify the foundation in stage combat: the 'Recipient' of the attacking action is always in control. Ensure students maintain a slow and fluid progression through the fight. Distance, targeting, eye contact, balance, and safe blade pathways must always be precise and controlled. However, even at this early stage of training, encourage the students' breathing to be free, even within the physical precision of this work.

A		B
1. Cut to right hip **(Half-note)**	→	Parry 2
2. Cut to right arm **(Half-note)**	→	Parry 3
3. Cut to left arm **(Full-note)**	→	Parry 4
4. React	←	Bind **(Full-note)**
5. Parry 2	←	Thrust right hip **(Full-note)**
Caesura		**Caesura**
6. Thrust right hip **(Half-note)**	→	Parry 2
7. Parry 3	←	Thrust right arm **(Half-note)**
8. Bind **(Half-note)**	→	React
9. En garde	–	En garde

After you have a thorough understanding of the safe execution of the mechanics, communicate with your partner and explore your own rhythms. Find those pauses or musical variations of longer or shorter length than what are listed above. What specifically occurs within a *relationship* between two people in a fight is what is compelling rather than what is happening to one person only. The theatrical revealing of the complications of human relationships is a primary task of the actor in scene work and within a fight.

Discussion

- How did the rhythmic variation affect your imagination within the fight?
- How does the rhythm affect your breath?

Connecting to thought

(I have been inspired by Scott Kaiser's excellent book, 'Mastering Shakespeare' within this series of exercises. For more information, refer to the Bibliography.)

The human body under the life-sustaining influence of adrenalin within the fight or flight response is capable of sustaining multiple wounds and injuries and still remain active and threatening. However, the effects of injury, pain, and the sight of blood are also able to create identifiable psycho-physical reactions that can also affect the breath and the voice. Often, the specific effects of safely and skilfully engaging the voice and the breath within the illusion of pain, fear, rage, and simulated kills is largely left to the actor to figure out. When choreography becomes devoid of the appearance of in-the-moment response and is learned as physical techniques only, there is little authentic humanity that can be revealed through the work.

A focus on technique is a natural response to learning the art and discipline of stage combat; however, your learning cannot stop there. As stage combat is a potentially dangerous activity, it is important that you learn the mechanics of the work with careful physical specificity and with a goal of ensuring the safety of yourself and your partner as the top priority. As you become more adept at learning these skills, drilling techniques, and honing the physical precision of the work, you may feel that your body is necessarily being placed into more and more control. However, even from the early stages of learning stage combat techniques, you will be aided in this development by fully integrating your physical acquisition of skill with your breath and expressively free vocal instrument. This integrated approach will further facilitate a more truthful human release of the choreography when your physicality is connected from the start to the imaginative thinking process of the character.

This does not mean that an audience needs to logically perceive every thought that might occur to a character within a fight, but it does mean that your development of physical storytelling skills are informed by a specificity of thought, in a similar way that is required when you are working on connecting specifically to text. Within text work, a new thought or a new discovery frequently results in a new breath. Likewise, a new realization within a fight, a new discovery of a target to attack, or a new decision to start or end a phrase, might include the possibility of a short or significant breath impulse that informs your action. Part of your task is to ask in what ways might your internal energy, including the breath and voice, specifically reveal the tactics and thoughts experienced within a fight. Each phrase within a fight, and potentially the individual attacks and parries within a choreographed phrase, might have specific thinking processes associated with them. These phrases of a fight can have titles as simple as:

> *Phrase 1: Test the waters*
>
> *Phrase 2: Get in, Get out*
>
> *Phrase 3: I'm in trouble*

The encouragement is to avoid performing 'choreography' as movement divorced from thought and story. Much of this is about taking the time that is needed before the fight begins, within the fight, and after the fight concludes to fully engage with the thinking process of the character rather than rushing into and through the violence as a physical exercise alone. The questions that are valuable to ask are:

a **Moments Before**: What is the *moment before* a punch, a kick, a stab, a slash, or a kill takes place? What are the images and specifically placed intentional, physical, and emotional responses prior to the action?

b **Moments During:** How is the moment characterized emotionally *as the action is taking place?* As the strike is landing, as the thrust is entering the body, as the head slash is evaded. What emotional experiences relate to the event as it is physically taking place?

c **Moments After**: What are the *results* of the action? What are the effects of not accomplishing your goal? What are the effects of seeing the injury or traumatic wound that you have inflicted? What is the specific nature of the pain that is experienced, as both an Attacker and as a Recipient of the illusion?

Choreographed violence can tell many diverse stories, including representing violence that is brutal, messy, explosive, and quick. However, it can be very helpful for actors to allow themselves to process experientially the subconscious workings of the human mind as it prepares and engages with conflict. It is helpful to remember that theatre is *heightened* reality. Every gesture and action on stage means something. Deepening your work through the 'inner monologue' that weaves throughout a theatrically violent encounter enables you to more fully bring depth into the representation of staged conflict. The specificity, and the level of care that is taken to fully establish, image, and play the specific moments of the action, is as important in stage combat as it is within the acting process of working on scene work. What your character *Expects, Hopes, Images, Realizes, Decides, Fears*, and *Intends* all affect your body, imagination, voice, and breath in ways that allow the choreography to be *lived through* rather than simply performed well.

Verbalize your responses to the prompts below while you work. Explore the possibility that, by speaking aloud, you can discover a greater depth of humanity within the physicality. Particular moments in which these questions can be verbalized are:

1   Before the text of the scene begins.
2   During the scene, add the answers to these prompts before you speak your line of dialogue.
3   Before the fight begins.
4   In extreme slow motion, between movements within the fight.
5   Between each phrase.
6   At the conclusion of the fight.

Expectations: The character in a fight has positive expectations. A head swipe, for instance, can look like it was meant to make contact with a partner. When the partner ducks, and the swiping blade passes harmlessly overhead, this potentially can be played as an action that was not expected. What do I *expect to happen* in the fight? What *actually does* happen?

A character speaking a monologue does not know they will end up speaking for a length of time but rather one thought leads to the next and by the end – what is called a 'monologue' has been *thought* through by the character speaking. In a similar way, a character's engagement in a choreographed fight is a result of intention. The fact that a 10–15 move fight occurs is the result of physical dialogue that is – at some level of conscious or unconscious discovery – responded to by the characters within the moment.

The actor who is able to authentically discover and enjoy the specific process of acting within fight work starts to reveal depths of how humans actually interact with real-life predicaments. Consider that specific well-placed moments of discovery and realization in a fight are not what the character expected to happen and must be dealt with accordingly.

Hopes: There are times when a character does not expect success but in such cases, there must at least be a *hope* that success can be achieved. What does my character *hope will happen* in the fight? In this phrase? This move? What *actually does* happen, and how does that potentially differ? Play for results *in your partner* of physical/psychological/emotional changes to occur. For instance, if you hope your partner will bleed from their forehead, and you see the results of that hope becoming manifest, your experience as a character changes within the success or failure of that goal.

Images: When confronted with heightened circumstances in real life, we often have vivid memories of the sights, smells, tastes, and sounds that were associated with the experience. A particular smell or hearing a specific piece of music on the radio will bring back memories long forgotten. Within a fight, being able to verbalize specifically what you *see, hear, taste, touch and smell* affects and transforms the work into becoming more specific and authentic. As an exercise, at your instructor's prompt ('*what do you see, hear, taste, touch, smell?*'), verbalize these images aloud to your partner before the fight begins, between each phrase and at the conclusion of the fight.

Realizations: Thought is action and behaviour. Within a fight scene, recognizing that new information and discoveries are being made allows the fight to be fresh and new within every performance while maintaining the integrity of physical consistency for safety. Ask yourself what *realizations* occur in the fight?

Allow the answers to these questions to affect your voice, your breath, and your connection to your acting partner. For example:

- *I realize* that a target is open to attack.

- *I realize* that I have accidentally left a target open to attack.

- *I realize* in this moment that my opponent is better/worse than I am.

- *I realize* that I am experiencing pain.

- *I realize* my pain is getting worse.

- *I realize* that I have caused blood to trickle down my partner's face.

- *I realize* that I should not have killed my opponent.

- *I realize* that my energy is waning.

- *I realize* that I'm not going to win but I am going to fight to the death anyway.

- *I realize* that I'm going to die.

Decisions: Thinking through a predicament and deciding on a course of action can be a powerfully theatrical moment. What specific *decisions* do I make in the fight? The fullness of the thought – the decisions – need to occur prior to the moment of physical engagement. It need not take long to decide, but human beings have thoughts, images, desires, needs, hopes, and fears that are based on thoughts which leads to speech and action, not the other way around. Decisions can come at the lightning speed of thought and may include:

- *I am deciding* to invite my opponent to attack a specific target.

- *I am deciding* NOW to make him bleed.

- This was a playful bout but now *I am deciding* to kill him.

- *I am deciding* to make him tell me the truth.

- *I am deciding* to give up.

- I can't win by playing fair, *so I am deciding* to cheat to win.

Fears: Allowing the possibility that the character is experiencing fear and doubt within a fight is always productive to explore. Doubt may be hidden or clearly apparent. Finding the specific opportunities of when and where your character gets into trouble within the context of a fight immediately humanizes the work in a way that is universal and recognizably human.

Within dramatic physical conflict, it must be remembered that there is the potential for a character to fear and be very wary of the possibility of painful injury or death. The weapons must be imagined to be lethal, which in turn affects the fight or flight response of the characters. Distance and blade positioning between partners must be 100 per cent safe and also reveal the reality of playing this intentionality. The actor's physicality needs to be specifically played and responsive to far, middle, and near distances between partners, prior to and during the course of a fight.

What hidden or exposed fears are experienced during the fight? Even in the case of a character that may not seem to experience fear, is it possible that this emotion has been buried and is lurking inside the character's psyche? What metaphorical 'mask' do you wear as this character that hides the inner reality?

- *I'm afraid that* I am going to die.
- *I'm afraid that* I am going to kill my opponent.
- *I'm afraid that* I am going to look foolish.
- *I'm afraid that* I have been wrong this entire time.
- *I'm afraid that* the pain of death will be intolerable.

Discussion

- In what ways might the exploration of these various elements (*decisions, realizations, images, intentions, etc.*) affect the breath when acting the fight?
- Within a fight or a scene, a new breath often precedes a new realization or a new discovery. These breaths can be very subtle or quite full. How can the breath be 'painted' within a fight scene in ways that are connected with the character's thinking process?

Aural story-telling in fights (1–2 hours)

(I am grateful for discussions with SAFD Certified Teacher and Associate Teacher of Fitzmaurice Voicework® – Brian Evans – from whom this exercise originated and was inspired.)

In this exercise, incorporating the explorations from this chapter, you will place the focus on the specificity of the aural storytelling aspects that are required to communicate within staged violence. Ensure you do not limit yourself to making a vocalized sound for every move in a fight. Within a fight sequence, vocal silence and the sounds of breathing can be as communicative as voiced responses.

1 With a partner, learn the choreography from the 'single sword rhythm' in this chapter.

2 Choose a specific scenario from the exercise 'Scenarios and Fights', also found in this chapter.

3 Explore specific vocal and breathing responses that may occur before, during, or after the fight. Explore vocal responses that support the specific storytelling requirements of your scenario.

4 In your fight, engage with your breath and voice but avoid using language or words.

5 In a class, each pair of students will show their fight with specifically chosen vocal and breath-based sounds. The students watching these fights will close their eyes and only *listen* to the sounds of the fights. The music of the blades, the rhythms, pitches, tempos, and volumes of the physical work will be heard. The actor's voices will specifically engage with the storytelling elements of their individual fights. Include explorations that have been covered in Chapter 3.

6 After you and your partner have shown your work with the remainder of the class only listening, discuss with the class what they heard. What story did they hear in your fight through the sounds of your breath and voice? What aural information did they receive that was particularly effective? What sounds seemed unnecessarily repetitive, confusing or unnecessary?

7 Repeat the choreography but this time have the remainder of the class open their eyes and watch the fight.

8 As a group, discuss what you heard and observed.

Discussion

- Does the story of the fight visually support the story that you and your partner communicated vocally?

- Are there areas in which the vocal choices in the fight can even more specifically support the physical language of the fight?

- Are there physical moments in the fight that are not fully supported by the vocal storytelling elements?

Engaged play

(I have been inspired from SAFD Fight Master David Brimmer, SAFD Fight Director Geoffrey Kent, and SAFD Certified Teacher Fulton Burns' writing. Refer to the Bibliography for more information.)

Pool noodles, cut down to four foot lengths to approximate a sword, are very helpful training tools for actors studying the connections between stage combat, acting, and voice/text work. They are forgiving physically and for this reason are valuable training tools. Nevertheless, care must still be strictly enforced to avoid any contact on or near the head and to also always avoid making any contact with the hard, bony areas of the body, including all joints.

Before any physical contact is made with pool noodles, it is a good practice to clearly establish areas that must be avoided:

1 Head/Face

2 Neck

3 Spine

4 Pelvis/Groin

5 Knees

6 Back of the Knees

7 Shin Bones

8 Wrists/Hands/Fingers/Thumbs

9 Elbows

10 Shoulders

11 Clavicles

12 Breasts

Areas that can be made contact with are only the major muscle groups, including such areas as:

1 Belly (avoiding the solar plexus)

2 Thighs (avoiding the groin and knees)

3 Calves (avoiding the shin bones)

4 Buttocks (avoiding the tail bone or spine)

5 Upper arms (avoiding the face, elbow, or shoulder)

Pool noodle killing cut (30 minutes)
(https://vimeo.com/132085881)

> ***Teaching Tip:*** Before all these drills, ensure the voice and body is effectively warmed-up and that your students are well hydrated. Refer to Chapter 2 for reminders of vocal and physical warm-ups.

Explore this physical exercise of exploring a killing wound with a pool noodle 'sword' in relationship to the breath and the voice. Allow the relative safety provided by the pool noodle to engage you within a release of specifically placed artistic choices. The temptations are to engage the work from the standpoint of purely a physical engagement. In this exercise, continue to explore the previous work connecting the breath, the voice, image placement, eye contact, and physical intentionality with this sequence.

1 Partner A – having established an eye contact cue with Partner B – brings their sword above their head in the preparation for a vertical cut downwards.

2 Partner B steps out to the left, removing his or her body completely off line from Partner A. This is accomplished by lunging with the left foot to the left. As always, ensure the knee is in alignment with the foot on this evasion and that the knee does not extend further over the foot than the ankle.

3   After seeing Partner B evade to their left, Partner A (holding the pool noodle with both hands in a double-handed 'Broadsword Grip') will step forwards bringing the pool noodle down to a horizontal level with the floor. It is important to ensure that Partner A presents a clear target of their belly for Partner B to safely place their pool noodle.

4   After Partner A has stopped their cut and the belly target is clearly and safely available, Partner B will place their pool noodle on the safe target of the belly, avoiding the ribs and the pelvis.

5   The placement occurs with the palm of Partner B facing down towards the floor (i.e., in 'pronation').

6   Once contact has been made, Partner A places their left hand on the pool noodle, firmly securing the pool noodle in place onto his or her own belly.

7   Partner A isolates their belly slightly over the noodle, ensuring that the head and torso remain relatively upright. The head of Partner A must not drop towards or near Partner B's head or shoulder. Keep the knees bent.

8   Both Partners A and B establish and maintain eye contact throughout the remainder of the exercise. It is imperative that at least two feet distance is maintained at all times between the heads of both partners. Both partners remain off-line from each other.

9   Partner B turns the hand holding the pool noodle into supination, with the palm now facing the ceiling. Partner A reacts with the breath and an open vocal response of a vowel that is preceded with a brief unvoiced /h/ sound to establish an open passage of breath and vibration.

10 Partner B removes the pool noodle down and away from Partner A. Partner B moves several paces away from Partner A as the removal of the pool noodle takes place.

11 Partner A isolates the belly forward as the pool noodle is removed. The knees buckling – ensuring to not fall to the ground – allows Partner A to more realistically engage with the physical experience of pain. Partner A isolates the sound of the weapons removal with an open vowel sound, again preceded by an open, unvoiced /h/ to preserve the free flow of air through the vocal passage.

Discussion

- How does maintaining eye contact after the pool noodle has been safely placed on the belly affect both the breath and the acted moment?

- In what ways does this technique connect to the voice and how is it possible to manage a killing thrust without adding vocal tension?

Pool noodle head and belly evasion (30 minutes)
(https://vimeo.com/132085882)

In the performance of evasions, a direction that is often used is that 'air does not bleed', meaning that a partner must have initiated the action of the evasion *prior* to the action of the swipe. After a clear 'cue' has been placed and seen by the 'Recipient', the action of the evasion may take place. Once the 'Recipient' has cleared the space, the partner performing the swipe can afford to freely release into the space that has been safely vacated by their partner.

With a pool noodle as a training tool, it can be valuable to explore a variety of evasions and their representative cues, in the development of a full and released physicality that is integrated with the breath and voice. Be aware that, while this exercise engages with more acted release, you must *always maintain complete control, balance and precision of the weapon and of your body*. Do not let the released action of the swipe allow you to be less precise with targeting, distance, cues or in your centred connection with your partner. Refer to Chapter 3 and the exercise, *Head swipe and evasion with voice*, as a reminder of the safety considerations.

1   Partner A establishes eye contact with Partner B.

2   Partner A cues the pool noodle to the outside of their left shoulder with the 'tip' pointing upwards towards the ceiling.

3   Partner B initiates a ducking evasion by lowering their centre downwards by bending the knees while continuing to visually be in contact with Partner A. Partner B will ensure the torso remains aligned in this evasive action rather than leaning forwards or bending over from the waist.

4   Once Partner A has ensured that Partner B has initiated the ducking action, he or she will continue looking at the target of where Partner B's head (ear-line) *used to be*. This is the area through which the swipe will horizontally travel. The swipe must travel perfectly horizontally – without turning the hand over. Do not 'track' Partner B's head visually and thereby bring the pool noodle close to Partner B's head during the evasive action.

5   Both partners recover back to neutral.

6   Partner B prepares the pool noodle to outside of their left waist with the 'tip' pointing upwards towards the ceiling.

7   Partner A performs an isolation of the belly retraction as he or she takes three steps to the rear that effectively carries the body backwards. On this evasion, the belly retracts to the rear, thereby creating the effect of removing the belly as the intended target.[8]

8   The hands and arms should be kept out of the trajectory of the path of the weapon. Either place the hands and arms up and out of the way or orient your hands and arms down and to the rear. In either case, it is important to ensure the hands and arms do not extend forward into the trajectory of the swipe.

9   As Partner B sees Partner A initiating the correct response, he or she will perform a small lunge and swipe perfectly horizontally across the space where Partner A's belly used to be.

10 Both partners return to neutral.

Once the basic Cue-Reaction-Action pattern has been safely learned, explore the full release of the body throughout the action. Engage with a free and supported release of the voice as it travels unimpeded out an open passageway on a vowel with a slight unvoiced /h/ release of air preceding the sound.

Explore the following vocal variations for their effects on the internal realities that are produced emotionally and intentionally within this training drill.

Vocal variation 1

1   ATTACKER: Release on an open vowel sound, avoiding a hard glottal attack by the inclusion of an unvoiced /h/ prior to voice.

2   EVADER: Release on an open vowel sound, avoiding a hard glottal attack by the inclusion of an unvoiced /h/ prior to voice.

Vocal variation 2

1   ATTACKER: Release on an open vowel sound, avoiding a hard glottal attack by the inclusion of an unvoiced /h/ prior to voice.

2   EVADER: Allow the body to breathe on the evasion with an audible inhalation. Ensure you are well hydrated before you begin.

Teaching Tip: At any point when the use of the voice is called for in extreme ways, it is important to limit the repetitions used and to carefully monitor any signs of vocal strain. Increased hydration is helpful for this work. At the first sign of vocal strain, ensure the student takes a break to rest and hydrate.

There are many other advantages of using pool noodles as additional training tools in the study of stage combat as it relates to the actor's process. Below are several applications to try. Explore what works best for you and your work, and adapt the basic foundations presented here to suit the requirements of your training or rehearsal needs.

Pool noodle combat (30 minutes)

The relative safety of the pool noodle as a training tool allows the use of exercises that help actors explore – in a controlled and safe way – the uncertainty experienced within real sword fights. The goal is to explore the following exercise physically as a mock duel and also to integrate the breath and the voice as a vital component of the exploration.

The concept of pool noodle improvised duelling often results in the initiation of the fight or flight response of a tightly held breath. As a reminder, it is possible to be physically engaged and also allow freedom within the breathing and vocal process. It can be useful to engage with any of the exercises from Chapters 1 and 2 prior to this exercise.

Teaching Tip: This exercise should never be attempted with any prop weapons other than soft pool noodles of approximately 3´–4´ long. Though all areas of the head and face are strictly off-limits, using protective eye goggles is required. This is an advanced exercise and is only intended for groups with significant skill level and maturity.

---

1   Armed with a sword-sized pool noodle, each partner enters the centre of the circle of students. The remaining students sit on the periphery of the circle, far out of distance from the two students in the centre of the circle.

2   Both partners Salute the other out of distance, while allowing the breath to be free.

3   One insult may be spoken from each partner, using the lists of insults from Chapter 3. Approach the exercise with a seriousness of intent and focus while remaining centred and safe.

4   Following the Salute, each partner attempts to make contact, *only on major muscle masses*, on their partner with the pool noodle. All areas of the head, face, neck, breasts, groin, and any hard, bony areas of the body are strictly off limits. Refer

back to the list of potential targets from earlier in this section ('Engaged Play') as a reminder.

5   When hits are received, they are played with utmost seriousness by exploring the true realities of what it is to experience the shock of pain and the complicated psychology of imagining the sight of wounds. The breath and the voice remain connected, free, and open to the physical stimulus received.

6   The exercise ends with the illusory death of one partner. Depending on the skill level and maturity of the group, this exercise can safely explore the complicated physical and emotional consequences of violence.

As the exploration continues, it can be helpful to remind students of the following:

- 'Where is your breath centred?'

- 'Where is the lowest place that you can literally feel your breath?'

- 'What temperature does the breath feel like between your lips?'

- 'Let your eyes go soft in your head.'

- 'Can you feel any movement of your ribs within your breath?'

- 'As you proceed into death, image your spine and watch its slow decay into dust.'

Discussion

- Explore a piece of choreography as only a set pattern of movement. Remove all intentionality while maintaining correct form and precise technique. Practice perfectly placed parries, perfectly targeted attacks, and a perfect maintenance of a safe distance. Allow the breath to be slightly held. In contrast, release your breathing and repeat the precision of the choreography (perfect parries, perfect cues, perfect targets, perfect extension and control, and perfect maintenance of distance) with only one added element to the choreography: an 'intention' or a single playable verb, that is, a 'tactic'. In what ways does even a small allowance of the imagination provide a framework of helpful cascading events that opens up greater release within the work without sacrificing physical specificity and safety?

Pool noodle scene work (45–60 minutes)

Pool noodles used to make light but firm contact with major muscle groups (not bones or joints) within scene work helps to viscerally engage text work with more active and playable choices. The use of light strikes on safe major muscle groups within scene work can greatly aid in the recognition that the process of acting and communicating through language is often much more visceral than we tend to allow. Tactic use becomes more varied when you safely explore this approach to the work. The use of these relatively safe 'weapons' is that they also permit the more full realization of both threatening and inductive tactics in the work. You can use this tool to not only safely and selectively make firm contact with each other at key points within text work, but their flexible nature also allows possibilities of drawing your scene partner in by seducing, encouraging, stroking, and charming each other tactically to achieve your character's needs. The question in scene work of 'What are you fighting for' becomes immediately more visceral when these playful but instructive aids are employed.

Follow-up

Reflective practice questions:

- Spend time watching the news. Observe carefully those individuals who are experiencing emotions from either tragic or happy events that they have faced. In what ways is emotion a by-product of 'thought' and 'imagery' and not an emotional state that is arrived at in isolation?
- With those real individuals experiencing emotion, what is their goal?
- In what ways do they want to be seen and heard despite the emotional obstacles that they are experiencing?
- In what ways can actors derive specific lessons from what real people do when faced with high stakes predicaments?

Envoi

Theatrical violence can be ugly, brutal, and disturbing as well as entertaining, comical, and thrilling. The artistic choices affecting the characters' inner lives within violence – from both the 'Attacker's' and the 'Recipient's' points of views – are to be respectfully explored and often need to be faithfully, though theatrically, reproduced. As always, ensure you explore with 100 per cent focus on safety, care, control, and respect.

It is highly recommended that you work with a recognized, experienced, and qualified teacher to develop your skills through an in-depth study of this art. The study of stage combat in relationship to acting and voice work holds great depth for your continued engagement as artists. Find the subtleties of what it means to connect as actors using the Stage Combat Arts as one of many paths towards your development of greater creative flexibility and artistic integration.

Notes

1   See the Bibliography for books authored by Robert Cohen.
2   This is the weapon used in the exercise 'head swipe and evasion with voice' in Chapter 3.
3   These basic questions are not new to authors or acting teachers. Many authors have described various similar approaches to this work. Refer to the following books for additional explorations:
    1   *A Challenge for the Actor* by Uta Hagen (pp. 256–285)
    2   *The Actor at Work* by Robert Benedetti (pp. 247–248)
    3   *Essential Acting* by Brigid Panet (pp. 95–97)
4   For additional instructions in the physical mechanics of safe blade pathways and safe distance practices, refer to authors Dale Girard, Gregory Hoffman, and Richard Lane in the Bibliography.
5   For a thorough description of the physical mechanics of these techniques ('bind', 'croise', and 'expulsion'), refer to SAFD Fight Master Dale Girard's book, *Actors On Guard*, pp. 279–292. See the Bibliography for more information.
6 · As additional preparation for this exercise, refer to SAFD Fight Director Emeritus Richard Lane's book, *Swashbuckling*. Specifically, Chapter 11 ('Swashbuckling with Broadswords') on pp. 211–244 provides an overview of basic training practices with this weapon. Refer to the Bibliography for more information.

7   See p. 90 of Carey, David and Carey, Rebecca, *Verbal Arts Workbook*, Methuen, London, 2008.

8   Under the instruction of a stage combat teacher, this backwards evasion is often more specifically characterized as a jumping backwards action, in which the feet can cross each other as the actor vigorously moves to the rear. The belly is particularly isolated rearward away from the horizontal swipe, at the same time as the body and feet move backwards.

Further reading

Berry, Cicely, *From Word to Play*, Oberon Books, London, 2008. Section One: Hearing Language, pp. 10–23.

Bogart, Anne, *And Then, You Act*, Routledge, New York, 2007. Chapter Three: Intention, pp. 30–50.

Callery, Dymphna, *Through the Body*, Routledge, New York, 2001. Section Six: The Physical Text, pp. 195–215.

Cohen, Robert, *Acting Power*, Routledge, New York, 2013. Chapter 2: Into the Other, pp. 37–98.

Hagen, Uta, *A Challenge for the Actor*, Scribner, New York, 1991. Part Four: Scoring the Role, pp. 256–290.

Mitchell, Theresa, *Movement from Person to Actor to Character*, Scarecrow Press, Oxford, 1998. Part Three: Character – Space, Time, Weight, and Action, pp. 95–97.

Potter, Nicole, *Movement for Actors*, Allworth Press, New York, 2002. Part Two: An Introduction to Laban Movement Analysis for Actors, pp. 73–84.

Suddeth, J. Allen, *Fight Directing for the Theatre*, Heinemann, Portsmouth, 1996. Chapter 3: Acting the Fight, pp. 155–181.

LINKS TO WORKING VIDEO

To view a particular video, please visit its URL below, or go to
http://vimeo.com/channels/stagecombatarts

APPENDIX: ADDITIONAL RESOURCES

This appendix offers a listing of training organizations and suppliers for stage combat worthy weapons. It is in no way a comprehensive list and there are many other suppliers and organizations not herein provided; however, the lists below represent an accurate foundation for your further research and study.

Fitzmaurice Voicework®:

- Fitzmaurice Voicework (www.fitzmauricevoice.com)
- Saul Kotzubei, Co-Director of the Fitzmaurice Institute (www.voicecoachla.com)

Stage combat/stunt training organizations and events:

- **United States of America**
  - Society of American Fight Directors (www.safd.org)
  - Dueling Arts International (www.duelingarts.com)
  - Academy of Theatrical Combat (www.theatricalcombat.com)
  - International Stunt School (http://www.stuntschool.com)
- **United Kingdom**
  - British Academy of Stage and Screen Combat (http://www.bassc.org)
  - British Academy of Dramatic Combat (www.badc.org.uk)

- **Canada**
  - ○ Fight Directors Canada (http://www.fdc.ca/the-academy /overview/)
  - ○ Paddy Crean Stage Combat Workshop (www.paddycrean .com)
- **Ireland**
  - ○ Irish Dramatic Combat Academy (www.idca.ie/)
- **Sweden, Denmark, Norway, Estonia, Finland**
  - ○ Nordic Stage Fight Society (www.nordicstagefight.com)
- **International**
  - ○ International Order of the Sword and Pen (http://www.iosp.org)

Suppliers for purchase and rental of stage weaponry:

- Vulcan's Forge (www.lewisshaw.com)
- Keen Knives (http://www.keenedgeknives.com)
- Rogue Steel (www.roguesteel.com)
- Preferred Arms (www.preferredarms.com)
- Baltimore Knife and Sword (www.imakeswords.com/index.htm)
- Starfire Swords (www.starfireswords.com)
- American Fencers (www.amfence.com)

Mask Suppliers:

- Theatre-Masks.com (http://www.theater-masks.com /neutral-masks)

BIBLIOGRAPHY

Stage combat and historical references

Amberger, Christopher J., *The Secret History of the Sword*, Distributed by Unique Publications, Burbank, CA, 1999. https://fencingclassics.files.wordpress.com/2015/01/the-secret-history-of-the-sword.pdf

Anglo, Sydney, *The Martial Arts of Renaissance Europe*, Yale University Press, New Haven, CT, 2000.

Baldick, Robert, *The Duel*, Barnes and Noble Books, New York, 1965.

Barry, B.H., *Fights for Everyone*, Self-published, 2013. http://www.lulu.com/us/en/shop/bh-barry/bh-barry-fights-for-everyone/paperback/product-21053694.html.

Barry, B.H., *Fights for Shakespeare, Book One*, Romeo and Juliet, Self-published, 2010. http://www.lulu.com/us/en/shop/bh-barry/bh-barry-fights-for-shakespeare/paperback/product-6519151.html.

Barry, B.H., *Fights for Shakespeare, Book Two, Macbeth and Hamlet*, Self-published, 2011. http://www.lulu.com/us/en/shop/bh-barry/bh-barry-fights-for-shakespeare/paperback/product-6519151.html.

Boushey, David, *Combat for the Stage and Screen Video*, Theatre Arts Video Library, Leucadia, CA, 1985.

Burns, T. Fulton, *A Violent Character (Stage Combat Character Analysis)*, The Cutting Edge (Editor Michael Mueller), March/April 2009, Volume XX, Issue 2. www.safd.org.

Burns, T. Fulton, *Beating the Punches (Scene and Fight Break Down Techniques)*, The Cutting Edge (Editor Michael Mueller), May/June 2009, Volume XX, Issue 3. www.safd.org.

Burns, T. Fulton, *The Games People Play (Rehearsal Games & Approaches for Fight Scenes*, The Cutting Edge (Editor Michael Mueller), September/October 2009, Volume XX, Issue 5. www.safd.org.

Burt, Payson, *What Makes for Good Fight Direction*, The Fight Master (Editor Margaret Raether), Spring/Summer 1996, Volume XIX, Volume 1, pp. 13–14. www.safd.org.

Capo Ferro, Ridolfo (edited by Jared Kirby), *Italian Rapier Combat*, Greenhill Books, London, 2004.

Cheatham, James, *Acting the Fight: A Series of Exercises*, The Fight Master (Editor Margaret Raether), Spring/Summer 1996, Volume XIX, Volume 1, pp. 15–19. www.safd.org.

Cohen, Richard, *By the Sword*, Modern Library, New York, 2002.

De Bazancourt, Baron Cesar, *Secrets of the Sword*, Laureate Press, Bangor, 1998.

De Becker, Gavin, *The Gift of Fear*, Dell Publishing, New York, 1997.

Dillon, Robert W., *Accounts of Martial Arts in Actor Training: An Enthusiast's Critique*, The Fight Master (Editor Linda Carlyle McCollum), Fall/Winter 2000, Volume XXIII, Number 2, pp. 18–22. www.safd.org.

Dillon, Robert W., *Beyond Acting in Fights: Stage Combat as a New Martial Art*, The Fight Master (Editor Margaret Raether), Spring/Summer 1994, Volume XVII, Number 1, pp. 17–19. www.safd.org.

Dillon, Robert W., *Pet Peeves in the Martial Arts, Part II*, The Fight Master (Editor Linda Carlyle McCollum), Fall/Winter 2004, Volume XXVII, Number 2, pp. 13–20. www.safd.org.

DuVal, Christopher, *An Interview with Drew*, The Fight Master (Editor Michael Mueller), Fall/Winter 2010, Volume XXXII, Number 11, pp. 17–25. www.safd.org.

DuVal, Christopher, *David Boushey: Closing Distance*, The Fight Master (Editor Linda Carlyle McCollum), Fall/Winter 2008, Volume XXXI, Number 2, pp. 23–26. www.safd.org.

DuVal, Christopher, *Erik Fredricksen*, The Fight Master (Editor Michael Mueller), Fall 2011, Volume XXXIII, Number 2, pp. 13–17. www.safd.org.

Ducklin, Keith and Waller, John, *Sword Fighting, A Manual for Actors and Directors*, Applause Theatre Books, New York, 2001.

Girard, Dale Anthony, *Actors On Guard*, Routledge, New York, 1997.

Girard, Dale Anthony, *The Sounds of Violence, A Detailed Look at the Process of Orchestrating Sound into the Staging of Fight Sequences for the Professional Theatre*, The Fight Master (Editor Linda Carlyle McCollum), Fall/Winter 2008, Volume XXXI, Number 2, pp. 14–21. www.safd.org.

Grossman, Dave, *On Combat: The Psychology and Physiology of Deadly Conflict in War and in Peace*, Warrior Science Publications, Millstadt, IL, 2012.

Grossman, Dave, *On Killing: The Psychological Cost of Learning to Kill in War and Society*, Back Bay Books, New York, 2009.

Hamill, Kyna, *They Fight – Classical to Contemporary Fight Scenes*, Smith and Kraus, Hanover, 2003.

Hobbs, William, *Stage Combat*, St. Martin's Press, New York, 1967.

Hobbs, William, *Fight Direction for Stage and Screen*, Heinemann, Portsmouth, 1995.

Hoffman, Gregory, *And They Fight* DVD Series. http://www.trueedgepictures.com/dvds/.

Houston, Hollis, *Combat as Actor Training, Parts I and II (Reprinted from The Fight Master, July 1982)*, Spring/Summer 2008, pp. 23–26. www.safd.org.

Howell, Jonathan, *Stage Fighting – A Practical Guide*, Crowood Press, Ramsbury, 2008.

Hutton, Alfred, *The Sword and the Centuries*, Greenhill Books, London, 2003.

Inouye, Kevin, *Cry Havoc and Let Slip the Sounds of War!*, The Fight Master, (Editor Michael Mueller), Fall 2012, Volume 34, Number 2, pp. 9–11. www.safd.org.

Inouye, Kevin, *The Theatrical Firearms Handbook*, Focal Press, Burlington, MA, 2014.

Kirkland, Michael J. *Stage Combat Resource Materials: A Selected and Annotated Bibliography*, Greenwood, Santa Barbara, CA, 2006.

Kreng, John, *Fight Choreography: The Art of Non-Verbal Dialogue*, Thomson, Independence, KY, 2008.

Lane, Richard, *Swashbuckling*, Proscenium Publishers, New York, 1999.

Langsner, Meron, *Acting the Fall: Adding Physical Narrative to Getting to the Ground*, The Fight Master (Editor Michael Mueller), Fall 2013, Volume 35, Number 2, pp. 4–5. www.safd.org.

Martinez, J. D., *Combat Mime*, Nelson-Hall Publishers, Chicago, 1982.

Martinez, J. D., *The Swords of Shakespeare*, McFarland Publishers, Jefferson, NC, 2013.

Morton, E.D., *A-Z of Fencing*, Queen Anne Press, London, 1988.

Nadi, Aldo, *On Fencing*, Laureate Press, Bangor, 1943.

Rector, Mark, *Medieval Combat*, Greenhill Books, London, 2000.

Sharon, Ted, *Battle Stories*, The Fight Master (Editor Linda Carlyle McCollum), Spring/Summer 2000, Volume XXIII, Number 1, pp. 20–21. www.safd.org.

Speaker, Dan, *Academy of Theatrical Combat – Basics Level I*, Academy of Theatrical Combat, Sylmar, 2012.

Steinberg, Zev, *The Three Things You Need to "Act the Fight"*, The Fight Master (Editor Jean A. Monfort), Fall 2014, Volume 36, Number 2, pp. 14–20, www.safd.org.

Suddeth, J. Allen, *Fight Directing for the Theatre*, Heinemann, Portsmouth, 1996.

Suddeth, J. Allen and Leong, S. David, *Unarmed Stage Combat 1*: Learning the Basics, *Unarmed Stage Combat 2: Perfecting the Fundamentals, and Unarmed Stage Combat 3: Mastering the Techniques*, Combat Masters International; Produced at GHS-TV Studios, Germantown, Tenn., New York, 1993.

Travers, Joseph, *The Reactor Game: An Exercise for Developing Specific and Dynamic Reactions*, The Fight Master (Editor Michael Mueller), Fall 2013, Volume 35, Number 2, pp. 6–7, www.safd.org.

Turner, Craig and Soper, Tony, *Methods and Practice of Elizabethan Swordplay*, Southern Illinois University Press, Carbondale, 1990.

Weitz, Stephen, *New Combatants, New Techniques*, The Fight Master (Editor Linda Carlyle McCollum), Fall/Winter 2005, Volume XXVIII, Number 2, pp. 18–20. www.safd.org.

Wetmore, Kevin J., *Song Duels and the State: Words as Weapons*, The Fight Master (Editor Linda Carlyle McCollum), Spring/Summer 2002, Volume XXV, Number 1, pp. 19–21. www.safd.org.

Wooten, Kara, *Acted Aggression*, Millenia Publishing, Toronto, 2003.

Wooten, Kara, *Developing a Course in Stage Combat: A Manual for Instructors and Students*, a Dissertation in Fine Arts submitted to the Graduate Faculty of Texas Tech University in Partial Fulfillment of the Requirements for the Degree of Doctor of Philosophy, May 2000.

Voice and breath

Barton, Robert and Dal Vera, Rocco, *Voice Onstage and Off*, Routledge, London, 1995.

Berry, Cicely, *Voice and the Actor*, Macmillan Publishing Company, New York, 1973.

Calais-Germain, Blandine, *Anatomy of Breathing*, Eastland Press, Seattle, WA, 2006.

Carey, David and Carey, Rebecca, *Vocal Arts Workbook and DVD*, Methuen, London, 2010.

Cook, Rena, *The Moving Voice*, Voice and Speech Trainers Association, Cincinnati, OH, 2009.

Dal Vera, Rocco, *The Voice in Violence*, Voice and Speech Trainers Association, Cincinnati, 2001.

Farhi, Donna, *The Breathing Book*, St. Martin's Griffin, New York, 1996.

Fitzmaurice, Catherine, *Breathing Is Meaning*, http://www.fitzmauricevoice.com/products.html.

Hendricks, Gay, *Conscious Breathing*, Bantam Books, New York, 1995.

Houseman, Barbara, *Finding Your Voice*, Nick Hern Books, London, 2002.

Kotzubei, Saul, *Why We Focus on Breathing*, http://www.voicecoachla.com/writing/.

Kotzubei, Saul, *To Breathe or Not to Breathe*, http://www.voicecoachla.com/writing/.

Kotzubei, Saul, *Stand Up and Express Yourself*, http://www.voicecoachla.com/writing/.

Kotzubei, Saul, *You're Getting Warmer*, http://www.voicecoachla.com/writing/.

Kotzubei, Saul, *Interview of Catherine Fitzmaurice*, http://www.voicecoachla.com/writing/.

Lessac, Arthur, *The Use and Training of the Human Voice*, 2nd ed., Rev., Drama Book Specialists, New York, 1967.

Linklater, Kristin, *Freeing the Natural Voice*, Drama Publishers, Hollywood, 2006.

McCallion, Michael, *The Voice Book*, Routledge, New York, 1988.

Rafael, Bonnie N., *Screaming without Suffering*, Voice Talk (Canadian Voice Care Foundation), Volume 1, Issue 3, Fall 1995.

Rafael, Bonnie N., *The Sounds of Violence, Part III*, The Fight Master (Editor Linda Carlyle McCollum), Fall 1989, Volume XII, Number 3, pp. 8–10. www.safd.org.

Rafael, Bonnie N., *The Sounds of Violence: Vocal Training in Stage Combat*, Theatre Topics. Published by The John Hopkins University Press, Baltimore, Maryland, Volume 1, Number 1, March 1991, pp. 73–86.

Rodenburg, Patsy, *The Right to Speak*, Routledge, New York, 1992.

Rogers, Janet (editor), *The Complete Voice and Speech Workout*, Applause, New York, 2002.

Saklad, Nancy, *Interview of Saul Kotzubei* (Voice and Speech Training in the New Millennium: Conversations with Master Teachers), http://www.voicecoachla.com/writing/.

Text work

Berry, Cicely, *Text in Action*, Virgin Publishing, London, 2001.

Berry, Cicely, *From Word to Play*, Oberon Books, London, 2008.

Carey, David and Carey, Rebecca, *Verbal Arts Workbook*, Methuen, London, 2008.

Houseman, Barbara, *Tackling Text [and subtext]*, Nick Hern Books, London, 2008.

Kaiser, Scott, *Mastering Shakespeare*, Allworth, New York, 2003.

Rodenburg, Patsy, *The Actor Speaks*, Palgrave Macmillan, New York, 2002.

Aikido and energy work

Dang, Phong Thong, *Advanced Aikido*, Tuttle Publishing, North Clarendon, 2006.

Gallwey, Timothy W., *The Inner Game of Tennis*, Random House, New York, 2008.

Herrigel, Eugen, *Zen in the Art of Archery*, Vintage Books, New York, 1971.

Hyams, Joe, *Zen in the Martial Arts*, Bantam Books, New York, 1979.

Leonard, George, *The Way of Aikido*, Penguin Group, New York, 2000.

Millman, Dan, *Body Mind Mastery*, New World Library, Novata, 1999.

Nachmanovitch, Stephen, *Free Play*, Penguin Putnam, New York, 1990.

Ozawa, Hiroshi, *Kendo*, Kodansha International, New York, 1991.

Rodenburg, Patsy, *The Second Circle*, Norton, New York, 2007.

Shifflett, C.M., *Aikido – Exercises for Teaching and Training*, Round Earth, Sewickley, 1999.

Stevens, John, *Abundant Peace*, Shambhala Publications, Boston, MA, 1987.

Stevens, John, *The Art of Peace*, Shambhala Publications, Boston, MA, 2002.

Tharp, Twyla, *The Creative Habit*, Simon and Schuster, New York, 2003.

Ueshiba, Morihei, *The Secret Teachings of Aikido*, Kodansha International, Tokyo, 2007.

Westbrook, A., and Ratti, O., *Aikido and the Dynamic Sphere*, Charles E. Tuttle Company, Tokyo, 1970.

Body work

Adrian, Barbara, *Actor Training the Laban Way*, Allworth Press, New York, 2008.

Appel, Libby, *Mask Characterization*, Southern Illinois University Press, Carbondale, 1982.

Bogart, Anne and Landau, Tina, *The Viewpoints Book*, Theatre Communications Group, New York, 2005.

Calais-Germain, Blandine, *Anatomy of Movement*, Eastland Press, Seattle, WA, 1991.

Dennis, Anne, *The Articulate Body*, Drama Publishers, New York, 1995.

Dymphna, Callery, *Through the Body*, Nick Hern Books, London, 2001.

Eldredge, Sears A., *Mask Improvisation*, Northwestern University Press, Evanston, IL, 1996.

Feldenkrais, Moshe, *Awareness Through Movement*, Harper Collins, New York, 1972.

Gelb, Michael, *Body Learning*, Henry Holt and Company, New York, 1981.

Juhan, Deane, *Job's Body – A Handbook for Body Work*, Barrytown/Station Hill Press, New York, 1998.

Lecoq, Jacques, *The Moving Body*, Routledge, New York, 2001.

Loui, Annie, *The Physical Actor*, Routledge, New York, 2009.

Marshall, Lorna, *The Body Speaks*, Palgrave Macmillan, New York, 2002.

Ohashi, Wataru, *Beyond Shiatsu*, Kodansha International, New York, 1996.

Potter, Nicole, *Movement for Actors*, Allworth, New York, 2002.

Sabatine, Jean, *Movement Training for the Actor*, Watson-Guptill, New York, 1995.

Simon, Eli, *Masking Unmasked*, Palgrave Macmillan, New York, 2003.

Acting

Bartow, Arthur (Editor), *Training of the American Actor*, Theatre Communications Group, New York, 2006.

Bogart, Anne, *And Then, You Act*, Routledge, New York, 2007.

Caldarone, Marina, *Action – The Actor's Thesaurus*, Nick Hern Books, London, 2004.

Chekhov, Michael, *On the Technique of Acting*, Harper Collins Publishers, New York, NY, 1991.

Cohen, Robert, *Acting One*, Mayfield Publishing Company, Mountain View, 1984.

Cohen, Robert, *Acting Power*, Routledge, New York, 2013.

Donnellan, Declan, *The Actor and the Target*, Theatre Communications Group, St. Paul, MN, 2002.

Hagen, Uta, *A Challenge for the Actor*, Scribner, New York, 1991.

Hlavsa, David, *An Actor Rehearses*, Allworth, New York, 2006.

Johnstone, Keith, *Impro – Improvisation and the Theatre*, Methuen, London, 1992.

Mamet, David, *True and False*, Pantheon Books, New York, 1997.

Oida, Yoshi, *The Invisible Actor*, Methuen, London, 1997.

Panet, Brigid, *Essential Acting*, Routledge, London, 2009.

Shurtleff, Michael, *Audition*, Bantam Books, New York, 1978.

Stanislavski, Constantin, *The Actors Work* (Translated and edited by Jean Benedetti), Routledge, New York, 2008.

Zarrilli, Phillip B., *Psychophysical Acting*, Routledge, London, 2009.

INDEX

Video Tutorials

Index of Authors and Teachers